GIVING BIRTH

GIVING BIRTH

Reclaiming
Biblical Metaphor
for Pastoral Practice

Margaret L. Hammer

Westminster/John Knox Press
Louisville, Kentucky

Book design by Susan Jackson

Cover design by Peggy Claire Calhoun

First edition

Published by Westminster/John Knox Press
Louisville, Kentucky

This book is printed on acid-free paper that meets the American National Standards Institute Z39.48 standard. ∞

PRINTED IN THE UNITED STATES OF AMERICA

9 8 7 6 5 4 3 2 1

Library of Congress Cataloging-in-Publication Data

Hammer, Margaret L., date.
    Giving birth : reclaiming biblical metaphor for pastoral practice
    Margaret L. Hammer. — 1st ed.
        p.   cm.
    Includes bibliographical references.
    ISBN 0-664-25137-4
    1. Childbirth in the Bible.   2. Childbirth—Religious aspects—
Christianity—History of doctrines.   3. Femininity of God.   4. Pastoral
theology.   I. Title.
BS680.C46H36   1994
220.8′61263—dc20   93-40601

To Jørgen, Sophia, Niels, and Anna,
who so richly bless my life.

Contents

Preface

While browsing in a bookstore a decade ago, I happened across a book titled *Lying-In: A History of Childbirth in America.*[1] Intrigued, I purchased a copy and took it home to read. The book was indeed fascinating, though at the time I had never given birth, nor was I planning to do so in the near future. A few months later, while studying the biblical and theological themes of "creation and fall," it occurred to me that childbirth and Gen. 3:16 might provide an interesting subject for a term paper. And indeed it proved to be a fresh and exciting subject: I found myself uncovering dramatic biblical imagery that I had no idea even existed. Why had I never heard of Isaiah's wonderful description of God shouting out like a birthing woman, turning the world upside down with her birthing labor? I loved this powerful, birthing God. That seminary term paper was eventually revised and published as an essay in a theological journal,[2] where it caught the eye of Westminster/John Knox editors and led eventually to the preparation of this book's more thorough exploration of the subject.

In the decade that has passed, my husband and I have been blessed by the birth of three children, and as a parish pastor, I have regularly ministered to women in their childbearing. As one result, I no longer imagine God the birthing mother marching quite so briskly across the stage of the world! I am more convinced than ever, though, that childbirth provides a metaphor of strength, endurance, and compassion that is illuminating and empowering—not only for those who give birth, but for us all; and that the graceful resolution of the spiritual challenges of childbearing have consequences for women, families, and communities today, and for generations to come. Thus, though this work is directed primarily toward pastors and chaplains, it is written as nontechnically as possible in the hope that the subject will pique the curiosity of a variety of readers. So, too, I hope that this study is not the last word on the subject—ample footnotes are provided so that readers may better pursue topics that can be only introduced here.

This book would not have been written without the encouragement and support of many people. Frederick Gaiser and Paul Sponheim encouraged my original work on the theme and suggested I seek its publication. Arland Hultgren of *Word and World* made helpful suggestions and accepted it for publication. I am indebted to these Westminster/John Knox editors: Cynthia Thompson, who first suggested developing the theme into a book; Walter Sutton, who saw its potential in its present form; Alexa Smith, who provided insightful reading of the manuscript; and Stephanie Egnotovich, who shepherded it through the publication process. So, too, I am indebted to the many pastors, parishioners, and friends who have shared their insights and experiences with me, and to the libraries of Luther Northwestern Theological Seminary, Vancouver School of Theology, and Western Washington University, and the public libraries of Bellingham, Washington and Vancouver, British Columbia. Finally, I owe immeasurable gratitude to my family. My parents, Roland and Marian Hammer, have given me lifelong encouragement and help. Our children, Sophia, Niels, and Anna, have been a joy and inspiration from their birth. Above all, my husband and coworker Jørgen Kappel Hansen has put up with and promoted my work, and has spent countless hours tending our three young children so that I could find time to think and write. To all of you, my many, heartfelt thanks.

Notes

1. Richard W. Wertz and Dorothy C. Wertz, *Lying-In: A History of Childbirth in America* (New York: Shocken Books, 1979).
2. "Birthing: Perspectives for Theology and Ministry," *Word and World* 4 (fall 1984): 391–400.

Introduction

Birth is one of life's fundamental miracles. The experience of birth may be exhilarating or awful; it is almost inevitably awe-inspiring. Women who give birth will often remember the scenario and details of the unfolding drama for years and even decades to come. As fathers and even siblings increasingly gain access to the birthing room, they too are moved by the age-old, yet ever-new agony and ecstasy of birth. Many of these parents will bring their children to the church to be baptized. Some will listen to many a sermon and participate in many a Bible study. Few will see or hear much in the church that directly addresses or lifts up this awe-inspiring, life-changing experience.

The baby boomlet of recent years has given rise to increasing interest in childbirth issues and to a burgeoning body of literature dealing with pregnancy and childbirth. One bookstore counts over 1,200 different titles or editions in its inventory of publications dealing with pregnancy, birth, and parenting;[1] most have been written or revised within the last decade. Titles range the gamut of possible topics—from diet and exercise to childbirth preparation philosophy and technique, from family relationships to infertility and stillbirth. In the midst of this abundance and variety, a recent catalog's annotated booklist shows only two titles that clearly deal with childbirth from a distinctly Christian or biblical perspective.[2]

Nor does a perusal of theological and religious works turn

up much that concentrates on birth per se. Theological studies dealing with human sexuality tend to focus on the relationship between sexual partners (marital status, sexual orientation, etc.) or on interventions in the procreative process (abortion, contraception, and more recently, the various artificial means of procreation). Devotional books do offer some support for new mothers,[3] and prayer books intended for clergy often offer prayers for birthing women.[4] Still, an anthology like *The Oxford Book of Prayer*, which is aimed at a general audience, includes a wide range of prayers—but none for pregnant women, women in childbirth, or families suffering the loss of an expected child.[5]

Can the church offer parents anything that they cannot find elsewhere amid the mounds of literature, and wealth of workshops and classes? Conversely, will the church gain anything important by focusing more attention on the experience of giving birth? In a word—yes!

What can the church offer expecting and new parents? First, the church offers a vocabulary. Childbirth, with all its attendant emotions and concerns, cries out for words. Very often, only religious language seems to do justice to the experience. Browsing through one county hospital's "birth journal" a few years ago, I was struck by the preponderance of religious expressions parents used to describe their child's birth. Perhaps the parents who chose to record their thoughts and feelings were predominantly "religious" persons. Perhaps, on the other hand, the words of that journal reflect the simple fact that childbirth is a prime moment of miracle in most people's lives, a moment of special openness to life's spiritual dimension. The Christian faith has tremendous resources to bring to this moment: words of praise, thanks, and wonder in time of joy; words of comfort, hope, and consolation in time of need.

Second, the church offers a context, a story in which the experience of childbirth can be understood and articulated: Its words of praise and lament are rooted in the multifaceted drama of God's ongoing involvement in the world. Within its first few chapters, the Bible reflects on the paradoxical coinciding of suffering and joy at the birth of a child. Less familiar Bible passages, too, like those in which God is depicted as giving birth, may lend new meaning to the human experience of birth. In addition, the church's varied efforts to comprehend the mystery and miracle of birth through the ages offer perspectives for today.

Third, the church has a long healing tradition and a tradition of raising up the dignity of the person—both of which can be extremely healthy and helpful for couples as they try to find their way through the contemporary maze of childbirth options and high-tech intervention at a vulnerable time in their lives. Church-affiliated hospitals and congregationally supported ministers of health are not found in every community. Local congregations, however, are to be found in most. The prayers, listening ear, and practical help offered by the local congregation can be a powerful source of life and health for the childbearing woman and her family. Most important, local congregations can offer expecting parents a continuity of support and care that extends from pregnancy into parenthood and beyond.

Similarly, while official representatives of the church are not regularly present in the birthing room, the church may well be present in the person and ministry of Christian midwives, doctors, and nurses. This presence is invaluable: health-care professionals' attitude, as well as their technical competence, can make the difference between a happy birth-day and a frustrating ordeal. The wider church, in turn, can contribute to this vital ministry by finding ways to encourage and inspire the health-care workers in its midst. Such support is particularly important today as the threat of litigation and the economic strains associated with expensive medical technology add to the stress level of health-care workers.

Fourth, the church offers wisdom and guidance that may assist persons as they face the challenges to personal identity and the changes in family relationships that accompany a new birth. The church is a living repository of insight into the nature and purpose of human life; thus it can lift the questions, aspirations, and anxieties of the childbearing year into a larger framework. Such counsel and guidance is important during every pregnancy and birth; it is particularly vital when a couple experiences grief or faces one of the difficult decisions that may arise as medical technology continues to break new ground. Technologies ranging from sperm banks to the artificial wombs of the neonatal intensive care unit pose a host of new ethical questions that the church may help a couple, and their caregivers, to face.

Fifth, the church offers rituals to celebrate the milestones of life. Childbirth is a point in life at which human beings sense a need for ritual. Rituals vary from one culture to another, but most cultures prescribe definite actions to ensure the health and well-being of mother and child. In the United States today, childbirth rituals are informed primarily by hospital routine and current obstetrical practice. Still, people turn to the church and its rituals to mark the birth of a child. Even families who are not active church members often bring their infants to be baptized or dedicated. Thus the church is in a position to set the experience of childbirth in an encompassing framework of meaning—to lift up the wonder of every birth and affirm each woman's passage through childbirth, even as it proclaims the miracle of rebirth in Christ.

The church has plenty to offer expecting and new parents. The church also stands to gain from focusing more attention on the experience of giving birth.

First, the church may gain fuller insight into what it means to be human. An adequate incarnational theology must seek to understand all human experience in the light of divine purpose. The Christian tradition affirms creation and procreation as good gifts of God and proclaims as Savior one who is both Son of God and son of a human mother. Still, theologians have treated the experience of birth warily, sketchily, and haphazardly, if at all. From a practical point of view, the very femaleness of this experience may explain its marginality as a source of insight in the Christian tradition: The male theologians who have written most Christian theology never carried a child in their belly, never labored to push a new little human being out into the light of day; many probably never even attended a birth. Moreover, male fear of this unknown and powerful female experience may have further limited theological inquiry into and appreciation of childbirth. The legacy of this marginalization ranges from disinterest to mistrust. Even today, childbirth is perceived as a special interest topic—of interest to expecting parents and some feminists, but less relevant to the average churchgoer or theologian than, say, abortion. This is quite astonishing, considering that we have all been on the receiving end of birth and that childbirth is such a dramatic and identity-shaping experience in the lives of at least half the population.[6]

Unfortunately, recent efforts to reflect theologically on childbirth, as well as creation more generally, have been met with mistrust. Lyman Lundeen, for example, warns against feminist theology's strong emphasis on "creation spirituality": "Concentrating on the birthing role of women brings an appreciation of the natural as a clue to theological interpretation. Just being a woman, with the mothering ability and instincts, can easily be elevated to a place where natural features of childbirth tend to diminish the need for a new birth in Christ."[7] Such concerns are troubling insofar as they suggest a zero-sum model of theology—as if attention to one aspect of theology necessarily implies diminishing another. A careful probing and pondering of the dynamics of birth is a *gift* to the church at large, not only because it helps "to unearth and to interpret women's religious experiences,"[8] but also because the issues that come to the forefront in childbearing are fundamentally human concerns—life and death, identity and vocation, creatureliness and creativity, self and other. Until the church deals with the implications of being born human, and of giving birth, or choosing or not being able to give birth, it will not have dealt adequately with the human condition.

Second, the church stands to gain a fuller and more adequate idea of God. The Bible's references to God as a birthing and nursing mother have been overlooked or ignored; although few in number, they make powerful statements about God's way of interacting with humanity. Other Bible passages prompt reflection on God's involvement in human fertility: Is God directly involved in every birth, or only in the extraordinary ones? What might Israel's impurity laws suggest about divine-human interaction in childbirth? Such questions, as well as the very unfamiliarity of biblical imagery of God as mother, can expand the church's understanding of the God who is unlimited by human definitions and envisionings. So too, medieval mystics challenge traditional conceptions with their startling visions of Jesus giving birth to the world on the cross and suckling Christians in Holy Communion.

Third, the church may learn something about itself as it comes to terms with both the affirming and the dubious elements in its dealing with birth over the centuries. The mainstay of Judeo-Christian teaching regarding sexuality is an affirmation of procreation as a God-given blessing that strictly avoids any tendency to worship fertility itself. Not infrequently, however, the desire to control sexuality and sexual processes has overpowered and obscured this healthy balance. Sifting through the church's legacy of thought and practice regarding the birth process may illumine issues for the church today as it seeks to articulate a wholesome understanding of sexuality.

Fourth, pregnancy and childbirth provide a powerful and virtually untapped source of imagery and symbolism for preaching and teaching, liturgical art and hymnody, thinking about God, the church, and the human condition. Giving birth is a powerful memory and source of associations for those who have experienced it in one way or another. Birthing, with its blood, sweat, and tears, is one of the most vital, life-and-death experiences that our convenient, mechanized, insulated environment still affords. The preacher or hymnist can tap this well of memory, emotion, and insight. Those who have not personally experienced any birth other than the veiled memory of their own can certainly imagine birthing at least as well as they can imagine marching off to war or prostrating themselves before a monarch.

Finally, pastoral and theological attention to childbirth provides a natural point of contact with young families, both inside and outside the church. The childbearing year is a propitious moment for the church to establish vital pastoral connections with people. Conscious and concerted attention to the questions, hopes, fears, and struggles of families adjusting to a new child may enrich and deepen congregational bonding and communal life, as well as benefit the expecting and new parents. Similarly, an engaging ministry to expecting and new parents and siblings can be an attractive and healthy form of outreach to the unchurched community.

There are, then, many good reasons for seeking to bridge the gap that currently exists between secular birthing literature on the one hand, and Christian theological studies on the other. This book is dedicated to beginning to build that bridge.

The task of the chapters that follow is primarily to gather bridge-building materials—from the Bible, from the church's history and thought, and from contemporary secular studies of the birthing year. These building blocks will include both reflections on the dynamics of human birthing and consideration of birthing imagery used to envision God. This study focuses on the resources that are part of the Judeo-Christian tradition, in contrast to more pluralistic explorations of the feminine aspects of the divine. A thought-provoking, consciously Christian example of this latter strategy is Sallie McFague's *Models of God.* McFague challenges readers to ponder what it might mean for our idea of God to think of God as mother (and lover and friend), but specifically avoids limiting her inquiry to the imagery found in Scripture and Christian tradition.[9] The present study is more limited, in that it focuses on the resources in the Judeo-Christian tradition, and in that it focuses on one constellation of maternal images, that is, those emerging from pregnancy, birthing, and (to a lesser extent) nursing. In other respects, this study is broader—exploring the dynamics and circumstances of pregnancy and birth, through the church's history and as experienced in late twentieth-century North America, and drawing out implications for Christian thought and ministry.

This study is intentionally broad, touching on a range of disciplines. It is written from the perspective of a parish pastor, who obviously cannot claim expertise in all these disciplines; the entire undertaking may seem overambitious. I have ventured into such a broad range of fields in order to introduce a subject as multifaceted as it is worthy. I do not pretend to have exhausted the resources of the various disciplines; rather, the intention is more modest: to sample, prod, and explore possible areas of inquiry and development.

My research for this project has benefited greatly from the insights of feminist theologians, historians, and sociologists who have been working to recover the contours and contributions of female experience through the centuries. At the same time, this study is based on a firm conviction that the Christian faith and scriptures are fundamentally liberating and life-affirming, although as we shall see, the church's teaching and practice have too often suggested the opposite. While I realize that a feminist perspective and Christian commitment are viewed as antithetical by some on both sides of the issue, I have found feminist scholarship indispensable to this project of Christian theology. Much of the ground covered here has been generally overlooked by more traditional theologians and historians. Furthermore, I view feminist questions and interpretations as part of the Spirit's ongoing reformation of the church, which challenges us to peel away preconceptions, that we may return to the heart of our faith with ever greater integrity.

Finally, this work has been filtered through my personal experience as a middle-class American Lutheran pastor and as a woman who has given birth once by cesarean section, once almost before the midwife arrived, and once under the influence of pitocin, amid a tangle of intravenous tubes and fetal monitoring belts and cords. My American and Lutheran background is evident in the predominance of Northern European and American viewpoints as well as in my theological emphases, including the primacy of scripture. My experience as pastor has provided insight into the practical application of the material gathered here and has supplemented my own fairly varied experience of childbirth. My personal childbearing experience is hardly normative—still, along with the the birth stories of women I know, it has served as an important guide and check in my efforts to explore the dynamics of childbirth from a theological perspective.

The wealth of fascinating material I have found appeals to the encyclopedist in me, but makes a simple, straightforward exposition something of a challenge. I have approached this wealth of material with three basic questions. First, what meanings are attached to childbirth and what effect might these meanings have on the childbearing woman? Second, how do religious and social structures form the circumstances of childbearing? Third, how does the experience of childbirth contribute to theology? These questions are considered in various ways throughout the book. Furthermore, the book is arranged in three parts, focusing in turn on the Bible, church history, and contemporary applications.

The section that considers biblical perspectives on birthing begins with Gen. 3:16, probably the first verse most people think of when asked what the Bible has to say about childbirth. This chapter seeks to clear away common mistranslations and misunderstandings of this influential passage and to recover its insights into the dynamics of childbirth and the divine-human relationship.

The second chapter gathers perspectives on the process and circumstances of childbirth from the Hebrew Bible. Hebrew naming practices, legal codes, laments and psalms of praise, and stories of extraordinary births are examined for their insights into divine-human interplay in birth, the value placed on childbearing, and its social structuring.

The third chapter explores the Hebrew Bible's metaphorical use of pregnancy, birth, and breastfeeding. Passages that describe God as a birthing or nursing mother are relatively few in number, but demonstrate surprising variety. These metaphors link God to humanity, drawing on female experiences of strength, creativity, and compassion, as well as tenderness and nurture. This chapter explores these metaphors and suggests reasons for their rare appearance in the Bible. It goes on to explore childbirth metaphors as applied to God's people, examining how the people's travail is both like and unlike that of God.

The final chapter of the biblical section will follow these themes into the New Testament, exploring the impact of Jesus' own birth, as well as the views he expressed on childbirth and motherhood, and New Testament writers' use of birthing and nursing imagery. This chapter asks whether Christian expansion of the definition of family implies a devaluation of divine activity and blessing in childbirth, grapples with 1 Timothy's reference to woman being "saved through childbearing," and finds that the travail of God's people and all creation has a new tone in the New Testament.

The second group of chapters turns to church history. The sheer volume of material that might be investigated presents a formidable task, and these chapters do not pretend to muster a complete collection of the church's views and practice regarding childbirth over the centuries. Three ages stand out as being of particular significance, however. First, the early church's reconsideration of the blessing of procreation; second, the medieval period, with its tradition of spiritual parenthood and its heightened sense of childbirth as a spiritually vulnerable occasion; and finally, the renewed appreciation of procreation that was ushered in with the Reformation.

The first of these chapters looks at the impact the ascetic movement in the early church had on views of procreation. This study focuses on the attraction of the celibate ideal, especially for women; the emergence of a two-tiered structure of the church in which celibacy occupied a more elevated position than marriage and procreation; and the doctrines of the virgin birth and infant baptism, and on Augustine's teaching regarding original sin, which had implications for the way sexuality in general, and childbirth in particular, were viewed for centuries to come.

The second chapter looks into the medieval traditions of spiritual motherhood, particularly as they blossom in devotional metaphors that address Christ as birthing mother, in some female saints' experience of mystic pregnancy, and in Julian of Norwich's trinitarian insights into the motherhood of God. This chapter also confronts the troubling legacy of the witch-hunts, which have their roots in this period. Of special concern is the connection made by witch-hunters between witches and midwives. Finally, this chapter looks into changing emphases and understandings of church rituals associated with childbirth, primarily infant baptism and rites for the churching of women.

The final chapter in this section surveys the changing conceptions of childbirth introduced by the Reformation. Martin Luther's life and thought is explored as an example of and spokesman for the sweeping changes of his time, changes that elevated the vocation of Christian motherhood at the expense of the celibate ideal. Cotton Mather and Anne Hutchinson are studied as varying examples of the Puritan tendency to see childbirth as an occasion to consider the state of one's soul. The chapter concludes with Søren Kierkegaard's reformulation of Augustine's doctrine of inherited sin, and his protest against the "familyism" that had emerged in the Protestant churches.

The third section lifts up childbirth's possibilities for theology and ministry. The first chapter explores how the dynamics of birth can illuminate the human condition. This inquiry begins with wonder and the sense of miracle, then deals with the perception and interpretation of birthing pain, and examines the physical, moral, and spiritual trial of pregnancy and childbirth.

The second chapter suggests ways the church can be a source of healing and meaning in childbirth and ways it can integrate childbirth more fully into its own communal life. These suggestions build on ministries and structures that are often already in place, including considerations for pastoral care, childbirth education and alternatives, devotional resources, advocacy, vocational support for health-care providers, and public worship. These ideas are presented in the hope that they may initiate a creative process in local settings. Important areas like church art and hymnody are missing, not because of a lack of appropriate applications, but rather because of the limits of this author's competence.

The final chapter begins to draw together the implications of the preceding chapters for our understanding of God. God our Mother is proposed as a biblically and theologically sound metaphor that complements more familiar metaphors and expands our appreciation of the God who cannot be limited to any one human formulation. I hope these reflections on the motherhood of God will empower our imagination, inspire our will and compassion, and overflow in celebration and sharing of the gifts of life and new life.

But as travail comes before joy, let us turn first to the difficult questions surrounding human birth. Why is the joy of childbirth overshadowed by suffering and danger? Why do human beings created in God's image bear young so messily and physically—are we just another animal after all? Throughout the ages people have struggled with such questions. And from the first pages of Genesis, God's people have brought those searching questions to God—and have received responses, if not always definitive answers. Let us turn, then, to the beginning, with the why of birth and suffering.

Notes

1. *Imprints: Birth and Life Bookstore's review newsletter/catalog* (7001 Alonzo Ave. N.W., Seattle, Wash. 98107: fall 1987), 2.

2. Ibid., 18. Both titles are by Helen Wessel: *Natural Childbirth and the Christian Family*, 4th rev. ed. (New York: Harper & Row, 1983); and *Under the Apple Tree: Marrying, Birthing, Parenting* (Fresno, California: Bookmates International, 1981).

3. For example, Augsburg Publishing House Supply Catalog, 1987–88, offers *Gift in My Arms: Thoughts for New Mothers* and *Meditations for the New Mother*.

4. For example, *Occasional Services: A Companion to Lutheran Book of Worship* (Minneapolis: Augsburg, 1982), 53–56. Compare Frank Colquhoun, ed., *Prayers for Every Occasion* (New York: Morehouse-Barlow, 1974), which includes eight prayers for childbirth.

5. George Appleton, ed., *The Oxford Book of Prayer* (Oxford: Oxford University Press, 1985). Compare *The Hodder Book of Christian Prayers* (London: Hodder and Stoughton, 1986), compiled by Tony Castle. Billed as "Over 1,000 prayers from 450 sources," this anthology offers numerous prayers for family, including one for a newborn child and none for or by pregnant or birthing women.

6. Whether or not we like it, childbearing, or the decision not to bear children, continues to have considerable impact on the way a woman is perceived and the way she perceives herself.

7. Lyman Lundeen, "Turning Points in Feminist Theology," *Word and World,* 8 (fall 1988): 354. Lundeen is not hostile to feminist theology—he describes himself as having "an interest in the feminist movement and a stake in its theological impact," 349, and concludes his essay hoping for honest theological partnership between the sexes, 356. His concerns reached a larger audience via Corinne Chilstrom, as quoted in *The Lutheran* 3, no. 12 (December 1990): 38: " 'Women speak of how the birthing experience, for example, opens up for them

new theological interpretation,' she said. 'They elevate motherhood and diminish the new birth in Christ.' "

8. Lynn N. Rhodes, *Co-Creating: A Feminist Vision of Ministry* (Philadelphia: Westminster Press, 1987), 14.

9. Sallie McFague, *Models of God: Theology for an Ecological, Nuclear Age* (Philadelphia: Fortress Press, 1987), 36f.

Part 1
Biblical Perspectives

1
Birthing and Suffering: Why?

Why is the joy of bringing new life into the world accompanied by pain and suffering? The majesty of God's creative work in Gen. 1 and the delightful love story of chap. 2 still resonate in the reader's mind as Eden begins to unravel in chap. 3. By Gen. 3:16, readers are confronted with conditions of existence that have troubled generation upon generation of the human race:

> To the woman he said,
> "I will greatly multiply your pain in childbearing;
> in pain you shall bring forth children,
> yet your desire shall be for your husband,
> and he shall rule over you."

Why this pain? Many a husband must have wondered this as he saw and heard his wife experiencing a difficult labor; many a pregnant woman has probably also wondered as she listened to some of the stories told by survivors of traumatic birthing experiences. Such experiences lead to a fundamental theological question: How could a loving, creative God order such pain?

Does the God of the Bible indeed order pain in childbirth? Writers as diverse as Christian childbirth educator Helen Wessel and feminist biblical scholar Carol Meyers agree that reading pain into Gen. 3:16 is a culturally conditioned misunderstanding.[1]

Thirty years ago, Wessel challenged traditional interpretations of the first half of this verse in her popular book, *Natural Childbirth and the Christian Family*. Her critique, based on the work of Samson Hirsch, a Jewish rabbi of the previous century, focused on the translation of the Hebrew *'iṣṣabon* in Gen. 3:16–17.[2] The Revised Standard Version (RSV) translates this word as "pain" when it applies to woman's childbearing in Gen. 3:16, but "toil" when it describes man's work in Gen. 3:17.[3] Wessel concludes that "when the same Hebrew word is translated as 'pain' for the woman and 'toil' for the man, it is clear that the translator's cultural beliefs have biased his judgment as a scholar of the text."[4] The cultural belief in question is the assumption that birthing is inevitably accompanied by severe pain. Does this quibble over a translation have any practical significance? According to Wessel, such "faulty translations do a great disservice by misleading women into expecting pain and trauma at birth." This expectation may, in turn, become a self-fulfilling prophecy, as a birthing woman's fear of the process leads to muscle tension and hence to increased pain.[5]

Meyers, too, rejects "pain" as an appropriate translation for *'iṣṣabon*—on the basis of a syntactic as well as a lexical study. She points out that the verb of the second phrase of Gen. 3:16 "nearly always involves a concept of numerical increase." Pain, however, "defies quantification" and is thus an unlikely object for this verb.[6] Furthermore, Meyers studies the meaning of *'iṣṣabon* that emerges from the only other instances of its use in the Bible: Gen. 3:17 and 5:29. In these passages, *'iṣṣabon* quite clearly refers to distressingly difficult labor, thus Meyers advocates translating all three instances "toil."[7]

But does "toil" adequately describe womankind's trials in birthing down through the generations? Toil implies prolonged and fatiguing labor, but falls short of conveying the acute physical distress that is part of most women's birthing experience. "Pain" may overemphasize that distress, but it would be foolish and counterproductive to pretend that the discomfort caused by strong uterine contractions is illusory or avoidable.[8]

Meyers, however, suggests that this discussion may be beside the point. Indeed, she rejects entirely the commonly held view that this phrase describes the conditions of human parturition. She shows that the Hebrew word *heron* (translated "childbearing" in the RSV in the second phrase of Gen. 3:16) refers not to parturition, but to pregnancy.[9] Moreover, Meyers does not believe that " *'issabon*" was intended to describe pregnancy. Instead she sees the two nouns as coordinate concepts that together aptly reflect the probable situation of early Israelite women pioneering in the marginally productive highlands of Palestine: much toil and many pregnancies.[10]

Equally plausible from a grammatical point of view, however, is the reading "your toil in pregnancy." This translation is less tied to the earliest context of the verse and better reflects the universal scope of the story in which the verse is embedded. It points to the increased toil involved in any pregnancy as ongoing daily tasks are compounded by the body's extra burden, and by practical and psychosocial preparations for the newcomer.

However the second phrase of the verse is read, *'issabon*'s parallel in the third phrase (*'eseb*, also translated "pain" in the RSV) is clearly intended to describe woman's procreative experience.[11] As the RSV translation indicates, *'eseb* is closely related linguistically to *'issabon*. The several other instances of *'eseb* in the Bible make it clear that here, too, "pain" is a faulty translation. Nowhere does *'eseb* refer unambiguously to physical pain. Only in 1 Chron. 4:9 is it linked to the birth of a child; there it is part of an etymology obviously based on Gen. 3:16. In most cases *'eseb* refers to hard physical labor, the fruits of which are ever in jeopardy. Proverbs 5:10, for example, exhorts people to steer clear of folly, "lest your labors [*'eseb*] go to the house of an alien."[12] The distressing quality of labor in most of these cases is probably linked to the meaning of the verb from which *'eseb* and *'issabon* are presumably derived. That verb, *'sb*, means "to grieve." This grief is not primarily associated with bereavement, rather, it is a moral sensibility. It can refer either to indignation or grief at being wronged, or to remorse at being in the wrong: the sons of Jacob were indignant [*'sb*] when they heard of Shechem's rape of their sister Dinah (Gen. 34:7); from the alternate perspective, Joseph counseled his brothers not to "be distressed [*'sb*], or angry with yourselves, because you sold me

here" (Gen. 45:5).[13] This verbal root is preserved in the King
James Version (KJV) translation of Gen. 3:16 and 17. There
both *'eṣeb* and *'iṣṣabon* are rendered as "sorrow." To distinguish
between the two forms, while maintaining the linguistic link
between them, we might translate Gen. 3:16c: "In distressing
toil you will bear your children."

In sum, then, neither *'eṣeb* nor *'iṣṣabon* refer to pain. Rather,
the bearing of children is described in Gen. 3:16 by associated
terms that point to arduous physical labor, the benefits of which
the laborer does not necessarily receive, and to the psychological
and spiritual anguish such a situation engenders. The Bible does
not say God orders pain in childbirth. Still the question, refor-
mulated, remains. Why this distressing, anxious toil? Unnecessary fear of pain may be removed, birth attendants may be
supportive and technological intrusions minimized, and still
birthing retains elements of danger and discomfort. Why is the
joy of birth overcast by distress of any sort?

Cultures around the world include stories that address the
origins of this situation.[14] Thus it is highly appropriate that the
Bible's chief response to this fundamental question is set in the
portion of the Hebrew Bible that is most universal in scope: the
primeval story of origins (Gen. 1—11). This response is generally
attributed to the biblical writer scholars call "J."[15] This writer saw
the ambivalent experience of sexuality as a basic human concern
with important theological dimensions and incorporated it from
the very start in the story of God's creative work and relationship
with all human beings. Genesis 2—3 celebrates human sexuality
and partnership as a God-given gift and attributes its distressful
dimensions to a breakdown in the relationship between human
beings and their creator.

Unfortunately, Genesis 3 has often been interpreted in
misleading ways. Its focus on humans acting *in community* has
been slighted, leaving Eve alone with the blame. Moreover, its
common label—"the Fall" into sin—has blocked comprehension of this multifaceted story.[16] Indeed, if we were not so
accustomed to hearing this story described in terms of crime,
rebellion, and sin, we would probably deem these quite exagger-
ated descriptions of the actions related in the Bible. In fact, the

word "sin" does not figure in this story at all, not even in God's own words of judgment. ("Sin" first appears in Gen. 4:7, in the story of Cain and Abel.) Genesis 3 does involve disobedience and punishment, but the story's explanation of the limitations and hardships of human existence is at least as important a motif. Thus Meyers terms the story a wisdom tale; it explains the origins of distressing aspects of human life and tells of the conferring of wisdom. Similarly, Tikva Frymer-Kensky describes Eve as a culture hero akin to Prometheus. Like Prometheus, Eve and Adam disobeyed the divine, brought culture to humanity, and as a result, suffer.[17] This story, then, interprets distress in childbirth (and work) both as a punishment for disobedience and as a corollary to the reception of knowledge.

The story leading up to the punishment is familiar: God completes the creation of the human being with the community of male and female; human beings in community then overstep the bounds God has set for them, and eat of the tree of the knowledge of good and evil. The story employs forms of speech that suggest both the intimacy of the family and the dignity and impartiality of the legal court.

The intimacy expressed here in the form of direct address between God and human beings is extraordinary. God addresses the prohibition directly to the human being, personally discovers the prohibition has been overstepped and calls the guilty to account, and personally addresses words of punishment directly to the man and to the woman. Such directness is not found anywhere else in the Bible.[18] The prose portions of the story will remind parents of the trials involved in getting to the bottom of children's misbehavior and of the unhappy task of imposing appropriate restrictions as punishment.

This mood of familial intimacy is disrupted by the somber, elevated rhetorical forms of the court. The sentences of punishment are delivered in poetry, corresponding to "the ancient legal pronouncements which are also presented in rhythmic and poetic form."[19] Genesis 3:16 is the second of three such speeches. These speeches (Gen. 3:14–19) are fitted into a story that already ended with a punishment that seemed sufficient for the transgression; that is, the human beings' expulsion from the garden in 3:23. The cumulative punishment that results may seem excessive for conspiring to eat a bit of forbidden fruit.

Note, however, that this punishment is not meted out by an angry ruler—nowhere in the primeval story is God described as angry. This stands in contrast to the Bible's descriptions of God in relationship to recalcitrant Israel and also in contrast to extra-biblical myths of origins (which often feature warring gods). Note, too, that these speeches contain some of the most realistic elements in the story. You and I may never meet a talking snake or taste a consciousness-raising piece of fruit; but we do know about toil in work and birthing, enmity between species, power plays between the sexes, thorns and thistles, and the dustheap that ends it all.

At some point in their history these divine speeches were probably independent etiological sagas, serving to provide explanations for the limitations and needs of human experience. Westermann points out that in the story as it stands, these primal experiences of need are taken up in a "convincing explanation of human existence as a whole and in its all-embracing ramifications, as having its origin in God, though disturbed by sin. The individual sentences in 3:14–19 lead to the expulsion from the garden. This means that every human limitation is in the context of alienation from God."[20] Thus the distress in the body and soul of the birthing woman becomes a symbol and reminder of the distressed relationship between God and humankind. Similarly, woman's continued desire for man, in spite of hardship in childbearing and man's domineering tendencies, attests to God's ability and desire to continue blessing human beings in spite of the obstacles introduced by human disobedience.

It could be argued that far from meting out excessive punishment, God is simply stating the obvious: when human beings ate of the tree of knowledge (and became self-conscious rather than simply instinctive creatures), discordant elements began to creep into their experience of life, not least into their experience of sexual relations and work. Their eyes were opened to life's ambiguities; anxiety came to accompany anticipation; human community with one another, God, and the world was disrupted. The individual speeches simply point out the nitty-gritty implications of being expelled from paradise.

God does pronounce these individual punishments, however, speaking directly to each actor in the drama. Thus the discord that has entered life cannot be written off as the impersonal working out of the ill effects of eating forbidden fruit. God involves Godself in the new situation. This is particularly clear in the punishment spoken to the woman and to the man. Contrary to prevalent and deeply ingrained suppositions, neither of them is cursed. This point cannot be emphasized strongly enough: In contrast to the snake and the earth, the human beings are not cursed. Both are held individually responsible for their actions and punished accordingly. The Bible does not describe the distress and toil of childbirth (much less the process of menstruation) as "the curse;"[21] no curse is even indirectly connected to the woman.[22]

The underlying traditions may have been in the form of curses at some point in their history;[23] as the text stands, however, the intertwining of curses and words of punishment serves to highlight the distinctiveness of the human beings. The nonhuman world suffers under a curse; the human beings are held personally accountable for their actions. Humans experience adversity and distress in moral terms, as a punishment. This punishment, in turn, stands as a reminder of human rights and responsibilities before God. This is particularly significant for woman. The word of punishment directed specifically to her attests to her standing as a person responsible before God. She is not consigned to moral or spiritual dependence on the man, in sharp contrast to the actual treatment of women in many times and places. Birthing, the point at which woman seems most governed by her biology, becomes the point at which woman is most vividly reminded that she is a spiritual being, related to and responsible before God.

In sum, this punishment reflects human dignity before God; it is pronounced by a God who cares enough about human beings to hold them personally accountable and to continue in relationship to them even when they disregard the one ground rule they have been given. Genesis 3 doesn't solve the mystery of human suffering; it does set this mystery in the context of alienation from God. In so doing, it transforms mundane toil and suffering into a reminder of human dignity and accountability amid the ambiguities of life as we know it.

Furthermore, Gen. 3:16 is not a wholly miserable punishment. The blessing of childbearing has been complicated, but not eradicated; its joys overshadowed, but not obliterated. As Leonhard Rost sees it, "Punishment is suggested only by the emphasis put on the labor and effort; the remaining statements on the contrary express in part a blessing." Rost sees a "formula of conferring" from the ritual of the initiation ceremony behind 3:16.[24] Similarly, some cultures still make a practice of telling a birthing woman a story to release her from difficulties in childbirth.[25]

Can we retell Gen. 3:16 in a way that highlights its expression of God's continuing concern and respect for woman and that becomes a source of healing and spiritual nurture for women as they give birth? Obviously such a retelling would need to be carefully done; the thicket of unfortunate interpretations that has grown up around this story presents a formidable obstacle. From the midst of this bramble, and in the midst of this very physical process, though, God's personally delivered message rings loud and clear: "I will greatly multiply your toil in pregnancy; in distressing toil you will bear your children." "Greatly multiplying" (literally "in multiplying I will multiply") may again seem excessive, but these words do lift whatever distress childbirth involves from the plane of animal suffering to the plane of punishment, and this punishment expresses (albeit in a negative way) human dignity and continuing relationship to God. Indeed, this particular construction of "multiply" resounds in God's *blessing* in the only other places it appears (of Hagar in Gen. 16:10 and of Abraham in Gen. 22:17). There, in the aftermath of life-threatening crises, God promises to multiply not distress but descendants.

And within a few chapters it will become clear that the distress that now characterizes human birthing and work is shared by the same God who pronounces the sentence: In Gen.

6:6 God sees the utter wickedness of humankind on earth and is grieved (*'sb*) at heart. God sorrowfully resolves to relieve the poor earth of human beings and the misery that has been wrought by their hand. A reprieve for the human race comes through Noah—the one whose name destines him to provide relief from the distress (*'iṣṣabon*) first described in Gen. 3:17.[26] Relief for woman's distress goes unmentioned for the time being; and for that matter, the relief Noah ended up providing was probably not quite what his aging father had in mind when he chose and explained Noah's name! Nevertheless, it is important to note that already as the ark bears the hope of a new generation through the flood's cleansing waters, relief from the effects of human disobedience is in sight.

Relief from the multiplied distress of birthing may not yet be on the horizon in the Hebrew Bible, but a reminder of God's continued blessing is only a few verses away in 3:20: "The man called his wife's name Eve, because she was the mother of all living." Let us now turn to the story of God's continued involvement in childbirth.

Notes

1. Helen Wessel, *Natural Childbirth*, 65ff., 172ff. Carol Meyers, *Discovering Eve: Ancient Israelite Women in Context* (New York: Oxford University Press, 1988), 100ff. Meyers writes in her preface that her book is "a project of the university" that benefited significantly from the seminars of the women's studies department. Wessel's work, on the other hand, emerges from the natural childbirth movement inspired by Grantly Dick-Read. (For the religious and social views of Dick-Read, see Richard W. Wertz and Dorothy C. Wertz, *Lying-In*, 183ff.)

2. Wessel, *Natural Childbirth*, 67. (Wessel subsumes *'iṣṣabon* and the closely related *'eṣeb* under one, slightly different transliteration: *etsev*.) Compare Rabbi Samson Raphael Hirsch, *The Pentateuch*, vol. 1, *Genesis*, trans. Isaac Levy (London: Isaac Levy, 1959).

3. Compare the *Good News Bible: The Bible in Today's English Version* (TEV) Gen. 3:16, which reads, "your *trouble* in pregnancy and your *pain* in giving birth"; 3:17 reads "you *will have to work hard*, (emphasis added). The *Jerusalem Bible* (JB) uses "pains" and "in pain"

in 3:16 and "with suffering" in 3:17. Unfortunately, the New Revised Standard Version (NRSV), which intentionally avoids unnecessary masculine translations, retains the RSV's gender-specific translation: "pangs" and "pain" in Gen. 3:16; "in toil" in 3:17.

4. Helen Wessel, "Childbirth in the Bible," Position Paper 4 (Fresno, Calif.: Apple Tree Family Ministries, 1988), 2; cf. *Natural Childbirth,* 65f.

5. Wessel, *Natural Childbirth,* 9. Might this mistranslation also reflect and contribute to a broader cultural expectation that woman is doomed to suffer physical pain, while man suffers primarily due to stressful work?

6. Meyers, *Discovering Eve,* 99f.

7. Ibid., 104 f.

8. Compare Sheila Kitzinger, *The Experience of Childbirth* (New York: Taplinger, 1972), 20.

9. Meyers, *Discovering Eve,* 102f. Meyers agrees on this point with TEV; cf. King James Version: "conceptions."

10. Ibid., 105, 118, cf. 62. Thus Meyers translates: "I will greatly increase your toil and your pregnancies." Meyers suggests that this increase of both toil and pregnancies reflects the particular situation of Israelite settlers, seen in contrast to the less demanding circumstances of their neighbors.

11. The verb in the third phrase (*yld*) is usually translated "beget" when the subject is male, or "bear children" when the subject is female. Meyers argues that *yld* refers to the status of parenthood when it is used transitively, as it is here. Thus in spite of the female subject, she translates *yld* "beget" here, in order to indicate that "it does *not* connote physical childbirth," Meyers, 106. I find this argument strained. It is well to expand our notion of *yld* to include more of motherhood than several hours of labor followed by delivery, but not at the expense of obscuring (under a masculine label, yet!) the profound, singularly female experience of childbirth.

12. Pslam 127:2 and Prov. 10:22 make clear that it is God's blessing, rather than human toil, that gives fruits and peace, but cf. Prov. 14:23. The oppressive circumstances in which this labor may be exerted are most clear in Isa. 14:3 and 58:3.

13. Other instances include Gen. 6:6; Neh. 8:10; Ps. 78:40; Isa. 54:6; 63:10.

14. Compare Claus Westermann, *Genesis 1—11: A Commentary,* trans. John J. Scullion (Minneapolis: Augsburg, 1984), 5, 54; Stith Thompson, *Motif–Index of Folk Literature,* rev. ed., vol. 1 (Bloomington: Indiana University Press, 1955), A 1351.

15. Short for Jahwist, based on the name for God this writer used. Most scholars believe that J wrote during the early part of the united monarchy (i.e., ca. 1000 B.C.).

16. Westermann sees the community of humankind (in making mistakes as well as in joyful companionship) as a central feature of this story (*Genesis 1–11*, 192, 194). He argues that "fall" is an inaccurate and deceptive label for the story (275f.), but still sees it as a story of "crime and punishment" (193f.).

17. Meyers, *Discovering Eve*, 87ff., esp. 91. Tikva Frymer-Kensky, *In the Wake of the Goddesses: Women, Culture, and the Biblical Transformation of Pagan Myth* (New York: Free Press, 1992), 109f. Frymer-Kensky notes that up until the first century B.C., exegetical tradition did not locate the origin of sin in Genesis 3, but rather in Gen. 6:1–4.

18. The closest parallel is in the world judgment scene of Matthew 25. See Westermann, *Genesis 1–11*, 193.

19. Ibid., 257.

20. Ibid., 195; see also 55f.

21. Nevertheless, Stith Thompson's index lists folktales linking the origin of menstruation to Eve and the serpent. Thompson, *Motif–Index* A 1355.1.

22. Phyllis Trible, *God and the Rhetoric of Sexuality* (Philadelphia: Fortress, 1978), 126; cf. Westermann, *Genesis 1–11*, 261.

23. Westermann, *Genesis 1–11*, 257.

24. Leonhard Rost, *Das Kleine Credo und Andere Studier zum Alten Testament* (Heidelberg: Quelle and Meyer, 1965), 62; translated quote in Westermann, *Genesis 1–11*, 263.

25. Sheila Kitzinger, *Women as Mothers: How They See Themselves in Different Cultures* (New York: Vintage, 1980), 86ff.

26. In Gen. 5:29, Lamech calls his son Noah, saying, "Out of the ground that the LORD has cursed this one shall bring us relief from our work and from the toil of our hands."

2

The Blessing of Childbirth: Old Testament Perspectives

It is ironic that Gen. 3:16, with its focus on the distressing aspects of giving birth, has become the Bible's best-known comment on childbirth. Genesis 3:16 is important, of course, not least in that it acknowledges and finds meaning in even these distressing aspects. But childbirth as blessing, source of joy, and sign of God's presence is the more prominent theme throughout the Old Testament.

The acclamation of childbirth is apparent as early as Gen. 3:20. There the first man names his wife in a way that seems to reflect parental joy at the birth of a child. He calls her Eve (which in Hebrew sounds very similar to the word for life) and explains the name as shorthand for an important title: mother of all living. The story of the man giving his wife this name comes before anyone has become a parent, indeed before the first couple has even learned that they are to be put out of the garden. The words come from the man's mouth, but they are spoken in God's immediate presence, while God fashions clothing suitable for human life outside the garden (3:21). Thus God's blessing of human life is reiterated following the prediction of death, and God's help is seen to continue, in spite of judgment.

This naming story anticipates God's continuing, usually indirect, involvement in childbirth, and it opens a new chapter in the relationship between man and woman. No longer are man and woman simply lovers immediately delighting in being made

28

for one another (2:23ff.). Here the man defines a new circumstance: Woman will become mother, and a new series of relationships and responsibilities will emerge for them both.

The complexity of this new chapter in the couple's life is illustrated by contrasting interpretations of this verse. Trible sees very negative implications in it: Its language "chillingly echoes the vocabulary of dominion over the animals in . . . 2:19. Now, in effect, the man reduces the woman to the status of an animal by calling her a name. The act itself faults the man for corrupting one flesh of equality, for asserting power over the woman, and for violating the companion corresponding to him."[1] Westermann takes the opposite vantage point and sees human naming of the animals in Genesis 2 as a positive sign of the close relationship between humankind and the animals. Thus "the meaning of man's naming the animals is not, as most interpreters think, that the man acquires power over the animals by naming them. . . . But rather that the man gives the animals their names and thereby puts them into a place in his world."[2] If the naming of the animals is not a matter of gaining power over them, but rather a means of articulating a relationship to them, certainly the naming of Eve should not be seen as a word of subjugation. Thus according to Westermann, the purpose of the name and naming of Eve "is to express joy over motherhood whereby life is protracted into the future."[3]

This very naming, then, bears witness to the ambivalence that now characterizes the relationship between the sexes. Adam incorporates the new experience of parenthood into his life by giving his wife a name that expresses a new father's joy; but this name also signifies new roles that will disrupt the two lovers' initial intimacy, as well as bind them together in the shared responsibility of parenthood. The naming puts woman in a particularly precarious position; she is "being put into a place" in man's world, and the former relationship of mutuality and equality is ever in jeopardy. The woman silently receives a title of great dignity, but also risks having her personal identity swallowed up in this new role and title.

A few verses later (4:1), Eve takes her turn at naming—on the occasion of her first child's birth. (If indeed naming is a prerogative of power, women would seem to be powerful in the Hebrew family structure. Otwell points out that "mothers name children more often than do fathers in the Old Testament narratives" and continues wryly, "yet scholars have not taken this as evidence that mothers exercised more authority within the family than did fathers."[4]) Both namings express the miracle human beings find in the otherwise utterly mundane matter of birth—a sense of miracle that centuries and scientific models have not diminished or explained away. The naming of Eve signals Adam's joy at the birth of their first child, and bears witness to God's continued blessing even in the midst of punishment. Similarly, Eve's naming of their son reflects her exultation and attributes this blessing to God's working in and with her. Elementary biology and the role of the husband is acknowledged in the first part of the verse: "Now the man knew his wife Eve, and she conceived and bore Cain," but Eve's exclamation clearly looks to God as the source of this blessing: "I have produced a man with the help of the LORD" (4:1, NRSV). One translator even has Eve boast, "I have created a man equally with the Lord."[5]

Eve's bold interpretation of her childbearing is not corrected. Instead this verse stands as a vigorous counterpoint to Gen. 3:16. As we have seen, that verse described the downside of childbearing—the taxing labor, the physical, emotional, and spiritual distress, the potentially problematic dimensions of desire and dominance between man and woman. Genesis 4:1 picks up the vocabulary of the earlier verse (the conceiving and the bearing) and goes on to articulate the empowering, cocreative dimensions of giving birth. Thus Gen. 4:1 transposes the themes of Gen. 3:16 from a minor to a major key, and sets post-paradise life off on a joyful, life-affirming note.

Moreover, Eve's exclamation sums up the Hebrew view of conception: Every new child and generation of children is a result of creative human partnership with God. The Bible clearly proclaims divine involvement in human fertility: God repeatedly blesses people with the promise of abundant progeny (for example, Gen. 1:22; 17:5; Deut. 7:14), and heals women of barrenness (see below, pp. 33f.).

Tikva Frymer-Kensky argues that it was particularly important for biblical monotheism to emphasize God's ability to assure the ongoing fertility of "his" people, because procreation had always been the realm of *female* deities. Thus, according to Frymer-Kensky, the Bible portrays God as "the master of human reproduction," exerting "divine control over all aspects of pregnancy and childbirth." She even goes so far as to assert that "childbirth itself was not considered an *accomplishment* of women or men, for the woman was considered the eager recipient of the baby, and only God could make women pregnant. The true maternal role of women commenced after birth."[6]

Just what is the nature of God's involvement in human reproduction? Is the biblical God a "master" who not only takes over the domain of the goddesses, but also practically obliterates the value of human participation in childbearing? Hardly—the Bible describes God's unseen action in the womb with metaphors that suggest a considerably more varied picture of God's way of working, and texts beginning with Gen. 3:20 and 4:1 reflect a much greater appreciation for the human contribution to the process.

Let us look first at the Bible's metaphors for God's intrauterine work. One constellation of images describes the gestation of the unborn child in terms recalling God's work forming the first human from the dust. Thus Isaiah likens God to a potter who has formed him from the womb (Isa. 49:5, cf. Jer. 1:5), and Job reminds God that God had made him of clay (Job 10:8f.). Job also uses many metaphors drawn from the workaday world of women to describe God's work in conception: God poured him out like milk and curdled him like cheese (10:10); clothed him with skin and flesh, and knit him together with bones and sinews (v. 11). There is, then, something of a balance between metaphors drawn from the work of the craftsman and those drawn from the domestic sphere of preserving food and making clothing.[7] Far from representing a masculine god's incursion into female territory, it seems that the biblical God's involvement in procreation called forth the womanly aspects of this same, multifaceted God.[8] In any case, all these metaphors display an intimate, hands-on quality to God's work. And, in turn, child-birth and the abiding mystery of God's work within the womb become a sign of a still greater mystery: the work of God in all creation (Eccl. 11:5).

This variety of metaphors and connnection with all creation are eloquently displayed in Ps. 139:13–16. In words that soar beyond the limits of logic, the psalmist extolls the mystery of conception and God's comprehension of it all:

> For thou didst form my inward parts,
> thou didst knit me together in my mother's womb.
> I praise thee, for thou art fearful and wonderful.
> Wonderful are thy works!
> Thou knowest me right well;
> my frame was not hidden from thee,
> when I was being made in secret,
> intricately wrought in the depths of the earth.
> Thy eyes beheld my unformed substance;
> in thy book were written, every one of them,
> the days that were formed for me,
> when as yet there was none of them.

This piling up of sometimes contradictory metaphors (for example, the baby's being both knit together in its mother's womb and wrought in the depths of the earth) is a reminder that these lines, like the other passages considered here, are not the Bible's attempt at a biology lesson. In most cases, biblical descriptions of God's action in procreation express something of the speaker's relationship to God; sometimes, as in Job 31: 13–23 (cf. 34:19), they represent the grounds of the human obligation to treat all other people justly. Given this emphasis on the relationship between God and human, it comes as no surprise that the Bible does not limit its evocation of the mystery of God's action in the womb to physical formation. In the psalm quoted above, for example, the psalmist sings of God's thorough knowledge of the shape that the unborn child's life will take. Similarly, in Isaiah, God's Servant describes being called, named, and formed for servanthood by God—all while still in the womb

(Isa. 49:1, 5). So, too, the Lord's word of call to Jeremiah reveals a long-standing relationship: God had formed him in the womb and consecrated him there for his prophetic task; indeed, God "knew" Jeremiah even before forming him (Jer. 1:5).[9]

The Bible's metaphors for God's work within the womb consistently point to God's relationship to (and often partnership with) human beings—it is unlikely that such a God would overpower people in their procreation and thereby rob them of any sense of accomplishment in it. The Bible does view God as the enabler and ultimate guarantor of human fertility, but this need not imply that the humans involved are simply marionettes or passive tools and vessels. A notion so removed from immediate experience would require considerable indoctrination, of which there is no sign in the Bible. Instead, woman's life-bearing powers are extolled (Gen. 3:20; 4:1), and parents are credited in numerous genealogies (for example, Gen. 5, 10, 36).

Even the Hebrew belief that God opened or closed wombs (which is a crucial element in Frymer-Kensky's argument for God's power over reproduction[10]) does not obliterate the value of human participation. This belief seems to have been generally accepted, though evidence is scanty and often indirect. Direct mention of God's opening the womb, giving conception, or sending a messenger to announce an upcoming birth is reserved for special cases, primarily the stories of women who had been barren.[11] The Bible mentions a variety of efforts made by these women in hopes of conceiving—efforts that bear witness to a belief that human action could enhance fertility. Thus Hannah prayed and made a sacred vow (1 Sam. 1:10f.; cf. 2:1) and Isaac prayed on Rebekah's behalf (Gen. 25:21). Rachel and Leah struggled to gain the advantage of more frequent intercourse with their husband and bartered with fertility-enhancing mandrakes (Gen. 30:1ff., esp. 14–16). The value attached to childbearing itself is especially clear in the story of Rachel. Although Rachel's maid served as a surrogate mother and bore children for her, Rachel did not feel truly vindicated until she had borne a child from her own body (Gen. 30:3–8, 23).[12] Similarly, Hannah sings a victory song after the birth of her son: "My heart exults in

the LORD; my strength is exalted in the LORD" (1 Sam. 2:1).
Like the warrior who attributes success in battle to the Lord, the
new mother can praise God's power without devaluing her own.
In all these cases, conception was eventually achieved, as it
was for Sarah (Gen. 16:1f.; cf. 18:10ff.), the mother of Samson
(Judg. 13:2f.), and in the New Testament Elizabeth (Luke
1:36). These stories highlight how highly childbearing was
prized in Hebrew society. Offspring were an important blessing
(cf. Deut. 28:11; Ps. 128:3f.), and a woman's status and security
were closely related to her childbearing ability.[13] At the same
time, these stories provide an important check on any tendency
to equate barrenness with divine punishment: Too many of
Israel's foremothers had the same problem, and nowhere does
the Bible fault the women involved.[14]

Still, sprinkled through the Bible's legal codes, ancestral
stories, and prophetic oracles is the warning that in some cases
human misbehavior will prompt God to close wombs. Thus
Leviticus prohibits certain types of incestuous intercourse, warning that it would result in childlessness for the people involved
(20:20f.). The story of King Abimelech (Gen. 20:1–18) presents
a somewhat different picture. In it God closes the wombs of all
the king's wives when he takes Sarah in as a new wife. The
women whose wombs were closed clearly were not at fault, and
even Abimelech erred only because he had been misled by
Abraham. Here, then, the closing of wombs was not a punishment (nor was it permanent). Rather, it served as a drastic
warning that prodded Abimelech to search out his unwitting
offense in time to avert catastrophe.

This story also highlights society's vital interest in maintaining fertility: Abimelech's sudden impotence threatened his dy-
nasty and ability to rule and, ultimately, the welfare of his entire
nation (20:9). Indeed, the Bible shows barrenness as much more
than a matter of personal disappointment and source of interpersonal tension: Issues of fertility were of urgent concern to the
entire society.[15] God's procreative blessing was crucial to the
survival of a people struggling to gain or maintain a foothold in
hostile territory. The very magnificence of God's promise (for
example, descendants as numerous as the stars in the sky, Gen.

15:5) accentuates the importance of abundant progeny.[16] These repeated procreative blessings also meant that the Hebrew people saw the birth of new babies year after year as basic evidence of God's continuing presence among them.[17] Imagine, then, the impact of Hosea's grim prophecy of "no birth, no pregnancy, no conception" (Hos. 9:11). This oracle of woe envisions collective barrenness as the punishment of an entire society, a punishment that strikes at the heart of any society's ability to survive, and that would be particularly devastating for the Hebrew people, who viewed childbirth as a vital sign of God's presence among them.[18]

In sum, the Bible depicts God as the gracious, unseen enabler of human reproduction. The occasional stories of barrenness being healed serve as reminders of the miracle of every human birth, offer hope to the childless, and check any tendency to blame infertile women for their condition. The isolated instances in which the closing of wombs expresses God's displeasure all serve as warnings, and point indirectly to the great personal and social value attached to childbearing in the Old Testament.

The personal and social significance of childbearing is reflected also in provisions of biblical law that strike most modern readers as quite foreign: the law of levirate marriage and the purity laws pertaining to menstruating and parturient women.

The custom of levirate marriage bears witness to the value society placed on offspring's carrying the family name on into the next generation. According to Deut. 25:5f., the brother of a man who dies before begetting a son is duty-bound to take the widow to wife and to beget a son on behalf of his deceased brother. Sexual relations between a man and his brother's wife are otherwise absolutely prohibited (Lev. 18:16; cf. 20:21); thus the very existence of this legal provision expresses an overriding concern for the continuation of the family.[19] This substitution of husbands, and ensuing surrogate fatherhood, served important social functions. It provided progeny (in name, and to some extent in genetic makeup, although not in actual conception[20]) for a man who died before begetting his own son. It also provided for his widow's welfare; thus the law contains a means for a widow to deal with her brother-in-law if he avoided his duty (Deut. 25:7–10).

Although the levirate law is phrased in terms of saving dead men from oblivion, both Bible stories that include its practice dramatize the levirate's importance to the childless widow. Both Tamar (Gen. 38:6–30) and Ruth take considerable risks to acquire the security that is rightfully theirs under the levirate obligation.[21] Moreover, it is the provision of progeny for Ruth's widowed *mother*-in-law that gives her story its happy ending (4:16f.)[22] Naomi takes Ruth's newborn baby to her bosom and nurses him—an action that supplies a deeply satisfying resolution to the story of Naomi's predicament as a childless older woman, always threatened by hunger. Naomi receives and nourishes a son, who will in turn support her. The story shows both the vital importance of offspring and God's working unobtrusively with and through people to provide for them.[23]

Hebrew purity regulations bear witness to the significance of procreation on a still more elemental level. The rules that make up the purity system touch on matters as diverse as diet and carcasses, diseases and discharges—and as in any purity system, they carefully regulate sexual matters. Of interest here are the rules dealing with menstruation (Lev. 15:19–24) and childbirth (Lev. 12).[24] A woman is unclean for seven days at the time of her "regular discharge of blood," during that time everything she touches becomes unclean. At the end of this time, she is to bring two birds to the temple to atone for her unclean discharge (15:29ff.). The time of purification following childbirth is longer: seven days of uncleanness followed by thirty-three days of purification in the case of a male baby, and two weeks of uncleanness followed by sixty-six days of purification in the case of a female baby. Regardless of the sex of the child, at the end of the purification time the woman is to bring an offering of a lamb and a bird (or two birds, if she cannot afford the lamb), that she may be made clean from the flow of her blood (12:6ff.).

Initially, this association of sexual processes with ritual uncleanness not only offends modern sensibilities, but also seems to be at odds with the Bible's own view of procreation as divine blessing. Closer inspection reveals, however, that these very rules bear witness to the awe-inspiring, sacred nature of procreation. Mary Douglas points out that the meaning of defilement is difficult for us to grasp because of the modern view that holiness and impurity are at opposite poles. In primitive cultures sacred rules are "merely rules hedging divinity off, and uncleanness is the two-way danger of contact with divinity."[25] Thus the "uncleanness" occasioned by menstruation, sexual intercourse, and childbirth need not imply denigration of sexual processes. To the contrary, the strict regulation of these processes may well reflect awe of the reproductive process.

The mystery and drama inherent in childbirth readily evoke awe, the birthing flow of blood could only intensify the perception of divine power at work. Indeed, Leviticus describes the parturient woman's uncleanness in terms of the blood shed in birthing (12:7), and for Israel, blood is sacred. Blood is life (Gen. 9:4; Lev. 17:11; Deut. 12:23), closely related to the living God. The use of blood was a vivid and integral part of Israel's sacrificial rituals.[26] Because of the sacredness of blood, not even the slaughter of animals was permitted without ritual (Lev. 17:4). The blood shed in bringing new life into the world must have been awesome and threatening, not only for the woman involved, but for the entire community. Thus the postpartum rituals defined by Leviticus were deemed important, both for the individual woman and for the entire community's protection.[27]

Moreover, these rules are taken up in a holiness code with its own internal logic. According to Mary Douglas, the Hebrew purity system reflects two related concerns: that individuals be whole and complete specimens of their kind; and that the categories of creation be kept distinct. Both concerns are rooted in an understanding of the Holy as separate and itself characterized by wholeness and completeness.[28] A holy people will do its best to maintain wholeness and the separateness of disparate kinds. The holiness code sets forth appropriate ways to rectify the situation when disruptions of this ideal wholeness and separation of categories occur.

Thus the uncleanness of menstruating and parturient women may be interpreted in terms of loss of wholeness. According to L. William Countryman, for example, when menstruating or giving birth, a woman's "normal wholeness and completeness is being violated by the loss of something proper to her. Any breach in the ideal wholeness of a being or of its place in ordinary processes thus occasions a diminution of its perfection." This rationale assumes that "the normal state of a woman is nonmenstrual, especially in an ancient family-oriented culture in which the ideal woman married at puberty and, from then on, remained more or less continually pregnant or nursing until menopause."[29]

A new mother has lost part of her pregnant self; her body does require time to recover its nonpregnant state of wholeness. However, a logic that explains a menstruating and parturient woman's uncleanness exclusively in terms of lost wholeness leads to the peculiar conclusion that a woman loses perfection precisely at the points where she fulfills her ideal role as childbearer: first when her menses signal her ability to bear children, and second, when she actually gives birth to a child. Thus an explanation based entirely on a loss of wholeness seems inadequate. The concern for restoring the wholeness of the parturient woman might be better understood as the female counterpart to the special requirements of physical health and wholeness expected of priests and warriors.[30] The priest mediating between God and the people, the warrior offering his life in a holy war, and the woman birthing a child are all specially engaged in God's work in the world;[31] therefore their wholeness is vital.

Along similar lines, Otwell suggests that "the woman who had just given birth to an infant may have been 'unclean' because she had been too closely involved with the work of the deity;" and further, that this may also be the reason for the double period of ritual uncleanness following the birth of a female, that is, a child who would most likely one day herself be the locus of divine activity in procreation.[32] Here the purity system's concern with maintaining distinctions between the categories of creation comes to the fore. From a Hebrew perspective, the reproductive process involves a mingling of divine and human, which is as potentially dangerous as it is obviously vital: thus the careful regulations intended to restore the appropriate distinctions. Adherence to these regulations was expected to promote the woman's return to full childbearing capability and to protect the entire community.[33]

In sum, the purity regulations respond to elemental awe of procreative powers, recognize parturition's cost to a woman's wholeness, and reflect respect for the dangerously intimate association of divine and human in childbirth. On a practical level, these rules would mean that the new mother would be left more or less alone with her baby for the first week or two of its life. The infant is not specifically described in the holiness code as unclean, but it would be "contaminated" by contact with its mother in her uncleanness (Lev. 12:2; cf. 15:19ff.).[34] After a week of seclusion with a male child, the woman's uncleanness is no longer contagious, and she is to have him circumcised. This religious ceremony seems to have taken place in or near the home.[35] In any case the mother was not to touch holy things or come to the sanctuary for several more weeks. There is no parallel religious rite for a female child,[36] though the extra week of seclusion with a female child and corresponding additional period of purification might be viewed as ritual cleansing on her behalf.[37] These regulations, then, would have been of practical benefit to new mothers: Limiting their sphere of activity for six to twelve weeks after birth (a time frame similar to modern maternity leave) would allow for physical and spiritual recuperation, as well as for establishing a healthy relationship between mother and child. On the other hand, these regulations did mandate the periodic exclusion of women from public, and especially cultic life; and as time went on, "unclean" began to carry increasingly pejorative connotations.

The Bible offers few other glimpses into the circumstances of childbirth for Hebrew women.[38] Midwives were known (Gen. 35:17; Ex. 1:16), but may not have been called on in all cases. The God-fearing Hebrew midwives Shiphrah and Puah saved many Hebrew baby boys by telling the pharaoh that Hebrew women were of such lively stock that they delivered their babies before the arrival of the midwife (Ex. 1:19). These two courageous women were hardly telling the pharaoh the whole truth. On the other hand, their story must have been within the realm of possibility: The ruthless ruler let them go. Perhaps the pharaoh was taken in by the midwives' reference to the delicacy of Egyptian women.[39] This was not the last time that cultured women would be depicted as suffering more in childbirth than their primitive counterparts. This continuing assumption may have some basis in fact; hard physical daily labor may be good preparation for the labor of birthing.

In any case, it is likely that Hebrew women, like women in many tribal societies, gave birth alone or were assisted by the women of their family, except in the case of difficult labors. Biblical evidence is slight and varied. Song of Solomon recalls an idyllic birthing under the apple tree (8:5). That allusion to an open-air, unattended birth provides a delightful counterpoint to Gen. 3:16, with its foretelling of childbirth under the sorry shadow of the forbidden-fruit tree. Elsewhere birthing women are assisted: Rachel was assisted by a midwife at the birth of Benjamin (Gen. 35:16ff.), as was Tamar at the birth of her twins (Gen. 38:28). The wife of Phinehas was assisted by women (1 Sam. 4:19ff.). These are all stories of complicated labors; Rachel and the wife of Phinehas died, in spite of encouragement and assistance from birth attendants. These are the only two deaths in childbirth noted in the Bible, and both occurred in unusually stressful circumstances. The death of the wife of Phinehas was closely related to the traumatic news of death and defeat that induced her labor. Rachel went into labor while she and her family were in the midst of a dangerous journey. Moreover, her theft of Laban's household gods, coupled with Jacob's subsequent words promising the death of the thief (Gen. 31:32) probably robbed her of peace of mind as she faced the challenges of her labor. It is sadly ironic that Rachel, the woman so desperate to bear children that she pleaded, "Give me children or I shall die" (Gen. 30:1), should end up dying in childbirth.

Thus the Old Testament presents childbirth in all its complexity—sorrow and joy, difficulty and triumph, deeply personal and inescapably social—a vital and varied expression of God's blessing. Moreover, this vital experience gave rise to powerful metaphors for God's way of working in human lives, as the next chapter will explore.

Notes

1. Phyllis Trible, *God and the Rhetoric of Sexuality* (Philadelphia: Fortress, 1978), 133.
2. Claus Westermann, *Genesis 1—11: A Commentary*, trans. John J. Scullion (Minneapolis: Augsburg, 1984), 228f.
3. Ibid., 268.
4. John H. Otwell, *And Sarah Laughed: The Status of Women in the Old Testament* (Philadelphia: Westminster, 1977), 18.
5. Umberto Cassuto, *A Commentary on the Book of Genesis*, trans. Israel Abrahams (Jerusalem: Magnes Press, 1961), 1:196, cf. 198ff. Also quoted in Choan-Seng Song, *Third-Eye Theology: Theology in Formation in Asian Settings* (Maryknoll, N.Y.: Orbis, 1979), 135. The verb in question (*qanah*) can be translated "form" or "possess"; when the subject is God, it is often translated "make" or "create." See, for example, Gen. 14:19; Prov. 8:22.
6. Tikva Frymer-Kensky, *In the Wake of the Goddesses: Women, Culture, and the Biblical Transformation of Pagan Myth* (New York: Free Press, 1992), 97f.
7. Carol Meyers suggests that even the metaphor of the potter may refer to women as well as to men, *Discovering Eve: Ancient Israelite Women in Context* (New York: Oxford University Press, 1988), 148.
8. See also the discussion of God as midwife and mother below, 46ff.
9. Bear in mind that this Hebrew "know" means a "recognizing as the result of an encounter," and thus often means sexual intercourse (as, for example, in Gen. 4:1), Westermann, *Genesis 1—11*, 288. Here it suggests the greatest possible intimacy and relationship betwen God and the individual human being.
10. Frymer-Kensky, *In the Wake of the Goddesses*, 98.
11. The Bible says only twice that God "opened" a woman's womb (Gen. 29:31; 30:22). Elsewhere God "remembers" Hannah (1 Sam. 1:19); "hearkens" to Leah (Gen. 30:17); grants Isaac's prayer (Gen. 25:21); and gave Ruth conception (Ruth 4:13). In Gen. 30:22f. God remembers, hearkens, and opens Rachel's womb; she proceeds to conceive and bear! Sarah and Samuel's mother received special messengers (Gen. 18:10; Judg. 13:3). In one case, God "heals" fertility problems (Gen. 20:17).

The Bible states twice that God had closed a womb (Gen. 20:18; 1 Sam. 1:6); more often it simply notes that a woman is barren or that she sees that she is not bearing children (Gen. 25:21; 30:1; 30:9; Judg.

13:2f.). Compare Jacob's interpretation of Rachel's childlessness (Gen. 30:2), and Sarah's interpretation of her own childlessness (Gen. 16:2).

12. Other instances of surrogacy: Sarah and Hagar (Gen. 16:4f.); Leah, who experienced a pause in her childbearing after bearing three sons, and her maid Zilpah (Gen. 30:9). Note that only after Rachel and Leah tempered their rivalry enough to trade their procreative advantages (mandrakes for an extra night with Jacob) did Rachel conceive and the pause in Leah's childbearing cease.

13. See Otwell, *And Sarah Laughed*, 49ff. for further discussion of this topic.

14. David's wife Michal is one possible exception: Otwell interprets the Bible's note of her childlessness (2 Sam. 6:23) as implying that "she was being punished for sin, although we are not told what the sin was" (Ibid., 57). A more mundane (and likely) explanation is that she remained childless because her estranged and politically astute husband avoided her bed. David could have little interest in begetting a child who would be the late King Saul's grandchild.

15. Note, for example, Deut. 7:13f; cf. Frymer-Kensky, *In the Wake of the Goddesses*, 97, and Otwell, *And Sarah Laughed*, 50.

16. The magnificence of the blessing should not obscure the indications of fairly modest family size. Abraham and Isaac had but two sons each; tribal father Jacob's two wives and their two maids bore a total of twelve sons and a daughter, thus averaging approximately three children each.

17. Compare Otwell, *And Sarah Laughed*, 61.

18. Hosea continues by envisioning a punishment still more horrible: times so difficult that a miscarrying womb and dry breasts could be a merciful lessening of misery (Hos. 9:13f.).

19. The practice of polygamy may be interpreted in like fashion (Otwell, *And Sarah Laughed*, 43). Biblical accounts of surrogate motherhood (Gen. 16:1ff; 30:1–13) reflect a similar concern for progeny on the part of the wife.

20. In discussing the evolutionary advantages of altruism, Stephen Jay Gould points out that the chances of siblings sharing the same genes are fifty-fifty: "Your brother shares half your genes and is, in the Darwinian calculus, the same as half of you." Gould, *Ever Since Darwin: Reflections in Natural History* (New York: Norton, 1979), 262. Even in purely genetic terms, then, a son via levirate is "half" a son, much better than none!

21. Neither story reports the use of the procedure as outlined in Deuteronomy. In both cases, the widow must resort to a risky, extralegal measure.

22. Concern for a woman's progeny is also reflected in Judah's plea for his half-brother Benjamin's life (Gen. 44:20).

23. Studies of tribal childrearing practices suggest that Naomi's ability to suckle her daughter-in-law's child might not require any extra divine attention. See Judith Goldsmith, *Childbirth Wisdom from the World's Oldest Societies* (New York: Congdon and Weed, 1984), 113f.: "Early reports of infants being nursed by their grandmothers, long past childbearing and menopause, mystified anthropologists." Goldsmith cites numerous reports from around the world, many of them from this century.

24. For a discussion of the entire range of Hebrew purity rules regarding sex, see L. William Countryman, *Dirt, Greed, and Sex: Sexual Ethics in the New Testament and Their Implications for Today* (Philadelphia: Fortress Press, 1988), 28. Compare Otwell, *And Sarah Laughed,* 176.

25. Mary Douglas, *Purity and Danger: An Analysis of Concepts of Pollution and Taboo* (New York: Frederick Prager, 1966), 7f.

26. D. J. McCarthy, "Blood," *Interpreter's Dictionary of the Bible: Supplementary Volume,* ed. Keith Crim (Nashville: Abingdon, 1976), 115.

27. Given the purity system's concern with blood and bodily discharge, it is surprising that the proper disposal of the placenta receives no mention.

28. Douglas, *Purity and Danger,* 51ff.

29. Countryman, *Dirt, Greed, and Sex,* 26.

30. Douglas, *Purity and Danger,* 51f; cf. Deut. 23:10–15.

31. Compare Goldsmith, *Childbirth Wisdom,* 86. In tribal societies around the world, "a woman in childbirth was treated with the same respect as a man in battle. In fact, in the tribal mind, there was a metaphysical equation between the two acts."

32. Otwell, *And Sarah Laughed,* 176.

33. The closest modern parallels may be the rho-gam treatment prescribed for an Rh-negative mother following the birth of an Rh-positive baby. Both the rho-gam injection and Hebrew postpartum rituals are actions meant to ward off the adverse effects of a mixing of types that has occurred in childbirth.

34. Contrast Ps. 51, in which the psalmist asks repeatedly for cleansing and traces his sinfulness all the way back to his birth, and indeed his conception (v. 5).

35. J. P. Hyatt, "Circumcision," *Interpreter's Dictionary of the Bible,* vol. 1, ed. George Buttrick, et al. (Nashville: Abingdon, 1962), 630.

36. Luther viewed the circumcision of the male sexual member as the parallel to the suffering that females would endure in childbirth. *Luther's Works*, (St. Louis: Concordia; Philadelphia: Fortress Press, 1955–76) 3:134.

37. The mother's psychic task of separating from a newborn may also be more demanding when the child is a female than when it is a male. Researchers have observed that women identify more strongly with their female infants, and conversely that their relationship to their male infants is characterized by an early respect for the child's autonomy. Nancy Chodorow, *The Reproduction of Mothering: Psychoanalysis and the Sociology of Gender* (Berkeley: University of California Press, 1978), 109f.; cf. Ann Oakley, *Women Confined: Towards a Sociology of Childbirth* (Schocken: New York, 1980), 165.

38. Raphael Patai seeks to fill the gap with a sketch of Hebrew birthing customs, based on a reading of biblical texts in light of twentieth-century Middle Eastern birthing practices. *Sex and the Family in the Bible and Middle East* (New York, 1959). Patai notes that after the birth, the child's navel cord was cut and tied, the child was washed, rubbed with salt, and swaddled. The cutting and tying of the navel cord seems to have signified the formal acceptance of the child into the family, 186. Ezekiel uses the alternative, i.e., the rejection and abandonment of the newborn, as a metaphor for utter degradation (16:4f.).

39. Compare Frymer-Kensky's translation of this verse: The Hebrew women "are female animals who give birth before the midwife can come to them," Frymer-Kensky, *In the Wake of the Goddesses*, 133. I propose: "They *are of such lively stock* that they give birth before the midwife comes to them." This translation both retains a form of "live" (which is key to the story as a whole) and flatters the pharaoh by hinting at a similarity between these slave women and the rest of his livestock.

3
Birthing Metaphors:
Old Testament Surprises

A brief glance through the Hebrew Bible readily uncovers a wealth of metaphors used to describe God—creator, king, rock, and redeemer among others. Descriptions of God as midwife or birthing mother are easily overlooked in the midst of this profusion, but they are treasure well worth the hunt. Before searching out these metaphors, however, let us pause a moment to consider reasons for their rare occurrence.

The predominance of masculine imagery in the Bible probably is not surprising, given the patriarchal organization of ancient Hebrew society. The surprise may be rather that the Bible includes any birthing metaphors at all, especially when its persistent polemic against polytheism is taken into account. A biblical writer who described God as "she" as well as "he" would have risked suggesting that Israel's God was not one, but a couple.

Furthermore, the Bible's distinctive view of sexuality militated against the use of any sexual metaphor for the divine. Tikva Frymer-Kensky points out that the Bible shows sexuality as human, not divine. Thus while the Bible describes God acting in a variety of traditionally masculine roles, it does not describe God as a male in sexual terms: "He is not at all phallic, and does not represent male virility."[1] This stands in sharp contrast to the religions of Israel's neighbors, which viewed sexual processes as a central point of correspondence between human beings and the gods. Their stories told of gods mating and birthing, as well as

45

fighting and dying; their religious practices included sexual intercourse ritually linked to agricultural fertility.[2]

Describing God in metaphors drawn from the realm of reproduction risked blurring the biblical distinction between human and divine and the distinction between the beliefs of the Hebrews and those of their neighbors. From this perspective, even the "Our Father" language now so familiar to Christians emerges as a daring metaphor. Claus Westermann explains that God is rarely called father in the Old Testament because "in the world in which Israel was set, the physical fatherhood of the gods was a basic feature of thinking in terms of myth. The Old Testament will have none of this. Man is not God's child, but his creature. God is never designated as father before the postexilic period, and even then it is only on the odd occasion."[3]

In spite of these deterrents, biblical writers ventured not only to speak of God as father, but also to depict God serving as birthing attendant, forming an entire people in utero, giving birth, nursing, and aching with womb-love for her people. In turn, these Bible passages challenge today's church to reclaim and lift up the birthing aspects of the biblical God—whose oneness encompasses male and female, as well as transcending both.

Many of the Bible passages examined in the previous chapter use vividly anthropomorphic metaphors to describe God's involvement in childbirth. References to God's opening or closing wombs, and forming the babe there, may reflect a prescientific people's attempt to explain factually the process of conception and birth. Some of these passages, however, point to a more metaphorical understanding of God's involvement in the process.[4] In the two individual lament psalms that liken God to a midwife, the metaphorical usage becomes unmistakable. Here the birthing attendant who helps the child safely into the world becomes an apt metaphor for the God who receives and helps human beings from beginning to end (Ps. 22:9; 71:6). This Midwife not only receives the child from the womb, but protects the vulnerable human being at its mother's breast, going far beyond a midwife's duty by initiating and sustaining a lifelong relationship with the child.

More often, procreative metaphors are used to express

aspects of God's relationship to the whole people. Thus Second Isaiah[5] takes up the idea that God forms each person in the womb and applies the idea to Israel as a whole. The result is an engaging introduction of the Lord who is about to speak a word of restoration and blessing to exiled Israel: The God who formed the entire people from the womb and calls them by name (and nickname!) will help them (Isa. 44:1f., cf. 43:1). The God who formed the people remembers them, and should be remembered by them (44:21). A few verses later, the prophet again introduces the Lord as the one "who formed you from the womb" (v. 24). The Lord's subsequent words of encouragement to a broken and disheartened people call to mind the creative power and mystery of God's activity in the womb. These childbearing-inspired titles for God circumscribe the chapter's more conventional royal and battlefield titles: Initially the Lord is described in terms related to childbearing (v. 2); next the Lord is introduced in terms that flank "[Israel's] Redeemer" with royal and battlefield images (v. 6), finally "your Redeemer" is described by a return to childbearing imagery (v. 24).

This unconventional picture of God forming Israel from the womb is well suited to Second Isaiah's purposes, because it suggests that God's way of caring for God's people is about to take a surprising turn. No longer would God's power be assessed in terms of battles won by Israel. According to Westermann, the criterion from this point on would be "the dependable and unremitting continuity between what a god says and what he does."[6] This metaphor looks back to the God who formed and called this people, and forward to the same God redeeming them. In the meantime, this metaphor encourages the people by extolling their Creator's incomprehensible majesty and power, even as it evokes the intimacy of the relationship God has established with them all the way from the womb.

Second Isaiah had burst out with a still more startling metaphor in 42:14, where God speaks in the voice of a birthing woman:

For a long time I have held my peace,
I have kept still and restrained myself;

now I will cry out like a woman in travail,
I will gasp and pant.

This speech is extraordinary: The voices of women in the
midst of birthing are not recorded elsewhere in the Bible.[7]
Moreover, according to Terence Fretheim, this is one of few
divine speeches in the Bible that does not have linguistic links to
hymns or laments of the people. Fretheim continues, "Had we
the full complement of Israel's lament language available to us, it
is probable that no such language would appear to be peculiarly
God's. The human cry becomes God's cry."[8] One wonders how
the parallel human cry sounded, and how it might have been
used: Was such a lament uttered by a woman or for her? Was she
expected to hold her peace throughout most of her labor, and
then encouraged by such a psalm to find new strength in
unleashing her voice as the birth drew near? Were the sounds and
exertion of birth perhaps called up to express the lament and
commitment of people struggling to make way for justice in an
oppressive situation?

As it is used here, the cry of the birthing woman is juxtaposed to the cry of the warrior that dominates v. 13. These two
verses belong together, though many editors and commentators
assign them to separate units. Both verses proclaim God's
powerful intervention on behalf of God's people. The coming of
God as man of war in v. 13 reverberates with the language of
earlier hymns celebrating God's dramatic coming to his people's
aid in their time of need.[9] Then something new happens (cf.
42:9). The familiar picture of God as warrior, crying out as he
strides into action (v. 13) is transposed in v. 14 into God the
birthing woman who also cries out, finally casting off self-
restraint as the delivery draws near. The entire creation dries up,
as the intensity of labor has God gasping for air (vv. 14f.); the
child who has seen nothing but darkness is guided via an
unknown and difficult passage to a new world of light (v. 16). All
of this is as inevitable as the ultimate exit of a baby from its
mother's womb. The God who had seemed so silent and so
distant from his people in Babylonian captivity now speaks, in a
way that points out how close and life-giving she has been all
along. The birthing is underway, and God has the strength to

deliver, no matter how bleak or chaotic the situation looks from Israel's limited perspective. In the aftermath, man-made gods and those who trust in them will be exposed and shamed in their uselessness (v. 17).

This cry of God as a travailing woman presents a sharp contrast to the cry of the Babylonian goddess Ishtar, who also cries out like a woman in travail in the Gilgamesh epic. For obscure reasons the gods called for a great flood, then were panic-stricken when it happened:

> Ishtar cried out like a woman in travail, . . .
> How could I bespeak evil in the Assembly of the gods,
> Ordering battle for the destruction of my people,
> When it is I myself who give birth to my people!
> Like the spawn of the fishes they fill the sea![10]

The biblical birthing God does not cry out of fear or helpless regret. To the contrary, her cry signals a new phase of creative intervention in the lives of her people.

Birthing imagery is well suited to the historical circumstances of this new divine initiative. The people Second Isaiah addressed were sitting in the "darkness" of exile, historical events were about to propel them into a new life in a country many of them had never seen. Between the limitations of life in exile and potential happiness in their own country lay an unknown passage—a chaotic political situation, a difficult journey, and more unknowns at their destination. For such a people, birthing imagery could provide both assurance and admonition. Thus Second Isaiah assures the people, reminding them that God has formed them, and promises to be with and protect them as they "pass through the waters," and "walk through fire" (43:1f.). While the birthing imagery here is not as clear as that of chap. 42, the assurance of 43:2 is phrased in a way that calls to mind a child's journey toward birth—its movement through the birth waters, and emergence through its mother's "ring of fire."[11] Read this way, the verse alludes to imminent new life, as well as to help facing trials along the way. On the other hand, Second Isaiah uses childbirth imagery to admonish doubters, by underscoring God's creative sovereignty and unfathomable wisdom. Thus in 45:10, God reprimands anyone foolish enough to ask a father what he is begetting, or a mother what she is birthing. Even an outside observer would be out of line asking a parent such a question; for the infant involved to do so is as absurd and insufferable as clay trying to teach its potter a lesson (45:9).

In sum, Second Isaiah's picture of God draws on the unfathomable miracle of procreation, the intimate relationship between mother and unborn child, and the childbearer's experience of endurance, release, and power. If this birthing God suffers, we hear little of it—instead we see a birthing mother who experiences the waves of contractions, but is not overcome by them. The accent is on her creative and redemptive capabilities: Her word directs the course of events, she exudes strength and stamina. Creation suffers as God's contractions turn it upside down; God's people may tremble in the face of dramatic change. God, however, has reached the point in labor when suffering is submerged in the strenuous, exhilarating work of bringing new life into the world.

Jeremiah's allusion to God as birthing mother tells a different story. This prophet uses the vocabulary of travail to express God's (and his own) anguish at the doom that the people have brought upon themselves: "My womb, my womb! My very heart travails," as the first part of Jer. 4:19 might be translated.[12] In the verses that follow, God sounds very much like a birthing mother suffering through wave after wave of hard contractions (v. 20), wondering how long this misery will go on (v. 21)—and all because of stupid children (v. 22)! Perhaps the obvious anguish of the speaker is the reason vv. 19–21 have so often been viewed as an interjection of the prophet's own viewpoint: God could not be so intensely affected by human wickedness and punishment—could she?

Hosea pushes this theme still further: "The pangs of childbirth come for him, but he is an unwise son; for now he does not present himself at the mouth of the womb" (13:13). Prolonged labor is often a function of fetal malpresentation; though to the mother laboring hard to get the baby out it may well seem like fetal recalcitrance or lack of wisdom! Today such labors usually

end safely in cesarean section. Before surgical delivery was an
option, however, such labors were life-threatening for the
mother and even more so for the child: The child might well
have to be sacrificed to save the mother's life. It is hardly an
accident that v. 14 finds God deciding whether to save the child
from death. The pathos of the situation is heartbreaking: The
hardships of a long, painful labor culminate not in the joy of
birth, but in the loss of the awaited child.

These prophets, then, use birthing metaphors to express a
wide range of messages—varying from Second Isaiah's joyous
words of encouragement, to Jeremiah's evocation of the suffering human sin causes God (and God's prophets), and to Hosea's
dire warning. In addition to these "present tense" birthing
metaphors, a number of Bible passages look back to God's earlier
giving of birth. Although these metaphors all point to the bonds
of affection and responsibility that originate in birth, they are
used in a variety of ways: lament, admonition, praise, and
assurance.

Thus Moses uses a childbearing metaphor to articulate his
lament in Num. 11:12: "Did I conceive all this people? Did I
bring them forth, that thou shouldst say to me, 'Carry them in
your bosom, as a nurse carries a sucking child, to the land which
thou didst swear to give their fathers?' " If Moses didn't conceive and birth this people, who did? The implication is clear:
Moses regards God as Mother of the bellyaching Israelites. With
his thinly veiled accusation, he testily suggests that God has been
shirking her maternal responsibilities. Thus this passage also
offers a glimpse of a divinely appointed leader sharing in God's
maternal responsibilities—in this case as a rebellious wet nurse.

In Deut. 32:18, Moses uses the opposite strategy in a final
attempt to admonish the people. He appeals to their heart-
strings, reminding them that from within God's own being, God
had given them life:

> You were unmindful of the Rock that bore (begot) you,
> and you forgot the God who travailed with you.[13]

The first line shows a self-giving God—Israel is not chiseled from
rock by a divine sculptor, but rather born from the Rock itself.

The second line goes on to intimate God's labor and suffering in bringing to birth. Moses' point is that the people should remember this self-giving and life-giving God, and behave accordingly. He makes his point with a memorable picture of a parent unlike any other: Israel's God is not just "the Rock" so often addressed as a bastion of stability and protection in the Psalms; this Rock is as living, self-giving, and intimately related to the people as any human mother is to her child.[14]

Psalm 90:2, also associated with Moses, uses the same verbs as Deut. 32:18, and similarly applies birthing metaphor to solid elements of the natural world. Here, however, the purpose is sheer praise of God the creator:

> Before the mountains were conceived,
> or ever you had travailed with the earth and the world,
> from everlasting to everlasting you are God (author's trans.).

This passage is unusually daring in its description of God's giving birth to the natural world: Elsewhere in the Bible, God's birthing of creation is only indirectly suggested.[15]

More often, biblical writers remind the people of God's birthgiving as a source of assurance. In Isaiah 46:3f., for example, God presents herself as a mother who has borne her child from the womb and will continue carrying it, even until the child has gray hair. So, too, a few chapters later, God asks: "Can a woman forget her sucking child, that she should have no compassion on the son of her womb?" Can a woman forget the child of her own body—one who stretched her womb and snuggled at her breast? The bond between mother and child is one of the strongest conceivable bonds between human beings, yet even this paragon of human compassion pales in comparison with God's steadfast love: "Even these may forget, yet I will not forget you" (49:15).

Indeed, Phyllis Trible shows that this uterine metaphor lies at the heart of common Hebrew words for compassion or mercy. This insight enables Trible to uncover the latent maternal imagery of Jer. 31:20. In her translation, God asks:

> Is Ephraim my dear son? my darling child?
> For the more I speak of him, the more I do remember him.

> Therefore my womb trembles for him;
> I will truly show motherly-compassion upon him.[16]

Here God's commitment to her child is expressed in terms of an almost physical remembering: The womb still trembles for the child it held and hugged and birthed.

Similarly translated, Isa. 63:15 displays a lamenting people's appeal to the birthing bonds of affection:

> Where are thy zeal and thy might,
> the trembling of thy womb and thy compassion?
> Restrain not thyself!

This lament (which most scholars believe arose during the difficult times following Israel's return from exile) recalls God's earlier birthing cry of action (Isa. 42:14). Not only are images of warrior and womb once again juxtaposed, the people's final cry here recalls God's earlier self-restraint in labor. In a new situation of despair, they call on God to once again break the silence and act according to the urgings of divine parental love.[17]

Biblical writers also employ imagery drawn from the world of mother and young child. Thus Hosea 11:1–4 shows us God remembering Israel's childhood: God loved Israel as a child, taught him to walk, took him up in her arms, and healed his hurts. God led the child with cords[18] of compassion, "was like those who lift infants to their cheeks,"[19] and bent down and fed them. These happy memories are clouded by memories of Israel's persistent wandering away into trouble, and God struggles within as she contemplates, then decides against punishing this beloved child (11:5–9).

This scene of divine remembering and deliberation is preceded by a warning of impending doom voiced in terms drawn from the realm of procreation: The prophet invokes memories of mothers and children being dashed to pieces and foresees the king of Israel's progeny completely cut off (10:14f.; cf. 9:16). In spite of this dire warning, and God's parental patience, eventually punishment becomes unavoidable. Finally God's passionate love for her children can only be expressed as the wrath of a mother bear deprived of her cubs (13:8, cf. 15f.). This is the one biblical depiction of God as a mother who is a threatening figure.

Here God is no human mother cuddling her child, but rather a
fierce and strong maternal animal who would protect her young.
This unsettling vignette interprets even the terrifying expression
of God's wrath in terms of a parent's passionate concern for her
child. Israel has become his own worst enemy—not only robbing
God of her beloved child, but sealing his own doom by refusing
to be born (13:12ff., cf. above pp. 50f.). Israel's recalcitrance
threatens even God's life, and with it, all hope.[20] It looks as if the
child refusing to be born will die—people falling by the sword,
little ones dashed to pieces, pregnant women ripped open (vv.
14ff.).

Even after this grim pronouncement, Hosea extends an offer
of hope through repentance and concludes with a word of
restitution, in which God again is portrayed in nurturing terms as
the one who answers and looks after you, the tree who is the
source of your fruit (14:8). So, too, in the last chapter of Isaiah,
God promises to comfort Israel, "as one whom his mother
comforts, so I will comfort you; you shall be comforted in
Jerusalem" (66:13). In Ps. 131, Israel accepts the offer:

> I have calmed and quieted my soul,
> like a child quieted at its mother's breast;
> like a child that is quieted is my soul.
> O Israel, hope in the LORD from this time forth and for
> evermore (vv. 2f.).

With this peaceful tableau, we near the conclusion of this
survey of the Old Testament's childbearing metaphors. We have
followed metaphors for God along the whole span of the
childbearing experience—from midwife to nursing mother, with
lots in between. Indeed, this survey reveals that though these
metaphors are relatively few in number, they display considerable variety. They range from the depiction of an exhilarated
birthing mother to that of an enraged mother bear, from words
of admonition to words of assurance, from oracles of liberation
to oracles of woe. They depict God's creative power, and
passionate commitment to her children, as well as God's tenderness in caring for them and her suffering for their sake.

Before leaving these biblical birthing metaphors, however, it should be noted that the Bible also uses birthing metaphors to describe people, nations, and even the land. The insistent, irreversible waves of birth contractions, and the anxiety that may accompany them, become a metaphor for the response of people faced with situations of extremity that they are powerless to change or avoid. Thus warriors may have a heart "like the heart of a woman in her pangs" (Jer. 48:41; 49:22); a king facing defeat or retribution may tremble or groan like "a woman in travail" (Ps. 48:6; Jer. 22:23; 50:43). Similarly, Isaiah not only foresees the travail of people facing the impending day of the Lord (13:7f.), but also experiences travail in his own body and soul as he receives the vision of judgment and destruction (21:3). Whole peoples tremble and experience pangs at the power of the Lord (Ex. 15:14); faced with the prospect of imminent destruction, they are seized by anguish and sorrow, as of a woman in travail (Jer. 49:24; cf. Jer. 6:24; Joel 2:6). It may also be that the fear and anxiety of human beings facing the imminent, powerful, and holy presence of their Creator is an underlying point of comparison between sinners facing God's judgment and women engaging in the dangerous divine-human intimacy of childbirth. The very real danger of such close contact with the Holy is evident in that even the land trembles and travails at the judgment its inhabitants bring on it (Jer. 51:29).

These analogies are drawn from the downside of the birthing experience: the danger and distress, the inevitability of the process, and the attendant feelings of powerlessness. The joy and purpose of childbirth are nowhere on the horizon. This stands in contrast to the birthing metaphors applied to God, which rarely dwell on the distress of childbirth, focusing instead on the endurance and purposeful suffering of the birthing woman, and the enduring bonds formed between mother and the child of her body. The contrast between God the birthing mother and Israel struggling to give birth is nowhere more clear than in the lament of Isa. 26:17f. as worded in the NRSV:

> Like a woman with child,
> who writhes and cries out in her pangs,
> when she is near her time,
> so were we because of you, O LORD;

we were with child, we writhed,
but we gave birth only to wind.

The people here express their experience of God's chastening as unproductive labor pains. Later, Second Isaiah would point out that God, too, was experiencing labor pains during this time—with one important difference: God's labor pains deliver new life, even from the grip of death (42:14ff.; cf. 26:19).

Jeremiah records God's response to a similar lament. God hears the people's cry of panic and terror (30:4), sees all the men acting like women in labor (their faces pale, their hands at their loins), and asks, "Can a man bear a child?" (v. 6). The question drips with irony, and might seem mean indeed, were it not for God's subsequent words acknowledging the gravity of the situation and promising deliverance (v. 7). So too, God's questions in Micah 4:9f. prod the people to reinterpret their situation in more hopeful terms. The people are apparently crying out, feeling abandoned and helpless, like a woman in travail with no birth attendants to help her (v. 9). God questions the people's assumption that they are alone, then speaks as a midwife who encourages the birthing woman to throw herself into her labor, in full confidence of her eventual delivery (v. 10).

Biblical writers describe restoration, too, in terms drawn from the realm of childbirth. Jeremiah 31:8 envisions the restoration of God's people as God gathering the people and helping them march home. The procession includes those who would have difficulty walking—the blind, the lame, and those bearing the promise of new life—pregnant and even birthing women! God will help them along, "for I am a father to Israel, and Ephraim is my first-born" (v. 9). Isaiah 54:1f. depicts the coming restoration still more radically as the reversal of infertility. Barren women should begin even now to sing for joy and make additions to their tents, for they will be blessed abundantly with children.

As if this were not enough, Isa. 66:7 envisions a transformation of the birthing process itself:

Before she was in labor
she gave birth;

before her pain came upon her
she was delivered of a son.

This extraordinary birthing parallels the extraordinariness of a nation being brought forth in a moment; the people hear that they are in the midst of extraordinary events:

For as soon as Zion was in labor
she brought forth her sons (v. 8).

In the verses that follow, God promises to see this birth through and calls people to rejoice with mother Jerusalem, to suck from her consoling breasts, to enjoy her abundance and loving presence, a motherly presence that finally is one with God's own (vv. 9–13).

With this extraordinary birth we conclude this survey of Old Testament birthing metaphors. For all their variety, the underlying message of all these metaphors is God's steadfastness. Some express this message directly, calling to mind the bonds of affection and responsibility that originate in birth. Others make a similar point by interpreting apparent disjunctions (God's silence, God's surprising initiatives, even God's wrath) as phases of a relationship that, like pregnancy, birth, and motherhood, embody both dramatic change and a fundamental connectedness. Note, however, that this continuity and connectedness differs markedly from the continuity represented by the "Great Mother" who both gives birth and envelops her children once again in death. In contrast, the biblical Mother God struggles to give birth to the people as a whole, giving them an identity and liberating them to a life of greater freedom and responsibility. Moreover, death is never associated with the biblical Mother God except in Hosea, and there the association is no reunion, but rather a grievous breakdown, a tragedy.

At the very least, these biblical birthing metaphors expand our theological imagination, challenging any habit of visualizing God as an old man with a flowing beard. In addition, they provide a helpful depiction of God as both immanent and transcendent: As an expecting mother encompasses, nourishes, and protects her unborn child, God is both intimately involved

with creation and well beyond its comprehension. Finally, I find
these metaphors particularly affective. They not only evoke the
intimacy of the child-mother bond, but also draw human beings
into God's experience. We not only delight in nestling into our
Mother's bosom and feeding at her breast, but also shudder at
the trauma and danger human hardheartedness causes our
travailing God, and we exult with her as she brings to birth.

In the New Testament, God displays still more intimate
involvement in creation—moving right inside the birthing process to be born of a human mother's womb. The next chapter
turns to the new views of childbirth that were to follow.

Notes

1. Tikva Frymer-Kensky, *In the Wake of the Goddesses: Women,
Culture, and the Biblical Transformation of Pagan Myth* (New York:
Free Press, 1992), 188.

2. See Frymer-Kensky, *In the Wake of the Goddesses,* 50–56, 91f.

3. Claus Westermann, *Isaiah 40—66: A Commentary,* trans. David
M. G. Stalker (Philadelphia: Westminster, 1969), 393.

4. For example, the mounds of contrasting metaphors for God's
intrauterine activity in Job 10; cf. Ps. 139, discussed above, 31f.

5. "Second Isaiah" refers to the author of Isaiah 40—55. This
anonymous author worked 150 years after the first Isaiah, and addresses
a very different situation—after many years in exile, Israel was about to
be allowed to go home. Second Isaiah's deft use of childbearing imagery
is extraordinary; perhaps this anonymous prophet was a mother herself!

6. Westermann, *Isaiah 40—66,* 15.

7. The voice of a new mother naming her child is heard fairly
frequently (for example, Gen. 29: 32–35; 30:23; 1 Sam. 4:21; 1 Chron.
4:9); a lament from the lips of a pregnant woman is recorded in Gen.
25:22. Genesis 35:17 and 1 Sam. 4:20 record attendants' responses to
birthing women struggling for their lives.

8. Terence E. Fretheim, *The Suffering of God: An Old Testament
Perspective* (Philadelphia: Fortress Press, 1984), 108.

9. Westermann, *Isaiah 40—66,* 104; cf. Judg. 5:4f.; Ps. 18:8–16.

10. "The Epic of Gilgamesh," XI: 116–123, trans. E. A. Speiser, in
James B. Pritchard, ed., *Ancient Near Eastern Texts Relating to the Old
Testament,* 2d ed. (Princeton: Princeton University Press, 1955), 94.

11. The prickly, hot sensation some women experience in the

moments before delivery, when the vagina is stretched to its utmost, has sometimes been called "the ring of fire."

12. The Hebrew translated by RSV as "anguish" (KJV: "bowels") is elsewhere often translated "womb" by RSV (Gen. 25:23; Ruth 1:11; Ps. 71:6; Isa. 49:1); cf. Phyllis Trible, *God and the Rhetoric of Sexuality* (Philadelphia: Fortress Press, 1978), 45. The verb RSV translates "I writhe in pain" often denotes the travail of birth (Isa. 13:8; 23:5; 26:17; 45:10).

13. Author's translation, cf. NRSV. The ambiguity of the first line is due to the Hebrew word *yld*, which suffices for both the female and the male roles in procreation. Normally the gender of the subject easily determines the appropriate translation into English. Since a rock is neither male nor female, however, the verb could be translated either way here.

The verb in the second half-verse (*chil*), however, denotes the exclusively female experience of labor and childbirth. The translation "gave you birth" (NRSV) is a tame rendition of the visceral engagement involved in birthing. On the other hand "writhed in labor pains" (Trible, *God and the Rhetoric of Sexuality*, 64) tends to overemphasize the pain that accompanies contractions.

14. Compare Isa. 51:1–2. According to Westermann, *Isaiah 40— 66*, 236, the metaphors of rock and quarry in v. 1 "are allusions to very ancient mythological ideas about the birth of mankind from a rock or quarry," rather than references to God. Deuteronomy 32:18, where a similar metaphor is unmistakably applied to God, suggests that a choice between these options is unnecessary.

15. Job 38:29; Isa. 23:4; 45:10f. Compare the birth of wisdom, Prov. 8:24ff.

16. Trible, *God and the Rhetoric of Sexuality*, 50f.; see also 33f., 38f.

17. Compare Isa. 64:12. The verb "restrain" links 42:14; 63:15; and 64:12; it is not found elsewhere in Isaiah. Between 63:15 and 64:12, the poet shifts from maternal imagery to intimate "our Father" language (63:16 and 64:8), which stands unparalleled in the Hebrew Bible (cf. Westermann, *Isaiah 40—66*, 393).

18. The Hebrew root here translated "cords" (*hbl*) has associations with birthing language; one of its meanings is travail or birth pangs. See H.-J. Fabry, "*hbl* IV," in G. Johannes Botterweck and Helmer Ringgren, eds., David E. Green, trans., *Theological Dictionary of the Old Testament* (Grand Rapids, Mich.: Eerdmans, 1980), 4:188f; cf. Hos. 13:13; Isa. 13:8; 26:17; 66:7; Jer. 22:23; 49:24.

19. NRSV, 11:4b.

20. Compare Fretheim, *Suffering of God*, 142: "We have seen how

Israel's rejection occasioned God's suffering; continued divine restraint in the face of continued rejection must have meant greater and greater intensification of suffering, a build-up of internal forces in God which finally (though not uncontrollably) burst forth in judgment. At the same time, this intensification of suffering is spoken of in terms of weariness. This must have something to do with a kind of exhaustion of life, a giving or expending of so much of the self for the sake of the relationship that, for the sake of the divine name (that is, the future of God), it must be brought to an end."

4
Fulfillment and Childbirth: New Testament Perspectives

Few birth stories are told in the New Testament—at its beginning are the intertwined birth stories of Jesus and John, near its end is the visionary birth story of Rev. 12. These birth stories form a dramatic arch around the events described in the New Testament, each in its own way signaling fulfillment—of Old Testament prophecy, of history, of human being, of the cosmos itself. Similarly, the theme of fulfillment pervades New Testament birthing metaphors. Moreover, the expectation of impending fulfillment cast traditional views of family and procreation in a new light, thus giving rise to new understandings of the relationship between personal and social fulfillment and childbirth.

The birth stories with which Matthew and Luke begin their Gospels are familiar and joyful. John's birth, in particular, follows in the tradition of extraordinary births in the Old Testament. His mother Elizabeth, like Sarah, had been barren throughout her childbearing years when she conceived in her old age (Luke 1:7, 18, 36); the birth was announced by an angel, with instructions that bring both Samson and Samuel to mind (1:13ff., 36). Furthermore, Elizabeth uses words that echo Rachel's, interpreting her pregnancy as a sign of God's favor, which would remove the reproach she had endured (1:25; cf. Gen. 30:23). Similarly, the turn of phrase that introduces Elizabeth's delivery (literally, "the time of her bearing was fulfilled") recalls Rebekah's delivery (Luke 1:57, cf. Gen. 25:24).

In various ways, then, Luke links John's birth with all the extraordinary births recorded in the Old Testament. In addition, Luke states explicitly what was only implied in the Old Testament birth stories—that the barren woman involved is not at fault. Luke emphasizes that Elizabeth and Zechariah were "righteous before God" (1:6), and that the reproach Elizabeth endured was of human origin (1:25). Even as it gathers these threads from the Old Testament, John's birth story signals the impending fulfillment of God's promises. The very description of his birth bespeaks fulfillment: The fulfillment language associated with Elizabeth's delivery recurs as John and his parents are "filled with the Holy Spirit" (1:15, 41, 67) and yet again as Mary gives birth to Jesus and the attendant birth rites are performed (2:6, 21, 22).[1] Thus a turn of phrase, which in Rebekah's story probably indicated simply that she had carried her difficult twin pregnancy to full term, becomes a refrain of fulfillment in Luke.[2]

Both Matthew and Luke present Jesus' birth as extraordinary, even by biblical standards. Not only was Jesus born of a virgin (Matt. 1:18; Luke 1:34), his birth was repeatedly foretold and interpreted—by angel both to Joseph (Matt. 1:20f.) and to Mary (Luke 1:30ff.), as well as by a prenatal prophet and his spirit-filled mother (Luke 1:41ff.). The birth itself was heralded by angel choirs and a special star (Luke 2:13f.; Matt. 2:1f., 9). This child would be revered by future generations as God Incarnate, his mother as "Mother of God." Precisely this extraordinariness, in turn, affirms the most ordinary of birth processes: The simple fact that God would undergo the danger, pressure, and mess of being born human imparts new dignity to every human birth. The incarnation of God in Jesus communicates on a very elemental, experiential level that God is indeed with us even in the very extremities of being human.

Of Jesus' actual birth, the Bible tells us little. Was the labor long or short, difficult or easy? Those details are not recorded. We do read, however, that the circumstances were far from ideal: Mary and Joseph were traveling when labor began and were reduced to seeking shelter among the animals (Luke 2:6f.).

Despite the difficulties, and the dangers yet to come, the joy and harmony that pervade the scene have touched hearts through the centuries. The onset of Mary's labor is not described in terms of travail and pangs, but (as in the case of Elizabeth) in terms of fulfillment: "The days of her giving birth were fulfilled" (v. 6). Despite the awkward circumstances, Mary carefully swaddles the baby and finds a safe place for him to rest. The manger (whether a feeding trough or a stall, in the open air or inside a cave or simple shelter) provides opportunity for visits from animals and stars as well as from traveling Wise Men and local shepherds.[3] The open setting calls to mind the harmonious birth picture of S. of Sol. 8:5, as well as the human vulnerability of the newborn and his parents.

The birth story toward the end of the Bible presents a harsh contrast to these peaceful scenes. In the portent recorded in Rev. 12:2 ff., a birthing woman not only cries out and travails to give birth, but also is threatened by a dragon that stands ready to catch her child and devour it. Traditionally this woman has been associated with Mary, the mother of Jesus. More likely she is Mother Jerusalem bringing forth the Messiah, and/or a personification of the church in time of persecution, bringing forth the messianic king (i.e., the second coming of Christ).[4] In any case, this frightening story starkly illumines God's saving presence at the most vulnerable point of this crucial birth. As soon as the woman gives birth to her child, he is caught up to God's throne, and the woman flees into the wilderness refuge God had prepared for her.

The New Testament is written to people living between the joyful births at its beginning, and the endangered birth at its end, i.e., between the incarnation and the second coming of Christ. For Christians living in this meantime, the birthing metaphor is endowed with new significance. In Revelations' portent, the distress of birthing labor, intensified by an external threat to the child, becomes an apt metaphor for the difficulties accompanying cosmic fulfillment. Similarly, Jesus had characterized the upheavals to be expected before the end as "the beginning of the birth pangs" (Mark 13:8; cf. Matt 24:8).

Indeed, according to Acts 2:24, Jesus himself experienced

birth pangs as his death and resurrection ushered in a new era: "God raised him up, having loosed the birth pangs of death, because it was not possible for him to be held by it."[5] The birthing imagery—unmistakable in the Greek original—is lost in most translations. "Pangs" or "pain" is usually all that remains of Peter's birthing metaphor, sometimes even that is dropped in order to produce a smooth, sensible translation. The phrase in question (*lusas tas ōdinas tou thanatou*) is not an idiomatic expression that is just difficult to translate. On the contrary, the antecedents of its syntax are few, and nowhere else are the elements put together quite like this.[6] The difficulty, rather, lies with the metaphor itself, as it pushes the boundary of our comprehension. What in the world does the "birth pangs of death" mean?

Peter's use of such an unusual figure of speech here can hardly be an accident. This curious metaphor is at the heart of the first Christian sermon, delivered on the spirit-filled "birthday" of the church. With it Peter aptly communicates the creative purpose of Jesus' terrible death: It was not a disgraceful dead end, but rather the travail of bringing forth new life. Moreover, this metaphor taps into the language of messianic expectation current in Peter's day. As noted in chap. 3, the Old Testament had used the distress associated with labor contractions to depict reactions of helplessness and fear, not least the helplessness and fear wrongdoers experience when confronted by the Day of the Lord.[7] By the late postexilic period, this travail imagery had acquired clearly apocalyptic overtones—thus rabbinic literature spoke of the "birth pangs of the Messiah,"[8] and Jesus himself spoke of the birth pangs of the end times. In this milieu, Peter's words ring forth as a birth announcement for the messiah and the messianic age.[9]

This birth announcement transforms the metaphor Peter inherited, by suggesting an equation between messianic travail and Jesus' death.[10] Old Testament writers had used the traumatic aspects of childbirth to describe human fear of an impending ordeal. This fear might well include fear of death (as well as fear of pain and defeat), but travail is not compared to death itself. Furthermore, these descriptions almost always refer to people who are God's opponents in one way or another.[11] The association of metaphoric travail and divine punishment continues in rabbinic usage, which focuses on exemptions from the travail that will precede the messianic era. For example, according to R. Eliezer (ca. 90), "If you observe the Sabbath (properly), you will be protected from three punishments: the birth pangs of the Messiah, the day of Gog and Magog, and the day of the great judgment."[12] In sharp contrast, Peter proclaims that Jesus, godly though he was, had not been exempted from the birth pangs of the Messiah. Instead, he had undergone the most harrowing travail imaginable: death itself.

What, then, are we to make of these birth pangs of death? The clearest point of comparison between death and birthing travail is the common element of suffering. Although we do not know what death itself is like, dying (like birthing) often involves obvious suffering, and humans have at times projected this suffering into the realm of the dead. Most translators have followed this line of interpretation, thus rendering the birthing metaphor as "pangs" or "pain." Medieval mystics, too, proceeded from this sense of the metaphor. In their hands it yields provocative insights into Christ's life-giving labor of love on the cross.[13]

Even if death does not mean hellish torment, it implies at least the suffering of imposed separation from life and loved ones.[14] Peter alludes to this sense of confinement when he describes God as having "loosed" the birth pangs of death, as the cords binding a prisoner might be loosed. The Septuagint's translation of Job 39:2 suggests that this picture also resembles labor and delivery. There the birthing contractions of the hinds are "loosed" (presumably by God), that is, their labor is resolved in delivery.[15] Contractions do resemble bands tightening around the abdomen. Moreover, while a birthing woman may not be bound externally, she is subject to the power of her womb for the duration of labor. Labor starts and progresses on its own timetable—without regard for carefully laid plans and schedules. Birthing contractions are involuntary and intense—they restrict a woman's accustomed mobility and seize her attention. Anesthesia may eliminate these intense sensations, but only at the expense of still greater physical restriction and deathlike mind-body dissociation.

A second point of comparison is related to the first. Suffering and confinement sound like punishment—and indeed, as discussed above in chap. 1, Gen. 3:16 does interpret the hardships of childbearing in terms of punishment. Moreover, from the very beginning this punishment was set in juxtaposition to death: The Bible depicts it as a merciful punishment that represented a reprieve from death, the penalty predicted in God's Gen. 2:17 warning. The Bible's metaphoric use of travail was also often associated with divine punishment. In such cases, however, it did not represent a reprieve. Rather, it served as a portent of God's dreadful wrath. In Peter's metaphor, these two punishments merge—the distress of birthing in its most drastic form is more than a portent, indeed it becomes the very death penalty that God had originally laid down.

Jesus bears this combined punishment, but is not destroyed by it. Instead, the distress of Jesus' travail gives way to the joy of birth. Jesus did not remain locked in travail: God raised him up, because death could not hold him. This is a powerful message: Jesus has gone before us through the very depths of birthing— and risen to its joys. I have seen how the simple presence of an experienced birthgiver can comfort and fortify a woman struggling to give birth. So, too, knowing that the Christ who is always by our side has lived through travail at its worst will surely encourage and strengthen women as they face the uncertainty and demands of their own birthing labor. What, after all, is the worst thing that can happen to a travailing woman? It cannot go on forever—sooner or later her travail will end, either in birth or in death. Jesus' travail gives his followers hope that even the worst case scenario—death—is not the end of the Christian story.

Jesus' birthing travail begins in solidarity with humans— sharing their punishment, their suffering, their death. In contrast to earlier instances of God's people's travail, however, Jesus' travail is productive (cf. Isa. 26:18), like that of a mother whose travail culminates in a healthy birth. The suffering of Jesus' death, like the distress of a birthing woman, is resolved and redeemed in the joy and fulfillment of having accomplished an arduous, but vital task. In this, Jesus' travail also resembles Old Testament glimpses of God's travail; it is a purposeful, productive travail that gives birth to new life, new hope, a new people. This convergence of Jesus' travail, and God's, points to God's place in this birth story. Indeed, it could be argued that this is God's birth story too. In it God "raises up" Jesus, as God had raised up Moses (Acts 3:22), or even as children could be "raised up" via the levirate (Matt. 22:24).[16] From this perspective, Jesus can be seen as the child being born, as well as the mother giving birth; God can be seen as the parent raising up a child, as well as the midwife who looses labor pangs. In any event, God has been involved in this birth from the beginning: Jesus' earthly power had its source in God (Acts 2:22); he was subjected to the travail of crucifixion and death with God's foreknowledge (v. 23). Jesus' suffering is presented as an unavoidable part of God's life-giving plan (v. 23, cf. Luke 22:42[17])—just as birthing travail of some sort is unavoidable for a woman great with child.

Jesus' birthing travail represents a turning point. It articulates succinctly the creative purpose of Jesus' death and sets out a new course for biblical travail imagery. In the New Testament, birth pangs continue to be related to the Day of the Lord, but they are no longer primarily related to the punishment of wrongdoers. Instead, the travail of birthing becomes a metaphor not only for Jesus' innocent suffering and death, but also for the temporary and worthwhile (albeit difficult) trial faced by the faithful as the Day of the Lord approaches. Used in this way, the metaphor provides a word of comfort. It assures the faithful that like labor contractions, the chaos and distress that threaten to overwhelm them are of limited duration and serve a creative purpose.[18]

Paul expands this birthing metaphor to cosmic proportions: "The whole creation is groaning together and travailing together until now" (Rom. 8:22, author's trans.). Even Christians, who have "the first fruits of the Spirit," experience these birth pangs (8:23). Like a birthing mother, creation and Christians both groan (v. 22, cf. 23) and wait with eager longing (v. 19, cf. 23). The "children," whom creation and Christians so eagerly await, are further signs of the messianic age: creation awaits the "revealing of the sons of God"; Christians await "adoption as sons," that is, the redemption of their bodies. Here, too, the birthing metaphor provides encouragement for Christians bearing "the sufferings of this present time" (v. 18) as they await ultimate fulfillment.

It may seem peculiar that Paul brings up adoption here, so close on the heels of his efforts to persuade his readers that they already have received the "spirit of sonship" (8:15), with its assurance that they are "children of God, and if children, then heirs" (v. 16f.). These are people who already have "the birth certificate of the Spirit" (8:23).[19] Why are they still longing to be adopted? Part of the confusion arises from the use of "adoption" to translate the Greek *uiothesian*. Like the English "adoption," *uiothesian* is a legal term. It is never used literally in the Bible, however, and the narrow legal sense of the word may be less important than the linguistic links between *uiothesian* and the Greek word for son (*uios*), with its multifaceted biblical associations. Indeed, *uiothesian* is often translated "sonship" (cf. RSV, Rom. 8:15; 9:4).[20] This translation allows for a more flexible, multilayered interpretation that better fits the meta-phorical structure of Paul's discourse.

In this discourse, Paul deftly combines metaphors derived from biological parenthood and from formal or legal parent-hood. Calling Christians "children (*tekna*) of God" (8:16f.) emphasizes the gut-level bonds and irreversible relationship between biological parent (especially mother) and child. "*Uio-thesian*," on the other hand, is a public category, involving a father's formal acceptance of an individual as his child. The inconsistency that "adoption" introduces into Paul's meta-phoric structure disappears if the usual definition of sonship is expanded to include the formal acceptance of an infant by its father. Such acceptance was the life-or-death prerogative of the head of the household in pre-Christian Rome: "The birth of a Roman was not merely a biological fact. Infants came into the world, or at any rate were received into society, only as the head of the family willed."[21]

Paul's discourse moves back and forth between these understandings of the parent-child relationship—the intimate, irrevocable condition in contrast to the public, chosen commitment. In 8:15ff., he reminds the Romans with an outward sign that they have received the spirit of sonship—their very prayer, "Abba, Father," bears preliminary witness that though they suffer and are despised, they *are* God's children (*tekna*). God knows this relationship exists, and with the help of the Spirit, Christians know it too, but the rest of creation does not yet see it: Creation still eagerly awaits the revealing of the sons of God (v. 19). Christians, too, long for this public revelation: As they share Jesus' suffering, they groan and eagerly await the redemption of their bodies, by which God will ultimately acknowledge them as heirs (v. 23). Finally, Paul returns to the biological metaphor, reminding his reader that God intends Jesus to be the firstborn of many siblings (v. 29). In so doing, Paul applies the Hebrew tradition of divine sonship to Jesus and his followers (cf. Ex. 4:22). As God gives birth to Israel at the time of the Exodus, so God gives birth to Christ Jesus, and through him to a multitude of siblings to follow.[22]

In sum, Paul weaves this passage together with childbearing imagery, applying it to God, to creation, and to Christians. Subtly undergirding the entire passage are the complementary parental metaphors for God—the biological metaphor intimating a God who has born first Jesus and subsequently (presumably through baptism) Christians; the legal metaphor pointing ahead to God's impending full acknowledgment of these offspring as rightful heirs. Between these two phases of the Christian birth story, Christians themselves mirror, and consciously participate in, the long drawn-out labor that human sin brought on creation. Helping them in this labor is the Spirit, who intercedes with groans that, like those of a birthing woman nearing delivery, are "too deep for words" (v. 26).[23]

Paul's vision of birth here is a magnificently intertwined, cooperative endeavor: God-in-three-persons, creation, and Christians are all intimately and integrally involved in this birth process. Again in Gal. 4:19, Paul employs birth imagery to emphasize the intimate bonds of suffering and love that knit

Christians together, exclaiming: "My little children, with whom I am again in travail, until Christ be formed in you!" Displaying tenderness unusual in this otherwise harsh letter, Paul addresses the wayward Galatians as "my little children" (*tekna*). And from Paul's perspective they are indeed *little* children—fetuses he once again struggles to birth. Paul's portrayal of himself as a birthing mother accentuates the extreme intimacy of his relationship to the Galatians, suggests that they are presently dependent on him for life, and vividly communicates the anguish they are causing him.[24]

Paul's anguish is compounded because this travail is a repeat performance. The Galatians are little *children*, not fetuses; Paul *again* travails to birth Christ in them. The Galatians seem to have crawled back into the narrow world of the womb, resembling in some ways recalcitrant Ephraim refusing to be born (Hos. 13:13). There, however, the birthing mother was God. Here it is Paul, another human being—a dramatic shift indeed. Paul's metaphor may, then, suggest a disturbing sense of dependence of Christians on their leader. Note, though, that Paul does not encourage dependency. The point of his whole letter is to encourage the Galatians to move out of the womb, to live in the freedom that is theirs as children of Mother Jerusalem (4:26, 31; 5:1).

The joy implicit in the interpretation of Christian suffering as birthing labor becomes most explicit in the Gospel and letters of John. There Jesus comforts his followers by referring to a birthing woman: "When a woman is giving birth, she has sorrow,[25] because her hour has come; but when she has borne the child, she no longer remembers the distress,[26] for joy that a human being has been born into the world. So you have sorrow now, but I will see you again, and your hearts will rejoice, and no one will take your joy from you" (John 16:21f., author's trans.). John's forward view emphasizes the joyful outcome of birth, while the distress of labor drops almost completely out of the picture. Rather than focusing on the birth pangs of the messianic age, John reaches into Hebrew tradition for a different birthing metaphor, that is, that which describes the king being begotten/born from on high at his anointing[27] and extends the possibility of that birth from on high through Christ to all believers. The Greek word John uses, like its Hebrew antecedent in Ps. 2, is a unisex term that may be translated either "beget" or "bear," depending on the sex of the subject. However it is translated, the starting point of the metaphor is the intimate, physical experience of birth. John barely finishes with the exalted Logos hymn of chap. 1 before he daringly describes God begetting/bearing believers (1:13). Raymond Brown accents the earthiness of the metaphor when he writes, "the crude realism of the begetting of eternal life is even more brutal in I John iii 9 where it is said that one begotten by God has God's *seed* abiding in him."[28]

John uses an equally vivid maternal version of the metaphor in Jesus' nocturnal parley with the Jewish leader Nicodemus. In response to a question from Nicodemus, Jesus alludes to the tradition of birth from above: "Unless one is born from above [or "anew"[29]] he cannot see the kingdom of God" (3:3). Nicodemus takes Jesus to mean "anew," and quite literally so: "How can a man be born when he is old? Can he enter a second time into his mother's womb and be born?" (v. 4). Jesus repeats his allusion, replacing the misunderstood word with a phrase that evokes a picture of the divine womb giving birth amid a rush of water: "Unless one is born of water and the Spirit, he cannot enter the kingdom of God" (v. 5).

Not surprisingly, this verse is taken as an allusion to baptism by Christians. The metaphor emphasizes God's gracious initiative and abundance: A baby need not ask to be born, and the cleansing amniotic fluid never runs dry. It also expresses the radicality of receiving new life in Christ: Rebirth is not a matter of "feeling like a new person" after a weekend retreat; the believer is figuratively pressed through a narrow opening, out of the dark into the light; whatever prominence and security has been achieved in the world is left behind as the individual begins anew as a babe in Christ.

John's use of birthing imagery would have been particularly shocking to contemporary Jewish sensibilities: "Giving birth, according to Leviticus, renders a woman unclean; yet John can even speak of God giving birth to the chosen (1:13). The waters of baptism, for John, are waters of birth, comparable to amniotic fluid; yet they convey not impurity but intimate association with God."[30] The first letter of John returns repeatedly to the birth metaphor of intimate association with God to describe the source of and impetus for the godly life (1 John 2:29; 3:9; 4:7; 5:1, 4, 18).

Peter, too, employs the birth metaphor to communicate Christian identity and hope in the face of suffering and death, and to provide motivation for shedding destructive habits (1 Pet. 1:3, 23; 2:1), and follows the metaphor a step further by envisioning Christ as a nursing mother (2:2f.). He counsels Christians to be like newborn babes, longing for the unadulterated spiritual milk Christ offers.[31] The analogy points to spiritual nourishment which is as ideally suited to newborn Christians as the milk that springs from a mother's breast is suited to the needs of her child, and suggests going to it with gusto. Peter uses very sensuous language—Christians are to *desire* this milk and have already *tasted* its goodness. You can almost hear those babies smack their lips in anticipation.

Such extensions of the birth imagery are sprinkled throughout the New Testament. Paul likens himself to a nurse tenderly caring for her children (1 Thess. 2:7) and to a mother giving her baby milk (1 Cor. 3:2). Before his death, Jesus likens himself to a mother hen lamenting the fate of offspring who foolishly refuse to take shelter under her wings (Matt. 23:37; Luke 13:34). Childbirth, itself, however, is clearly the central image. It is used to interpret Jesus' death and resurrection as the fulfillment of messianic expectation and to provide comfort to Christians suffering for their faith. It provides a memorable picture of the source of Christian identity and of the bonds of affection and responsibility that bind Christians to one another, to God, and to all creation.

At the risk of stating the obvious, it is important to note that all these metaphors take for granted that childbirth is a blessing despite the distress involved. Even Jesus' words to the lamenting women he passes on his way to Calvary speak of the grim days ahead for them, rather than of the intrinsic worth of childbearing. In words that call the lament of Hos. 9:14 to mind, Jesus foresees a day people will say, "Blessed are the barren, and the wombs that never bore, and the breasts that never gave suck!" (Luke 23:29). The barren woman is at least spared the agony of seeing her child suffer. Similarly, Jesus mourns for those who are pregnant or nursing when the great tribulation comes (Matt. 24:19), presumably because they would have greater difficulty fleeing, just as everyone would if they needed to flee during the winter or on the Sabbath (v. 20).

Such words would have shocked Jesus' hearers: He was, remember, born into a world in which "blessed" and "barren" were opposites, a world in which women experienced childlessness as a disgrace, at least "among men" (Luke 1:25; cf. Gen. 30:23). These few verses are hardly a celibate manifesto. Still, they did raise a new question: Are there situations in which childbearing is not the highest good? Similarly, Jesus' responses to questions of family law often point to a subordination of the traditional obligation to procreate. His rejection of divorce, for example, implied that the bonds of marriage are more important than the duty to have children—in contrast to the prevailing Jewish view of his day that considered divorce a right and sometimes an obligation essential to procreation.[32] Similarly, Jesus taught that the coming resurrection of the dead means that arrangements like levirate marriage, intended to ensure the continuation of a man's name into posterity, lose significance (Luke 20:28–36). Moreover, Jesus deflated any tendency to assess a woman's blessedness in terms of her procreative ability:

> As he said this, a woman in the crowd raised her voice and said to him, "Blessed is the womb that bore you, and the breasts that you sucked!" But he said, "Blessed rather are those who hear the word of God and keep it!" (Luke 11:27f.)

Such passages imply that childbearing is not a woman's sole or even primary source of fulfillment—an unsettling proposition in Jesus' day and age. At the same time, it is important to note that Jesus does not demean childbearing as in any way shameful or unclean. Rather, Jesus breaks down the barriers between clean and unclean: He makes a point of including and lifting up those despised in his society for their inability to bear children (cf.

Matt. 19:12; Luke 23:29), just as he included those despised as unclean (cf. Mark 2:15ff.; Matt. 11:19; 21:31). A peculiarity in Luke's reference to the process of purification following Jesus' birth suggests that Jesus began expressing solidarity with the ritually unclean right from the start. The holiness code required a new mother to bring an offering to the temple and be cleansed from the birthing flow of blood, but Luke refers to "*their* purification" (2:22). Given the special divine involvement in Jesus' birth perhaps it should not be surprising that Jesus joined his mother in fulfilling the time of postnatal purification.[33]

To repeat, Jesus' reservations regarding family ties were never expressed in terms of the impurity associated with child-bearing. Rather, he voiced a practical concern that family ties might present an impediment to the urgent demands of pro-claiming the coming of God's kingdom, and he counseled his followers to keep dependents to a minimum. Even so, Jesus himself took time to minister to society's dependent and power-less members—children and the sick; and he expected his disci-ples to do the same (Matt. 18:5; Mark 9:36f.; Luke 9:48). This point is made particularly clear in Matthew, where Jesus barely finishes affirming eunuchs "who have made themselves eunuchs for the sake of the kingdom of heaven" (19:12) before turning to admonish his disciples, "let the children come to me and do not hinder them" (v. 14).

This radical challenge to forego traditional family life was soon joined by more conservative voices—notably those articu-lated in the pastoral letters. The extreme of this tendency is to be found in 1 Tim. 2:12–15:

> I permit no woman to teach or to have authority over a man; she is to keep silent. For Adam was formed first, then Eve; and Adam was not deceived, but the woman was deceived and became a transgressor. Yet she will be saved through childbearing, provided they continue in faith and love and holiness, with modesty (NRSV).

This passage has offended writers as diverse as contemporary Canadian novelist Margaret Atwood and nineteenth-century Søren Kierkegaard's pseudonym Judge Wilhelm. Atwood draws out the grotesque possibilities implicit in this passage in *The Handmaid's Tale,* where she depicts a harshly regimented dystopia in which women are quite literally saved from death if they are able to bear a healthy child.[34] The Bible itself is kept locked up, and women are not allowed to read anything, much less such an "incendiary device." Periodically, however, male "Commanders" read aloud selected Bible passages (including a number pertaining to procreation) to reinforce their control over their women.[35]

Judge Wilhelm's comments are less grotesque, but telling nevertheless, coming as they do from the pen of an utterly traditional male head of household. He takes the apostle Paul to task for the possible implications of these verses:

> And when in one place the Apostle Paul admonishes woman with a good deal of severity to receive learning in silence, with all submissiveness, and to be in silence, and then, after having gagged her, humiliates her still more by adding: she shall be saved through childbearing, I truly never would have forgiven the apostle for this contempt, if he had not made it all right again by adding: if they (the children) remain in faith and love and holiness with discipline.[36]

The judge agrees that woman shall submit to the man,[37] and himself describes her as "silent," but he is offended by the suggestion that woman should be saved by her reproductive function alone. Only Paul's inclusion of the morally and spiritually challenging work of childrearing makes the passage acceptable to Wilhelm.

Even if we accept Wilhelm's reading of that final phrase,[38] the passage is problematic. William Countryman points out:

> It is difficult in the extreme to coordinate this "reliable saying" with another from the same author which insists that God has saved us "not as a result of works of righteousness which we ourselves have done, but according to his own mercy through a washing of rebirth and renewal of Holy Spirit" (Titus 3:4–8) . . . our author has brought us a long way from Paul—not in his demand for subordination

or in his appeal to the order of creation, both of which are found in Paul, but in his astonishing and unprecedented theology of childbearing.[39]

What is the thoughtful Christian to do with this passage? Are there but two options: either accept its "unprecedented theology of childbearing" at face value or dismiss the passage as a hopeless intrusion of resurgent patriarchal tendencies? Interpretation of this verse in light of the rest of the Bible rules out the first option. Jesus himself points out that a woman's blessedness is not determined by her procreative functions. What is more, the central Christian message of salvation as God's gracious gift through Jesus Christ obviates any notion of salvation through childbearing.

On the other hand, difficult Bible passages must never be lightly dismissed as socially conditioned impurities. Ironically, the most problematic verse (v. 15) reads like an addendum intended to blunt the force of the preceding verses in which the writer advocates restricting women's behavior and sphere of influence (vv. 9–12) and uses a dubious argument to support his point (vv. 13f.). Perhaps the writer realizes that he has little warrant for using the story of Adam and Eve to argue for gender-determined social roles—nowhere else in the Bible does this occur.[40] At any rate, it seems that his mention of Adam and Eve reminds him of some unfinished business left over from their story. Adam's sons had received something of a reprieve from their sentence of punishment (Gen. 3:17f.; cf. Gen. 5:29 and 8:21–9:3); and it has been suggested that the manger in which Jesus was laid, too, signified a restoration of harmony between Adam and the beasts,[41] but the issue of woman's sorrow in childbearing had not yet been fully addressed. From this perspective, the writer of 1 Timothy might well write of woman being saved (i.e., preserved) *through* (not by virtue of) the hardships of childbirth, much as Noah and his family were saved through the waters of the flood (1 Peter 3:20). These persons were not saved by virtue of the water, but by virtue of God's patience, which allowed Noah time to build an ark.[42] Admittedly, this "saved through a danger" meaning occurs much less frequently than the "saved through (i.e., by virtue of) someone or something" meaning. However, "saved through a danger" makes the best Christian sense of 1 Tim. 2:15. Read thus, this passage indicates that the coming of Christ makes a healing difference in the experience of childbirth—at least for the Christian woman or couple who abides in faith, love, and holiness, with self-discipline.

This final word, in particular, provides a counterpoint to the multiplied sorrow that has attended birthing since Gen. 3:16. Although the Greek (*sōphrosunē*) may be translated "modesty" when applied to women, it is better translated here as "self-discipline." "Modesty" tends to unnecessarily narrow the meaning of the word by alluding to sexuality, whereas the Greek range of meanings is typically related to a more general sense of mental health, morality, moderation, and good judgment. From this perspective, 1 Tim. 2:15 promises that the embodied moral grief and brokenness of Gen. 3:16 distress may be overcome by a spirit of self-discipline similar to that received by Timothy through the laying on of hands (2 Tim. 2:7). This does not mean that physical distress and danger disappear for the Christian woman in childbirth; nor does it mean that Christian women will never need pain medication or medical assistance. It does mean that the distress of childbirth need no longer be received as a reminder of punishment and human mortality. Rather, in the light of Christ, even this distress may be received as an experience of grace, given the assurance of God's saving presence through life and death, and as an experience lending insight into God's labor of love in bringing a new creation to birth. And in this light, the earthy experience of birthing may be received as a spiritual gift and offered up as a disciplined prayer that fully integrates body and spirit in a work of love and life.

History reveals, however, that Christians have not always interpreted this passage, or childbirth in general, in these terms. The next chapters will explore some of the burdens and resources church history bears with regard to childbirth.

Notes

1. In all six instances, as in 1:57, the Greek is *pimplēmi*, cf. also 1:23. This verb also points ahead to the spirit-filled birth of the church in Acts—cf. Acts 2:4; 4:8, 31; 9:17; 13:9.

2. Matthew, too, describes Jesus' birth in terms of fulfillment: see Matt. 1:22; 2:15, 17, 23.

3. Raymond E. Brown, *The Birth of the Messiah: A Commentary on the Infancy Narratives in Matthew and Luke* (Garden City, N.Y.: Doubleday, 1977), 399, cf. 401. For Brown's comments on the significance of the manger, see below, n. 41.

4. See G. B. Caird, *A Commentary on The Revolution of St. John the Divine*, 2d ed., (London: A & C Black, 1984), 149; and Rosemary Radford Ruether, *Mary, The Feminine Face of the Church* (Philadelphia: Westminster, 1977), 31.

5. Author's translation. *Ōdinas,* translated by RSV as "pangs," like the related verb (*ōdinō*), refers specifically to birthing labor and its pangs (cf. 1 Thess. 5:3, Gal. 4:27; Rev. 12:2). Even when used metaphorically, the associations with birthing remain (cf. Matt. 24:8; Mark 13:8; Gal. 4:19). When the noun is singular, it (like the English "labor") refers to the entire birthing process, beginning with the first contractions and lasting until delivery (cf. 1 Thess. 5:3). The plural form, as here, refers to birth pangs.

6. The Septuagint translation of Job 39:2 offers a close parallel: *ōdinas de autōn elusas.* Here the loosing of *ōdinas* (labor pangs) means delivery at the end of labor; cf. "luō," Walter Bauer, *A Greek-English Lexicon of the New Testament and Other Early Christian Literature,* trans. William Arndt and F. Wilbur Gingrich (Chicago and London: University of Chicago Press, 1979).

Another possible antecedent lies in the Septuagint's translation of Ps. 18:4f. There the Hebrew root *hbl* (which has several possible meanings, including both *birth pangs* and *cords,* cf. above, chap. 3, n. 18) is translated *ōdines:* Cords (*ōdines*) of death encompassed me . . . cords (*ōdines*) of Hades entangled me. Compare Ps. 116:3.

7. See pp. 55f.

8. A. Bauman, "*hyl,*" in G. Johannes Botterweck and Helmer Ringgren, eds., David E. Green, trans., *Theological Dictionary of the Old Testament* (Grand Rapids, Mich.: Eerdmans, 1980), 4:347.

9. According to Wilcox, this metaphor's context in Peter's speech also points to an eschatological interpretation (note esp. the phrase, "in the last days," Acts 2:17; cf. Isa. 2:2). Max Wilcox, *The Semitisms of Acts* (Oxford: Clarendon Press, 1965), 47f.

10. The genitive construction ("birth pangs of death") leaves the exact relation of travail and death open to discussion. Bertram, for example, sees the metaphor involved in this phrase as the womb of the underworld releasing the Redeemer: G. Bertram, "*ōdin,*" in Gerhard Friedrich, ed., Geoffrey W. Bromily, trans. and ed., *Theological Dictionary*

of the New Testament (Grand Rapids, Mich.: Eerdmans, 1974), 9:673, cf. 670. I do not find this interpretation persuasive. The underworld is not mentioned here (although "Hades" does appear as a variant in some later manuscripts). Nor is birth from the womb of the underworld a biblical theme. (The passages from the Septuagint that Bertram cites as alluding to "the womb of death" are few and unconvincing: 2 Sam. 22:5f; 2 Kings 19:3; Isa. 37:3; Hos. 13:13f.) Moreover, such a reading leaves us with death (a concept that is the antithesis of life and, as Paul put it, "the last enemy to be destroyed") as the Messiah's mother! It makes much better sense to read travail and death as coordinate concepts in this phrase, as readers naturally do with the parallel construction in Heb. 2:9: "the suffering of death." The point there is that Jesus' death was suffering, just as the point here is that Jesus' death was birthing travail.

11. The exception is the sympathetic suffering of Isaiah, Isa. 21:3, and Jeremiah, insofar as Jer. 4:19–21 is taken as an interjection of the prophet's own voice.

12. Quoted in Hermann L. Strack and Paul Billerbeck, *Kommentar zum Neuen Testament Aus Talmud und Midrash* (München: C. H. Beck, 1956), 1:950; author's trans.

13. See below, pp. 104ff. The imagery Anselm and these mystics develop is strikingly similar to that of Acts 2:24, yet this passage has escaped attention in discussions of the biblical antecedents of the medieval imagery.

14. The Old Testament offers no formal doctrine of the fate of the dead. Its scattered depictions suggest a realm less desirable than that of the living, but nowhere is the realm of the dead depicted as a place of torment. Theodor H. Gaster, "Abode of the Dead," in George A. Buttrick, ed., *Interpreter's Dictionary of the Bible: An Illustrated Encyclopedia* (Nashville: Abingdon, 1962), 1:787. "The concept of an infernal 'hell' developed in Israel only during the Hellenistic period," ibid., 788.

15. See above, n. 6.

16. The Greek is *anistēmi*, which means both to cause to be born or appear and to raise from the dead.

17. Jesus' willingness to go through the birthing travail of death can be seen as redeeming Ephraim's failure to present himself at the mouth of the womb (Hos. 13:13).

18. The one exception is the analogy Paul draws between labor contractions and the destruction the Day of the Lord will bring to the complacent (1 Thess. 5:3). Even here, Paul's point is to admonish the faithful: Like a pregnant woman, who knows that labor contractions will start sometime soon, but never knows exactly when, Christians do well to be prepared for the sudden and irreversible coming of that day.

19. Alternate translation of *aparkhēn;* see Bauer, *Greek-English Lexicon.*

20. The RSV translates "sonship" in Rom. 8:15 and 9:4, "adoption as sons" in Rom. 8:23 and Gal. 4:5, and "to be his sons" in Eph. 1:5. Unfortunately, sonship is not as gender-neutral as adoption, which is probably the reason NRSV translates "adoption" in Rom. 8:15, 23; 9:4, and "adoption as children" in Gal. 4:5 and Eph. 1:5.

21. Paul Veyne, "The Roman Empire," in *A History of Private Life,* vol. 1: *From Pagan Rome to Byzantium* (Cambridge: Harvard University Press, 1987), 9.

22. In Rom. 9:4, Paul again alludes to the Ex. 4:22 divine begetting/bearing, this time in reference to Israel. Moreover, he uses *uiothesian* to do so—a further sign that Paul means "sonship" rather than "adoption" when he uses *uiothesian.*

23. The word for the groans (*stenagmois*) of the Spirit is the same noun that the Septuagint uses to translate *heron* (pregnancy) in Gen. 3:16. The corresponding verb appears in Rom. 8:23 and in modified form in v. 22.

24. In light of this imagery, Paul's enraged cries elsewhere in the letter (for example, 1:6ff; 3:1ff.) might be interpreted as the anguished cries of a birthing mother. Compare also the reverberations of birthing travail that color Paul's Rom. 9:2 description of his feelings toward the Israelites who have rejected Jesus as Christ. His great sorrow (*lupē*) recalls Gen. 3:16 (see n. 25); his anguish (*odunē*) is so similar to birthing travail (*ōdinō*) that it is found in a variant reading of Matt. 24:8 (see "*odunē*" in Bauer, *Greek-English Lexicon*).

25. This phrase, (*ē gunē otan tiktē lupēn ekhei*) recalls the Septuagint translation of Gen. 3:16: "In sorrow [*lupe*] you shall bring forth [*tiktein*] children." The Greek *lupe* means grief or sorrow, an anguish of mind or spirit, rather than physical pain.

26. The Greek word *thlipsis* (translated "distress" here) literally means "pressure"; it also is used figuratively of the tribulation of the last days: Matt. 24:21, 29; Mark 13:19, 24; John 16:33; Rev. 7:14.

27. Compare Ps. 2:7. The verse is quoted directly with regard to Jesus (Acts 13:33; Heb. 1:5; 5:5).

28. Raymond E. Brown, *The Gospel According to John I-XII: Introduction, Translation, and Notes,* vol. 29 of The Anchor Bible (Garden City, N.Y.: Doubleday, 1966), 138.

29. The ambiguity of *anōthen* is key to Nicodemus' misunderstanding. It can mean either "from above" or "anew." RSV puts "anew" in the text and "from above" in the margin; NRSV does the opposite.

30. L. William Countryman, *Dirt, Greed, and Sex: Sexual Ethics in*

the New Testament and Their Implications for Today (Philadelphia: Fortress Press, 1988), 93.

31. Peter goes on to describe Christ as a living stone, thus calling to mind the birthing rock of Deut. 32:18.

32. Elaine Pagels, *Adam, Eve, and the Serpent* (New York: Vintage Books, 1988), 14.

33. Brown admits that "there is no Jewish tradition for the purification of the father," and yet maintains that the plural refers to Mary and Joseph (*Birth of the Messiah*, 436). This seems unlikely, particularly considering Joseph's lack of involvement in the birth.

34. Margaret Atwood, *The Handmaid's Tale* (New York: Ballantine Books, 1985), 35, 79, 163.

35. Ibid., 112, 114, 286, cf. 146.

36. *Søren Kierkegaards Samlede Værker*, 1st. ed., Drachmann, Heiberg, and Lange (Copenhagen: Gyldendal, 1901–06), 2 [*Either/Or II*, 1843]: 64. Translations my own.

37. Ibid., 2:84.

38. The second verb of v. 15 is indeed in the plural, but it is unclear whether the plural refers to the children, to childbearing women, or to husband and wife.

39. Countryman, *Dirt, Greed, and Sex,* 227.

40. Second Cor. 11:3 is the only other mention of Eve in the New Testament; there she is compared to all Christians, not just women. Leonard Swidler points out that in Rom. 5:12–14 and 1 Cor. 15:21–22 Paul refers to the first sin in Eden, but ascribes fault to Adam. This is in contrast to much Jewish interpretation prevalent at the time, which blamed Eve for sin and death. *Biblical Affirmations of Woman* (Philadelphia: Westminster Press, 1979), 323f.

41. Brown, *Birth of the Messiah*, 419, notes that the manger is referred to as a sign, and is mentioned no less than three times by Luke (2:7, 12, 16). He summarizes Derrett's suggestion as to the symbolism: "For instance, in a midrashic tradition about the curse on Adam in Gen. 3:18, Adam asks, 'Shall I be tied to the manger to eat with my donkey?' If this tradition were in Luke's mind, he might be portraying Jesus as a second Adam, fulfilling the situation feared by Adam, but turning it to salvific purposes." Compare J.D.M. Derrett, "The Manger: Ritual Law and Soteriology," *Theology* 74 (1971): 569–71.

42. Compare 1 Cor. 3:15. There the person who loses his work by fire suffers loss, but he himself will be saved, but only as through fire. Here, too, the subject is saved through a danger, not by virtue of it.

Part 2
Church History: Burdens and Resources

5
The Blessing of Procreation Reconsidered

The Christian vision of a family that is not determined by bloodlines, and blessedness that is not determined by procreative status, opened traditional reproductive obligations to discussion. Early Christians began drawing out the practical implications of Bible passages that challenged the supremacy and enduring value of natural kinship ties (Luke 18:28ff.; 20:34ff.) and that suggested that in some cases childlessness might be a blessing (Matt. 19:12; Luke 23:24) and celibacy preferable to marriage (1 Cor. 7:8, 32ff.). They did so in a world distant in many respects from twentieth-century North America. Theirs was "a world in which many learned and serious people, Christian and pagan alike, tended to distrust the physical world and their own physical being."[1] Moreover, the ever-present possibility of martyrdom must have affected early Christians' view of life and family commitments in ways we can barely imagine. In such an intellectual climate, passages such as those mentioned above were readily taken as exhortations to sexual renunciation.

A great variety of meanings were attached to sexual renunciation during these formative years.[2] For some, it was a practical measure enabling Christians to proclaim the coming of the kingdom unimpeded by family responsibilities.[3] For others, celibacy was an equal opportunity, physical form of witness that could distinguish Christians, much as their fearlessness in the face of death did.[4] Celibacy was seen as an effective technique for achieving clarity of the soul[5] and as a physical expression of the preexisting purity of the soul, an oasis of human freedom.[6] The most radical saw "the boycott of the womb" as a way of bringing the "present age" to a halt, and even as a way of undoing the sin of Adam and Eve.[7]

The church never wholeheartedly embraced such ascetic views, definitely not in their most radical forms. In the pastoral epistles, the Bible itself includes early voices intent on reining in the disruptive tendencies of ascetic ideals.[8] Similarly, the emerging Christian orthodoxy condemned the teachings of Christian Gnostics, who generally rejected creation and despised procreation.[9]

Curiously enough, this era's most elegant defense against such ascetic views was put forth by the Greek church father Clement of Alexandria (ca. 150–215), whose thought otherwise shows considerable affinity with Christian Gnostic teachings.[10] One element of Clement's affinity to Christian Gnosticism is particularly pertinent here. Like many Christian Gnostics, Clement freely intertwines feminine and masculine metaphors for God: "The Word is everything to the child, both father and mother, teacher and nurse . . . the Word alone supplies us children with the milk of love, and only those who suck at this breast are truly happy . . . . to those infants who seek the Word, the Father's loving breasts supply milk."[11] As we have seen, such imagery is utterly biblical, yet Clement is the only orthodox Christian teacher of the patristic period to draw on it. We have yet to determine why leaders of the emerging Christian orthodoxy left this evocative biblical imagery to the Gnostics. Had these metaphors become too closely associated with the Gnostics and their questionable teachings? Was this imagery simply overlooked by male church teachers, or were these men somehow threatened by such sensuous and female metaphors?

In any case, when it came to procreation, Clement parted company with Gnostics and radical ascetics. He firmly asserted that sexual intercourse and legitimate procreation are blessed by God from creation. In doing so, however, he insisted "that marriage find its sole legitimate purpose—and sexual intercourse its only rationale—in procreation."[12] This latter view was not unique to Clement or to Christian circles: according to Paul Veyne, "the Christian Clement of Alexandria was influenced by Stoicism to the point of copying out the conjugal precepts of the Stoic Musonius, without mentioning the true author."[13] Clement, however, writing in a climate of increasingly vocal ascetic radicalism, insisted on procreation as the goal of sex with a thoroughness not found in pagan literature. Still, though Clement insisted on procreation as the only goal of sex, he did not view procreation as woman's only goal. Instead, Clement emphasized the equality of men and women: "Men and women share equally in perfection, and are to receive the same instruction and discipline."[14]

Clement's focus elevated birth in one sense—it was the end that justified the means. Unfortunately, his product-oriented ideal left no room for "the 'graciousness' created by intercourse—that indefinable quality of mutual trust and affection gained through the pleasure of the bed itself—which even the dignified Plutarch took for granted."[15] So, too, this low view of intercourse left birth open to guilt by association, especially when the unruly experience of sex failed to conform to Clement's sober guidelines. For all its regrettable tendencies, however, Clement's teaching did represent an effort to claim the most intimate aspects of human life for Christianity and to defend at least a narrow definition of good sex in an era increasingly inclined toward complete renunciation.

It soon became clear that even Clement's strict Christian ideal of married sexuality would not be able to redirect the momentum of the increasingly vigorous ascetic movement. In other Christian communities, the church was already accepting teachers who questioned the very legitimacy of procreation. Clement's Latin contemporary Tertullian (ca. 155–220), for example, asserted that marriage and fornication "are not intrinsically different, but only in the degree of their illegitimacy."[16] Despite this harsh judgment, however, even Tertullian did not regard marriage and parenthood as a permanent spiritual liability. Indeed, Peter Brown describes Tertullian's picture of ideal church leadership as a "Spirit-filled gerontocracy" of elderly widows and widowers who had a long experience of life, including the begetting and rearing of children "before the sexual urge had 'fizzled out' with the approach of age."[17]

Throughout the first centuries of the church, all this concern with sexual status and degrees of procreation's legitimacy fades away in the presence of courage in martyrdom. This point is exemplified by Perpetua and Felicity, whose Christian witness coincided with motherhood, but was not determined by it.[18] Both were young mothers at the time they were martyred in 203 and were widely admired for their courage and dignity in the face of their terrible death in the arena. Neither indicated that she saw motherhood as in any way antithetic to her Christian calling, although it did present special challenges. While in prison, Perpetua was inspired by visions, and emerged as leader and spokesperson for her companions (including her catechist, the priest Saturus). At the same time, her diary shows that she was both happy to suckle her son in prison and thankful for God's help in weaning the child when he was eventually taken from her and placed in her father's care.[19]

Perpetua's companion Felicity, who was eight months pregnant, faced a particularly trying obstacle—Roman law prohibited the execution of pregnant women. She did not want to die alone or with common criminals, so two days before their ordeal in the arena, the entire group poured forth their distress in prayer. As soon as the group prayer was finished, Felicity went into labor. After intense suffering (attributed to the eighth-month delivery), she gave birth to a healthy baby girl, who was subsequently raised by "one of the sisters." Felicity's premature labor and safe delivery were viewed as divine intervention that enabled her to undergo her martyrdom alongside her companions and strengthened the group's assurance of God's presence with them.

Felicity herself was "glad that she had safely given birth so that now she could fight the beasts, going from one blood bath to another, from the midwife to the gladiator, ready to wash after childbirth in a second baptism."[20] Her difficult birthing experience did not leave her weak or worn, but rather exhilarated and empowered to face the still more difficult ordeal awaiting her. Here the blood of childbirth is not a source of defilement, but a reminder of God's presence and a preparation for the bloodbath of martyrdom. The physical evidence of recent motherhood touched even the spectators who had come to enjoy the gory show. When the group was stripped in the arena, the crowd was horrified to see that one was a delicate young woman, and the other obviously fresh from childbirth, milk still dripping from her breasts.

For these early Christians, "motherhood was not especially relevant to holiness. . . . The biological demands of motherhood, accepted in the ancient world as marks and determinants of female incapacity, were not allowed to stand in the way of the martyrs' witness. Motherhood was not in itself redemptive, but neither did it preclude participation in the most sacred vocation."[21] If anything, their new motherhood added poignancy to their fate—highlighting how much they were willing to give up in order to remain true to their faith and winning them the sympathy of a hostile crowd. Here Christian witness in its most demanding form makes clear that neither motherhood nor celibacy is the crucial determinant of Christian discipleship, and that God's glory can show forth not only through visions and inspiring speech, but also in the earthy details of giving birth and nursing and weaning.

This remarkable combination of motherhood and martyrdom remained an inspiring exception. Although ordinary married Christians could still face martyrdom in the years that followed, the Christian imagination was increasingly drawn to virginity. Thus the imagined inviolate virgin Thecla quickly became more popular than the real woman, wife and mother Perpetua.[22]

What prompted the growing enthusiasm for renunciation is not completely clear. It was probably at least partly due to the desire of young people to choose their own futures, rather than accepting the social entanglements entailed in the marriages that were arranged for them at an early age by their families.[23] Celibacy may have been particularly attractive to Christian women. Although embracing celibacy meant renouncing an important aspect of female identity, it did offer women (especially those of independent means) "practical benefits often

denied to them in secular society. They could retain control of
their own wealth, travel freely throughout the world, . . . devote
themselves to intellectual and spiritual pursuits, and found
institutions they could personally direct."[24]

In contrast, woman's role as childbearer and rearer imposed
enormous burdens on her in the ancient world. She was usually
married young, died young, and probably mourned the loss of
children who died before her;[25] childbearing and rearing duties
would have left her little if any time for learned pursuits.
Treatises on virginity made these advantages of the celibate life
abundantly clear to young girls; in so doing, they spoke in public
on the physical state of the married woman in a way educated
Greeks and Romans had never done. The dangers of childbirth,
possible difficulties of nursing, and the shame of infertility were
publicly acknowledged—though this acknowledgment did little
to alleviate the suffering of women who were already (or would
soon be) committed by marriage to childbearing.[26]

Whatever the reason, within the first two centuries of the
Christian church, celibacy had become first an acceptable and
then an admired choice of lifestyle. In the meantime, married
couples were counseled to demonstrate their Christian identity
by adherence to strict codes of marital morality.[27] By the
beginning of the fourth century, a tacit truce was reached
between the two different views of Christian sexual and social
relations that had emerged. The resulting two-tiered structure
would endure for centuries: the uncommon, almost angelic
spiritual elite practiced celibacy, while the more humble and
human Christian continued to marry and have children.[28]

In spite of the enthusiasm for asceticism, full-fledged ascetics remained uncommon; during the century following Con-
stantine's conversion, there were probably no more than one
desert hermit per thousand Christians.[29] Those who stayed
home and continued to propagate the human race and rear
children in godly ways were viewed, at least to some extent, as
second-class Christians. The birth of children had lost its position of honor as a prime sign of God's blessing; instead it was
relegated to the legitimization of sexual relations for those too
weak to live a celibate life. On the other hand, this reevaluation

of procreation meant that an alternative to the traditional family-dominated life was visibly possible for women, as well as for men.[30] There is little written record of how the married majority of this era viewed themselves—by the sixth century, literacy was limited largely to monks and nuns.[31] Thus we may never know how the vivid exhortations to virginity affected childbearing women. Did they benefit women by publicly acknowledging the sacrifices many women made bringing children into the world or simply increase women's suffering by accentuating the danger of labor while demoting the prestige of motherhood? For that matter, we may never know to what extent married Christians perceived parenthood to be demoted and to what extent the ascetic ideal actually overshadowed the joy of bringing new life into the world. Pictures on Roman sarcophagi showing Adam and Eve with their hands joined in the symbol of Roman marriage suggest that a silent majority "believed as firmly as did their Jewish neighbors that God had created humanity for marriage and childbirth."[32]

Such views were occasionally also voiced among church leaders, at considerable personal risk. For example Jovinian, himself a celibate Christian monk, argued on scriptural grounds that celibacy in itself is no holier than marriage. Jerome (ca. 374–419) vigorously opposed these views, however, and eventually Jovinian was condemned as a heretic. Even so, Jovinian was supported by some of Rome's leading Christians, and the vehemence of Jerome's *Against Jovinian* was a source of embarrassment even to those who agreed that virginity surpassed marriage.[33] Indeed, the loathing for the flesh that colors Jerome's rhetoric in this work is a burden for the church to this day. In it, the barriers between clean and unclean that Jesus did so much to dismantle reappeared in new form. Jerome writes, for example, "Although I know that crowds of matrons will be furious at me, . . . I will say what the apostle [Paul] has taught me. . . . indeed in view of the purity of the body of Christ, all sexual intercourse is unclean."[34]

It is no wonder that by expressing such views in such language, Jerome could expect to incur the wrath of "crowds of matrons." It may be more difficult to understand why the majority of Christians continued both to marry and to assert the primacy of renunciation. Pagels sees this assertion of the primacy of renunciation as "resistance to conventional definitions of human worth based upon social contribution" and finds in this resistance "the source of the later western idea of the absolute value of the individual—the value of every human being, including the destitute, the sick, and the newborn—quite apart from any consideration, real or potential, to the 'common good' "[35] Thus the same matrons who were furious at Jerome's "dirty" labeling of sex also could be attracted to Christianity's respect for each individual, a respect that was reflected not only in the affirmation of renunciation, but also in the rejection of practices like the exposure of unacceptable infants.[36]

Then too, married people may have felt themselves graced by the presence of representatives of another way within their midst. Just as modern city dwellers may take comfort in the fact that wilderness areas continue to exist, even if they never have the opportunity to experience them firsthand, so, too, women struggling to bear and bring up their children might be strengthened by the simple existence of dedicated virgins who did not suffer "the consecutive dislocations of marriage, childbirth, and bereavement."[37] Confronted with childbirth or fertility problems, they might seek the aid of celibate holy men;[38] unable to dedicate themselves to a life of celibate devotion, they might console themselves by making such a life possible for their children.[39]

These ascetics were surely appreciated for the spiritual insights that they received and communicated. Thus, too, in spite of the mistrust of sexuality and the body (not least the female body) that is an unfortunate legacy of the ascetic tradition, we may also glean from this tradition unexpected insight into the integration of body and soul. For example, the desert hermits, for all their humbling of the body and their exhortation's stress on the opposition of pure spirit and sensual body, reached an appreciation of the inextricable interdependence of body and soul: "In the desert tradition, the body was allowed to become the discreet mentor of the proud soul. . . . Of all the lessons of the desert to a late antique thinker, what was most 'truly astonishing' was 'that the immortal spirit can be purified and refined by clay.' "[40]

Taking a clue from this desert tradition of spiritual development in a situation of physical extremity, might women, more prone to self-doubt than pride, find in their birthing bodies an available and capable mentor for the encouragement of their souls? Childbirth, too, is a situation of physical extremity, which has probably often yielded personal insights—take, for example, the woman who said of her childbearing experience, "I never knew I was so strong."[41] For the most part such insights have remained private, and perhaps have been half forgotten amid the numerous duties and delights that follow in the wake of childbirth. Although it might sometimes be tempting, few mothers are likely to drop everything and head for the desert. As a more practical alternative, church women's groups might find ways to provide "desert" opportunities for mothers of all ages to reflect together on the personal and theological significance of their birthing experiences.

The insights into the integration of body and soul expressed in the best of the desert wisdom tradition did not become the dominant force shaping Christian views of sexuality. It is, rather, the complex legacy of Augustine (354–430) that has had the greatest effect on Western society's understanding of sexuality. In his *Confessions,* Augustine laid bare his turbulent experience of his own sexuality, an experience that left an unfortunate residue in his theology, particularly his formulation of the doctrine of original sin. It should be noted, though, that Augustine was not unduly concerned with sexual sins. Peter Brown points out that Augustine "was content with the most banal exhortations to restraint" in his sermons to married persons. In those days, "when a bishop preached, he was expected to preach, rather, against *sclera,* against violence, fraud, and oppression, not on sexual sins."[42] Nor was celibacy a prominent issue for Augustine: he "wrote to African nuns, warning them never to look down on married women . . . 'For a virgin of the church may not yet be able to be a Thecla, while she [the married woman] may have been called by God to be a Saint Crispina.' "[43] Indeed, according to Brown, Augustine managed to defend marriage and to find a place for virginity in the church "by making them both magnificently social." Marriage and virginity both represent human concord; one form of friendship happened to produce children, and was therefore physical, while the other did not; but both pointed to the heavenly city.[44]

Against radical ascetic sects like the Manicheans (who could see no good whatsoever in sexual intercourse, and to whom Augustine had been attracted before his conversion), Augustine clearly proclaimed the goodness of God's whole creation. This affirmation is weakest, however, when it comes to sex.[45] Like Clement and others before him, Augustine viewed the goodness of sexuality solely in terms of procreation: "The cohabitation for the purpose of procreating children, which must be admitted to be the proper end of marriage, is not sinful." Still, desiring "carnal pleasure," even in marriage, involves venial sin.[46] Moreover, Augustine increasingly focused on human sexuality as the arena in which the warping effects of sin (which affects all human endeavors) were most clearly expressed. In particular, he saw the limits of rational and volitional control over sexual relations as a sign of the grave disorder introduced by sin.[47] From this perspective, spontaneous sexual desire offered prime evidence of the effects of original sin, precisely because of the physical spontaneity involved: The sexual members "are rightly called *pudenda* [parts of shame] because they excite themselves just as they like, in opposition to the mind which is their master, as if they were their own masters."[48]

Nowhere does Augustine's ambivalent attitude toward sexuality cast a darker shadow on the goodness of procreation than in his theory that original sin is physically transmitted from one generation to the next. One may heartily endorse the point of this teaching, that is, the solidarity of human sin and the universal human need for God's grace, and still deeply regret the way in which Augustine saw fit to explain it. For in his struggle against what he viewed as the moral optimism of the Pelagians, Augustine went well beyond pondering the contradictions of sexuality as a symbol of how sin warps the human being. Indeed, he took it upon himself to describe how original sin continued to be spread throughout the human race—through the sex act. He argued that even the embrace that is "lawful and honorable" in marriage "cannot be effected without the ardour of lust," i.e., concupiscence, hence "whatever comes into being by natural birth is bound by original sin."[49] Furthermore he declared that ever since Adam, semen itself, " 'shackled by the bond of death,' transmits the damage incurred by sin. Thus Augustine concludes that every human being ever conceived through semen already is born contaminated with sin."[50] This astonishing theory means not only that the lack of volitional and rational control over sexual drives amounts to sinfulness, even in the case of a lawfully wed and loving couple, but also that original sin is transmitted at conception to the child born of such love. Although this theory focuses on conception rather than on birth as the source of contamination, the whole process falls under a shadow. And although Augustine focuses primarily on sexual arousal, impotence, and intercourse as signs of body/soul disharmony, similar conditions can be seen to apply during childbirth. Then, too, the body leads the way, with little deference to the conscious will and its directives. It may be, however, that upon reflection, the body-soul relationship in childbirth may provide a positive corrective to negative aspects of the model Augustine describes, for in childbirth, the body leads the way in one of the more selfless of human acts.

For Augustine, though, the suffering involved in procreation was but another sign of original sin. He pointed to the nausea, illness, and pains of pregnancy; the painful contractions of parturition; the even greater agonies of miscarriage; "tortures inflicted by doctors; or the shock and loss of giving birth to an infant stillborn or moribund;"[51] not to mention birth defects and the vulnerability of even those children who are born healthy.[52] Augustine refused to accept that such suffering could be part of human nature as created by God: "Suffering *proves* that sin is transmitted from parents to children: 'If there were no sin, then infants, bound by no evil, would suffer nothing harmful in body or soul under the great power of the just God.' "[53]

In sharp contrast to these depictions of unruly passion and childbearing distress, Augustine envisioned the Virgin Mary as having a completely harmonious experience of conception and birth. Not only did Jesus' birth from a virgin mother eliminate contamination by semen, Augustine believed that "Mary had felt not the slightest eddy of uncontrolled feeling at the moment when she conceived Christ: the physical sensation associated with the sexual act had been fully consonant, in her case, with the untroubled movement of her will."[54]

Augustine was not the first to find doctrinal significance in the tradition of the virgin birth. The ascetic ideal had increased interest in Mary's virginity; and in the writings of Augustine's mentor Ambrose (339–397), the idea of a causal connection between Mary's virginity and Jesus' holiness was firmly established.[55] Ambrose described Mary's womb as sacred, unviolated space and went on to teach that she had remained a perpetual virgin.[56] Augustine, however, emphasized the body-soul dynamics of conception, rather than physical boundaries. Thus for Augustine, Mary's virginity was not primarily that her body had not been entered by a man's, but rather that in her conception of Christ, Mary "recaptured the ancient harmony of body and soul, in which the will was not the maimed thing that it so soon became."[57] Augustine's belief that Mary retained her virgin wholeness even through childbirth was a logical corollary. The ancient harmony of body and soul embodied by Mary at Jesus' conception thus also characterized his birth; Mary simply did not experience the distress that had accompanied birthing ever since Eve.[58]

Unfortunately, this theory of Jesus' extraordinary birth tends to put more ordinary birthing in a rather dubious light, leaving some wondering if Augustine and Ambrose feared that the blood and mess of normal birth might have contaminated Jesus.[59] And so, ironically, the birth of Christ, which can be seen as hallowing all human birth, was instead interpreted in a way that would for centuries do precisely the opposite—demeaning instead of hallowing the messy miracle of childbirth.

These ideas did not go unopposed. The Pelagian bishop Julian was appalled at the Manichean tendencies he saw in Augustine's thought. He rejected Augustine's depiction of sexual drives as permanently corrupted and his claim that birthing pangs are the result of sin. Julian argued that the labor contractions that women and other female animals experience are a natural part of the birth process and that the suffering involved in that process was not instituted, but only amplified in Eve's case as punishment for sin.[60] Julian's views may seem much more wholesome and reasonable to a modern reader than those of Augustine. Yet, after much controversy, the church of the fifth century eventually accepted Augustine's views, rejecting Julian's as heretical.[61] Why? Pagels suggests that one of the reasons Augustine's views prevailed was that they were psychologically compelling: "Many people need to find reasons for their sufferings . . . people often *would rather feel guilty than helpless*. . . . Augustine, like the Hebrew author of Gen. 2—3, gives religious expression to the conviction that humankind does not suffer and die randomly, but for specific reasons."[62]

Moreover, Augustine's views provided a satisfying explanation for the church's practice of infant baptism. If all are not born sinful and in immediate need of regeneration, why was the church baptizing infants? Origen (185–254), too, had grappled with this question, finding a tentative solution in the traditional association of impurity with birth: How else could the baptism of infants for the remission of sins be understood, "unless in accordance with the idea that no one is clean of filth, not even if his life on earth has only been for one day? And because the filth of birth is removed by the sacrament of baptism, for that reason infants, too, are baptized."[63] Origen might well see infant baptism in terms of the Hebrew purification rites associated with the birthing process; at this time baptisms were often performed on the eighth day of birth, following the Jewish timetable for circumcision. This timetable emphasized baptism as the Christian rite of initiation, differing primarily from its Jewish counterpart in that it was available to female as well as male children. As the correlation between infant baptism and the emerging doctrine of original sin became more pronounced, teachers like Cyprian urged that infants be baptized still earlier.[64] Augustine gathered the thoughts of Origen and Cyprian on infant baptism, Ambrose's emphasis on the virginal aspects of Jesus' birth, and his own insights into the dynamics of sexuality into an imposing doctrine of original sin that would shape Christian attitudes toward sexuality and procreation for generations to come.[65]

This doctrine of original sin would contribute to the urgency of infant baptism in centuries to come, although the belief that the devil has special powers for inflicting physical evil on an unbaptized child, or for snatching it away, is probably equally important.[66] These popular conceptions of baptism reflect the same sense of vulnerability at the time of childbirth that is reflected in Hebrew provisions for the ritual purification of parturient women and in the Hebrew custom of rubbing the newborn with salt. The issue had changed from a theological point of view, however. In the Hebrew purification rites the issue was the uncleanness associated with the dangerous divine-human intimacy of the reproductive process; ritual purification was primarily a means of reintroducing the *mother* into society. The Hebrew birth rite for (male) infants was circumcision, a rite of initiation whose sacrificial and sexual overtones suggest a symbolic sacrifice of the infant's body and virility rather than a need for purification. After Augustine, the issue was sin—a universal, salvation-threatening birth defect rather than an occasional, remediable condition. Thus the focus of ritual cleansing shifted increasingly to the *infant,* although the first Christian mention of purification rites for parturient women also date from about this time.[67] As baptism increasingly became a kind of birth rite, performed by an exclusively male clergy, the seeds were sown that would develop centuries later into a suspicion that baptismal "rebirth" might be a patriarchal religion's attempt to improve on and to diminish the importance of natural birth.[68] The more immediate impact of this era's reevaluation of procreation was an increased sense of vulnerability at the time of birth, and a tradition of spiritual parenthood that was to blossom in medieval celibate communities.

Notes

1. Clarissa W. Atkinson, *The Oldest Vocation: Christian Motherhood in the Middle Ages* (Ithaca: Cornell University Press, 1991), 70.

2. Peter Brown provides a fascinating account of these varied understandings in *The Body and Society: Men, Women, and Sexual Renunciation in Early Christianity* (New York: Columbia University Press, 1988).

3. This is the tendency of the apostle Paul's reasoning.

4. Peter Brown calls attention to this aspect of Justin Martyr (ca. 100–165) and his contemporaries. *Body and Society,* 60f.

5. Thus Tertullian, and many to follow. Brown, *Body and Society,* 78.

6. For example, Origen. Brown, *Body and Society,* 170.

7. Among the Encratites (radically ascetic Christian Gnostics), married intercourse was regarded as the linchpin of the present age, thus men and women alike were called upon to undo the mistake of Adam and Eve and to reject further participation in procreation. Brown, *Body and Society,* 96–99.

8. Compare above, 74ff.; 1 Tim. 2:11–15; 3:2–5; 2 Tim. 3:6f; Titus 2:4–6; Eph. 5:23f.

9. See Jaroslav Pelikan, *The Christian Tradition: A History of the Development of Doctrine* (Chicago: University of Chicago Press, 1971), 1:87ff. Compare W.H.C. Frend, *The Rise of Christianity* (Philadelphia: Fortress Press, 1984), 371, 390f., n. 23.

10. Indeed, Pelikan asks if Clement (and his successor Origen) should be regarded "as the right wing of Christian Gnosticism rather than the left wing of Christian orthodoxy." After discussing this possibility, Pelikan finally rejects it. Pelikan, *Christian Tradition,* 1:96.

11. Clement Alexandrinus, *Paidegogos,* ed. O. Stählin (Leipzig, 1905), 1.6; quoted in Elaine Pagels, "What Became of God the Mother? Conflicting Images of God in Early Christianity," 107–119 in *Womanspirit Rising: A Feminist Reader in Religion,* ed. Carol Christ and Judith Plaskow (Harper & Row: San Francisco, 1979), 116f. Pagels points out that the writings of the Christian Gnostics abound in maternal symbolism for God. The coincidence of maternal symbolism for God and rejection of biological parenthood among Christian Gnostics is intriguing, but beyond the scope of this study. Brown suggests that in the thought of Tatian (associated with the Encratites) images of the soul's marriage to Christ's Spirit and of the Spirit as mother of the soul "were so powerful that they blocked out the possibility of sexual joining in ordinary marriage," *Body and Society,* 92.

12. Elaine Pagels, *Adam, Eve, and the Serpent* (New York: Vintage Books, 1989), 28. Compare Brown, *Body and Society,* 133.

13. Paul Veyne, "The Roman Empire," in *A History of Private Life,* vol. 1: *From Pagan Rome to Byzantium* (Cambridge: Harvard University Press, 1987), 47.

14. Clement, *Paidegogos,* 1, 4; quoted in Pagels, "What Became of God the Mother?" 117. Pagels points out that in this, too, Clement more closely resembles Christian Gnostics than his orthodox contemporaries.

15. Brown, *Body and Society,* 133.

16. Tertullian, *Castit.* 9 (*Corpus christianorum. Series latina* [Turnhout, Belgium, 1953] 2:1027–28), quoted in Pelikan, *Christian Tradition,* 1:288. John Irving's fictional character Jenny Fields begins her autobiography with a surprisingly similar sentiment: "In this dirty-minded world, you are either somebody's wife or somebody's whore—or fast on your way to becoming one or the other." *The World According to Garp* (New York: E. P. Dutton, 1978), 112.

17. Brown, *Body and Society,* 79, cf. 80.

18. According to Pelikan, Tertullian may have written or at least edited their story. Pelikan, *Christian Tradition,* 100. It is available as "The Martyrdom of Saints Perpetua and Felicitas," in *Acts of the Christian Martyrs,* ed. Herbert Musurillo (Oxford: Clarendon Press, 1972).

19. Brown, *Body and Society,* 74; Atkinson, *Oldest Vocation,* 20.

20. "Martyrdom of Saints Perpetua and Felicitas," chap. 18, 127; also quoted in Atkinson, *Oldest Vocation,* 21.

21. Atkinson, *Oldest Vocation,* 21f.

22. Brown, *Body and Society,* 158, cf. 154f. Thecla's story is told in the apocryphal *Acts of Paul and Thecla,* which began circulating around the middle of the second century. It is not clear whether there was an actual person at the heart of the many legends that grew up around her. Pagels, *Adam, Eve, and the Serpent,* 18ff.

23. Pagels, *Adam, Eve, and the Serpent,* 20, 80. Compare Brown, *Body and Society,* 6, 191. Even so the family continued to exert considerable control over its young, cf. *Body and Society,* 360.

24. Pagels, *Adam, Eve, and the Serpent,* 88f.; cf. 96, and her bibliography of recent research in this area in note 31, 166.

25. Brown assembles evidence that suggests the median age of Roman girls at marriage may have been as low as 14 and that half the married women recorded on North African gravestones had died before the age of 23. It appears that during this short span each woman would need to bear an average of five children, if the population of the Roman Empire were to remain even stationary. *Body and Society,* 6.

26. Brown, *Body and Society,* 25.

27. Ibid., *Body and Society,* 206ff.

28. Eusebius sketched these two ways of life given to the church in *Demonstratio Evangelica* 1.8, *Patrologia Graeca* 22:76 C, in W. J. Ferrar, trans. *Eusebius: The Proof of the Gospel* (London: SPCK, 1920), 1:48. Quoted in Brown, *Body and Society,* 205. Pressure began to build for total clerical celibacy, though Brown points out that it was not until the late sixth century that bishops were drawn solely from the ranks of lifelong celibates, *Body and Society,* 432.

29. Pagels, *Adam, Eve, and the Serpent*, 82f.

30. Brown believes that Christian encouragement for continence among women as well as men was directly related to women's prominence in the early Christian church (*Body and Society*, 145). Also, if the alternative presented by the ascetic movement had not prevailed, Christian sexual morality might well have hardened into a form much like that which prevails today along the Islamic shores of the Mediterranean (206).

31. Compare Atkinson, *Oldest Vocation*, 64.

32. Brown, *Body and Society*, 401. Brown also tells of a funeral witnessed by Jerome as an example of the "cheerful impermeability of the many. . . . A husband, the veteran of twenty wives, buried a wife who had, in her time, got through twenty-two husbands. The husband led the procession around her bier, crowned and carrying a palm of victory, with all the people of the City in attendance, to the chant of 'Lay 'em out in hundreds.' " *Body and Society*, 430, quotation from Jerome, *Letter* 123.10: *Patrologia Latina* (Migne) 22:1052–53.

33. Pagels, *Adam, Eve, and the Serpent*, 91–96.

34. Jerome, *Adversus Jovinianum* 1, 10; 20, quoted in Pagels, *Adam, Eve, and the Serpent*, 94. It was Jerome, too, who "praised marriage because it was the way virgins were brought into the world." Pelikan, *Christian Tradition*, 1:289.

35. Pagels, *Adam, Eve, and the Serpent*, 96.

36. In pre-Christian Rome, "Infants came into the world, or at any rate were received into society, only as the head of the family willed. Contraception, abortion, the exposure of freeborn infants, and infanticide of slaves' children were common and perfectly legal practices." Veyne, "The Roman Empire," 9. Christianity's rejection of the exposure of infants may have been an aspect of the gospel especially attractive to many pagan women. Martin A. Hansen suggests that this was the case in the later Christianization of Scandinavia, *Orm og Tyr* (Copenhagen: Gyldendal, 1956), 242.

37. Brown, *Body and Society*, 298, cf. 271.

38. Ibid., *Body and Society*, 327.

39. Macrina's mother, having experienced a vision of the virgin St. Thecla during labor, resolved that Macrina should be free to pursue the celibate life, Brown, *Body and Society*, 278. Similarly, "Theodoret's mother was only one of many women known to us who plainly felt that only a child marked out for a sacred life would redeem their own loss of virginity and exposure to the remorseless physical disruption of childbirth," ibid., 325.

40. Brown, *Body and Society*, 237. Brown's quote is from "the

undisputed masterpiece of Byzantine spiritual guidance," i.e., John Climacus (579–649), *The Ladder of Divine Ascent,* 14:868C; p. 169 in the English translation by C. Luibheid and N. Russell (New York: Paulist Press, 1982).

41. Not all women will have such affirming experiences. Indeed, Ann Oakley believes that modern obstetrical practices too often make childbirth a disempowering experience; see her *Women Confined: Towards a Sociology of Childbirth* (New York: Schocken, 1980), 272f. In such experiences, too, there is much to be learned, as well as a significant opportunity for healing.

42. Brown, *Body and Society,* 424.

43. Brown, *Body and Society,* 397f. Thecla was a well-known heroine (cf. above n. 22), while Crispina was a married woman and mother who had been martyred.

44. Brown, *Body and Society,* 402.

45. David Nikkel, "St. Augustine on the Goodness of Creaturely Existence," *Duke Divinity School Review* 43 no. 3 (fall 1978):185f.

46. Augustine, "On Marriage and Concupiscence," 1.16, *A Select Library of the Nicene and Post-Nicene Fathers,* ed. P. Schaff and H. Wace (New York: Christian Literature Company, 1886–1890), 5:270. See also chap. 17.

47. Compare James Nelson, *Embodiment: An Approach to Sexuality and Christian Ethics* (Minneapolis: Augsburg, 1978), 54; Nikkel, "St. Augustine," 186; Brown, *Body and Society,* 407, 416.

48. Augustine, *De Peccatorum Meritis et Remissione* 2, 2; quoted by Pagels in *Adam, Eve, and the Serpent,* 111.

49. Augustine, "On Marriage," 5:275.

50. Pagels, *Adam, Eve, and the Serpent,* 109; cf. Augustine *De Civitate Dei,* book 13, chap. 14 *Corpus Christianorum. Series latina* 48:395f.

51. Augustine, *Opus Imperfectum Contra Julianum,* 4, 114, quoted in Pagels, *Adam, Eve, and the Serpent,* 133.

52. Pagels, *Adam, Eve, and the Serpent,* 134.

53. Pagels, *Adam, Eve, and the Serpent,* 135. Citation is from Augustine, *Opus Imperfectum,* 6, 26. Compare Peter Brown, *Augustine of Hippo* (Berkeley: University of California, 1967), 396.

54. Brown, *Body and Society,* 40f.

55. Pelikan, *Christian Tradition,* 1:288f.

56. Brown, *Body and Society,* 354.

57. Brown, *Body and Society,* 407.

58. Compare Leonardo Boff: "Mary embraced her sorrow, and integrated it into God. What we live in a disintegrating, threatening,

merely passive way, Mary actualized in an integrating way, and it became an opportunity for growth, a grace-filled encounter with God. . . . Thus, Mary was genuinely free not from pain itself, but from the *way* we have pain, the *way* we experience the breach to which we are still subject, incapable as we are of integrating our negativity with God in a personal way." Leonardo Boff, *The Maternal Face of God: The Feminine and Its Religious Expressions,* trans. Robert R. Barr, and John Diercksmeier (San Francisco: Harper & Row, 1987), 148.

59. Paul Jewett, *Man as Male and Female* (Grand Rapids: Eerdmans, 1975), 105.

60. Pagels, *Adam, Eve, and the Serpent,* 136f., and Brown, *Body and Society,* 412–415.

61. Pagels, *Adam, Eve, and the Serpent,* 143.

62. Ibid., 146f.

63. Origen, *Homilies on Leviticus,* 8.3, quoted in Pelikan, *Christian Tradition,* 1:291.

64. Pelikan, *Christian Tradition,* 1:291.

65. Compare Pelikan, *Christian Tradition,* 1:291f., and Brown, *Body and Society,* 352f.

66. E. S. Hartland, "Birth," *Encyclopedia of Religion and Ethics,* ed. James Hastings (New York: C. Scribners, 1908–1927), 2:643.

67. Cheryl Kristolaitis, "From Purification to Celebration: The History of Service for Women after Childbirth," *Journal of the Canadian Church Historical Society* 28 no. 2 (October 1986):56.

68. I hear this concern voiced among women inside the church, as well as by those who have distanced themselves from it. For a published example, see Elizabeth Gray, ed., *Sacred Dimensions of Woman's Experience* (Wellesley, Mass.: Roundtable Press, 1988), 60f.

6
Divinity and Demons

One of the intriguing surprises of recent medieval scholarship is the existence of "a minor but persistent and theologically responsible tradition which experiences God and especially Jesus as Mother and Sister as well as Father and Brother."[1] It is surprising that people who generally viewed women as both physically and morally weaker than men would even conceive of calling the supreme being by female names, particularly in a society that continued to view virginity as holier than motherhood. And yet this was also an era intensely interested in the incarnation; baby Jesus in the flesh becomes an increasingly prominent theme in religious art, as does the exposed body of the suffering Christ.[2] Thus it may be precisely because the female was conventionally viewed as the earthier sex that female attributes were employed to proclaim the earthiness of Christ incarnate in Jesus and in the sacrament of the altar.[3]

It may come as a surprise that these images were not initially developed by or for women.[4] Bishop and theologian Anselm of Canterbury (1033–1109) seems to be the first medieval writer to take up and expand upon the New Testament's maternal metaphors for Christ. In his devotional writing, Anselm addresses Jesus as the Mother who gathers and comforts her children, as a hen gathering her chicks under her wings;[5] and as the Mother whose giving birth is characterized by acceptance of all:

Truly, Lord you are a mother;
for both they who are in labour
and they who are brought forth
are accepted by you.

Anselm continues by describing Christ's birthing labor and sacrifice as a source of empowerment to Christians in their own birthing labor:

You have died more than they, that they may labour to bear.
It is by your death that they have been born,
for if you had not been in labour,
you could not have borne death;
and if you had not died, you would not have brought forth.
For, longing to bear sons into life,
You tasted death,
And by dying, you begot them.[6]

Thus Anselm moves easily back and forth between mother and father language, declaring a few verses later: "Then both of you [i.e., Saint Paul and Christ] are mothers. Even if you are fathers, you are also mothers."[7]

The motif of Christ as mother reappears in cosmic proportions in the meditations of Marguerite d'Oingt, thirteenth-century prioress of a convent of Carthusian nuns. She addresses Jesus as a woman giving birth:

Ah, who has seen a woman give birth thus!
And when the hour of birth came, they placed
You on the bed of the Cross. And it is not astonishing
your veins ruptured, as you gave birth in one single day,
to the whole world![8]

Indeed, Marguerite viewed Jesus' entire life as a bringing to birth: "Are you not my mother, and more than my mother. My mother carried me and laboured to give birth a single day or a single night. But you laboured for more than thirty years. And when the time of giving birth approached, you sweat as with drops of blood."[9]

Other medieval mystics drew on the motif of the nursing

mother. Mechthild of Hackeborn, a thirteenth-century German nun, speaks of God's love as a Mother at whose breasts she sucks.[10] Catherine of Siena, a fourteenth-century nun famous for her care of the sick and her diplomatic efforts as well as for her spiritual insight, refers to Christ as a nursing mother "who takes medicine instead of her suckling, because she is grown up and strong and the child is not fit to endure its bitterness."[11] The monk of Farne, a fourteenth-century British recluse, speaks of Christ on the cross suckling faithful souls with the blood from his side.[12] He compares Jesus to a mother who loves us as children and gives us to drink his health-giving blood. "Do not wean me from the breasts of thy consolation as long as I live in this world."[13]

This and similar references to suckling Jesus' blood may well seem grotesque to modern readers. The image would have been less shocking to medieval people because current medical theory held that breast milk was transmuted blood.[14] Still, the sacrificial image is potent, and the connections to the Eucharist unmistakable. Late medieval art made a similar connection between lactation and the Eucharist, whether it be the lactating Virgin Mary, or less frequently, the suggestion of the lactating Jesus.[15]

Twelfth-century Bernard of Clairvaux, who was an influential Cistercian abbot, preacher, and mystic, also speaks of Jesus as nursing mother: "Suck not so much the wounds as the breasts of the Crucified. He will be your mother and you will be his son." More frequently Bernard uses the metaphor of a nursing mother to lift up the nurturing aspects of religious leadership, applying it to male figures including Moses, Peter, and Paul, as well as abbots in general, and himself in particular.[16] Similarly, Francis of Assisi wrote "to his friars with respect to their work as pastors and preachers, bidding them to be mothers, to bear Christ and to give birth to Christ in others;"[17] and Catherine of Siena counseled a cleric to "guard your own soul and body so you can nourish other souls and give birth to them."[18]

These and other examples lead McLaughlin to observe that "the 'people language' of medieval piety is also less limited and more androgynous [than its twentieth-century counterpart]. In particular, men were able to see themselves as mothers, sisters, nurturers, persons who give birth to God and who are as midwives to the birth of God in other souls."[19] Throughout this period, the weakness and dependence associated with the female and the child could be appropriated by members of both sexes to express something of their relationship to God. The experiences of birthing and nursing could be taken as expressive both of a spiritual leader's relationship to the souls in his or her care and of God's salvific work in Christ: Christ's humanity and creative suffering, as well as Christ's ongoing nurture of humanity through the Eucharist.

We may take issue with the notion that the female is particularly weak and still appreciate the imaginative freedom that allowed male leaders to think of themselves in terms of female life experiences. The drawback of the increasing use of parental language to define relationships within celibate communities was its tendency to elevate spiritual parenthood at the expense of the more mundane begetting and bearing, birthing and rearing of flesh and blood children. So, too, the idea of spiritual parenthood could be used to lend legitimacy to a hierarchical church structure.[20]

For fourteenth-century mother-saints like Birgitta of Sweden, however, giving birth to Christ had less to do with church hierarchies than with a personal sense of vocation and a joyous communion with God. Like other mother-saints, Birgitta experienced a mystical pregnancy: "With a great burst of joy in her heart, she felt as if a living child were moving in her heart."[21] Birgitta had borne and raised eight children before widowhood freed her to devote herself fully to her spiritual vocation; thus she was one of a new era of saints. After centuries in which the models for female holiness were virgin martyrs, religious vocations began to open up to married women in the later Middle Ages;[22] and the experience of physical motherhood began to shape perceptions of spiritual motherhood. Increasingly, nuns like Birgitta had mystical experiences of giving birth to and suckling the infant Christ. According to Atkinson, this new tradition of spiritual motherhood "incorporated an enhanced appreciation of biological and social motherhood, which had acquired its own numinous characteristics. The recognition and acknowledgment of the necessity and holiness of suffering, believed to be intrinsic to all motherhood, contributed a sacred dimension to physical motherhood."[23]

Not only did Birgitta experience a mystical pregnancy and a long and intimate relationship to the holy mother Mary, she freely employed the imagery of birth—both in relation to actual births (physical and spiritual) and as a metaphor to clarify theological meaning. In her *Revelations,* for example, Christ compares sinners to stillborn children and himself to a mother (VI.28): "Just as a stillborn child does not taste the sweetness of the mother's milk, nor the comfort of her words, nor the warmth of her breast, just so thou [sinner] shall not be comforted by my words, nor feel the warmth of my love." Similarly, Christ speaks as a mother whose sufferings have been needlessly increased by her unappreciative son (VI.19); such a son may justly be reproached, "for I brought him from darkness to light by my Passion, and fed him with the milk of my sweetness."[24]

Meanwhile, across the North Sea, maternal imagery for God also was blossoming in the visions and meditations of Julian of Norwich. Julian begins in the spirit of the tradition that sees Jesus as the mother who gives birth to Christian souls:

> But our true Mother Jesus, he alone bears us for joy and for endless life, blessed may he be. So he carries us within him in love and travail, until the full time when he wanted to suffer the sharpest thorns and cruel pains that ever were or will be, and at the last he died. And when he had finished, and had borne us so for bliss, still all this could not satisfy his wonderful love.[25]

For Julian, the picture of Jesus as mother is not a fleeting devotional metaphor, but rather an enduring, Christ-centered insight that enabled her to see the motherhood of all three persons of the trinity:

> I understand three ways of contemplating motherhood in God. The first is the foundation of our nature's creation; the second is his taking of our nature, where the motherhood of grace begins; the third is the motherhood at work.[26]

Christ's motherhood begins in the womb of Mary, at the moment God takes on human flesh. The point of reference is not primarily the travail of childbirth compared to travail on the cross. Christ's motherhood is expressed in the incarnation itself, which is "a kind of *creation* of us, as a mother gives herself to the foetus [*sic*] she bears."[27]

Even while some Christian thinkers and mystics were employing female images to communicate something of God, and unprecedented numbers of women were being canonized as saints,[28] the tendencies of other aspects of medieval theology combined with social changes to put women at increasing risk. The Middle Ages were dangerous centuries in which to be born: The plague worked its dreadful decimation of the population for almost a century (1348–1430), many of the survivors lived in extreme poverty. Infant mortality was high during the plagues; infanticide ceased to be rare after 1348 and became even more common in the next century.[29] The word "foundling" had its origins in the fourteenth century as impoverished parents increasingly abandoned their children, and hospices were established to care for them. The centuries that followed were marked by social upheavals as medieval structures began to give way to modern ones.

A most appalling characteristic of these times was the fear of witches that spread across the European continent. A full inquiry into the origins and excesses of the struggle to vanquish witchcraft are beyond the scope of this study.[30] It is, however, important to note here that fertility in general, and the birthing chamber in particular, were seen as especially vulnerable to the witch's evil intent. Witches were thought to cause impotence and barrenness, as well as excessive passion and miscarriage.[31] *Malleus Maleficarum* [Hammer of the Witches], the classic witch-hunter's guide published in 1486, draws special attention to the dangers of witch-midwives, with their access to unbaptized infants. It warns that the most powerful witches "are in the habit of eating and devouring the children of their own species. . . . But these are only children who have not been re-born by baptism at the font, for they cannot devour those who have been baptized."[32] The authors observed that even when witch-midwives "do not kill children, then, as if for some other purpose, they take them out of the room and, raising them up into the air, offer them to devils."[33] A few pages later they warned that even baptized children were vulnerable, "especially when they have not been protected by the sign of the Cross and prayers,"[34] that is, when they have not been properly baptized. According to some, even the mother's soul was at risk at this critical time: "The mother is no longer a real Christian until she is churched, for she has been despoiled of her Christianity by the child in the act of birth."[35] Krämer and Sprenger advise that given the dreadful nature of their possible crimes, witch-midwives are to be condemned and sentenced like other witches, even if their only known crime is to "remove spells of witchcraft superstitiously and by the help of devils; for it can hardly be doubted that, just as they are able to remove them, so can they inflict them."[36]

The misogynist flavor and implications of this work haunt the church to this day. The concluding directive concerning witch-midwives has emerged as particularly problematic. Within the theoretical framework of the day it was logical; the theory of the demonic pact (an implicit or explicit arrangement with the devil by which a person received supernatural powers) had abolished the traditional distinction between magic intended to help and that intended to harm.[37] The effect of this logic, however, was to open the way for prosecution of any midwife who might employ folk remedies deemed superstitious by the ruling authorities. And at least to modern eyes, many medieval obstetrical customs seem superstitious indeed. Among other things, women drank potions of pulverized rocks, deer's horn, dragon's blood, and turpentine; they held stone amulets in their hand or wore them tied to their thigh; they wore verbal charms around their neck, and even drank the words rinsed off a piece of paper![38] In addition, midwives of this period, at least in rural areas, were often poor and ignorant, their position lowly and even despised.[39] That even well-meaning midwives might rely on questionable practices to aid the birthing process seems quite likely.

The witch-hunters' special interest in midwives has fueled

suspicion that the witch-hunt represents an attempt by the emerging medical profession, supported by church and civil leaders, to eliminate competition. Some exponents of this theory practically suggest that "witches" were simply organized female peasant healers.[40] Indeed, there was considerable practical overlap in official and unofficial medicine at the time of the witch-hunts. The sharpest distinction between the two was their authorization, and thus also their gender: "All official healers were male; most unofficial healers were female."[41] Still, there are difficulties with the theory that the witch-hunt was primarily an attack on female healers. For one thing, the church had traditionally displayed ambivalence toward medical practice of any sort: "The relationship between the cure of the soul and the care of the body was too close for most active adherents of Christianity to remain neutral to the potential of medicine for good or for ill."[42] Moreover, Christina Larner points out that men also were arrested for unofficial healing, and that "most of the women who were arrested for witchcraft were more often accused of harming than of healing—white magic alone rarely brought anyone to the stake." Larner also notes that "the masculinization of healing was only beginning during the period of the witch-hunt. By the eighteenth century, when professionalization was rapidly increasing and midwifery also taken over by men, the witch-hunt was already finished."[43] Midwifery, which concerned even the earliest witch-hunters, turned out to be the sphere in which women retained their healing role longest.

Why, then, this focus on midwives? To some extent it probably arose out of celibate males' fear of female sexuality in general, and the unknowns of the birthing room in particular. It may also have roots in the mythical Diana's reputation as a midwife—as Jeffrey Russell points out, many of the characteristics attributed to witches can be seen as embodiments of the Diana myth.[44] In part, the focus on midwives probably reflects an age-old human ambivalence toward any healer; those with the power to heal also can withhold their help or turn their knowledge to harm.[45] Midwives' involvement in such a vulnerable point in people's lives put them in a particularly precarious position.[46] Furthermore, many midwives were also at risk because they were single, elderly, and poor. Most of the women prosecuted as witches were older "masterless" women, and one of the occupations whereby such women could eke out a living was midwifery.[47]

Then, too, some midwives may actually have thought of themselves as witches. In his study of medieval midwifery practices, Forbes observes that "ignorant, unskilled, poverty-stricken, and avoided as she often was, it is small wonder that the midwife could be tempted, in spite of the teachings of the church, to indulge in superstitious practices or even in witchcraft."[48] Whether "witchcraft" was as nefarious as its victorious opponents depicted is less clear; the very words "witchcraft" and "devil worship" are obviously dangerous labels. Modern scholars have discredited Margaret Murray's once-popular theory that those who were accused of witchcraft were in fact members of a pre-Christian fertility religion that met secretly at the old festivals.[49] Still, the beliefs and customs of an earlier era probably lingered at least until the time of the Reformation and the accompanying emphasis on Christian education of the laity. The midwife who secretly raised a newborn into the air and mumbled an incantation may have been a culturally conservative friend, rather than a demonic foe. Indeed, she might have seen her actions as providing extra protection for the child.

What, then, of the persistent grisly reports of child sacrifice? Were they polemic or paranoid excesses, or did they reflect a genuine problem? It is still difficult to know.[50] Whatever the actual case may have been, the intellectual zeal of demonologists like Krämer and Sprenger was more than matched by the increasing anxiety of the general public.[51] One can only begin to imagine the anxiety that must have attended birth in such circumstances. The inherent distress of birthing itself could hardly be eased by the possibility of evil intentions on the part of one's birthing attendant. Nor was such an atmosphere likely to encourage wise women to practice midwifery.

This is a dark chapter in the history of the church. From the vantage point of a later century, the myriad trials and executions stand as an outrageously misguided response to a widespread experience of vulnerability, suffering, and social dislocation, and as a sobering witness to the church's human fallibility. Church and civil authorities, along with the general populace, bear responsibility for this holocaust, which began in the Middle Ages and continued well into the "Age of Reason." The church also must live with the disturbing fact that most persons burned as witches were women, although the extent of the church's responsibility for this focus is not clear.[52] The association of women with magic is found in traditional societies the world over. Widespread, too, are myths like the unbiblical Pandora's box, which associates women with the introduction of evil into the world. In addition, views of women were changing in medieval culture as a whole: At a time when woman was idealized as loftier and more spiritual than man in theories of courtly love,[53] secular authorities demonstrated a new willingness to prosecute women, at least for newly criminalized offenses like witchcraft and infanticide.[54]

Given this complex context, the average parish pastor's concern for events in the birthing room, the female domain so essential to society, may well reflect not only mistrust and fear of women but also some measure of pastoral concern. How could clergymen hope to fulfill the vital task of protecting weak women and newborn children from the assaults of the evil one, when the doors of the birthing room were closed to them? This sense of concern for the welfare of mother and child during childbirth may be the only mitigating quality in the entire episode. Still, it is shocking—and sobering—to see how readily a highly respected sixteenth-century churchman can shift from sharing compassionate insights into the childbearing woman's needs to talking of the bonfires awaiting the "troll woman" who "persists in using blessings and magic formulas."[55]

Medieval clergy expressed their pastoral concern first and foremost by urging speedy baptisms to minimize the infant's vulnerability. The increasingly close connection between birth and rebirth is pictorially clear in a thirteenth-century depiction of childbirth scenes that moves directly from the birthing stool behind closed doors and the nursing of the newborn to the church and baptism. The bulging maternal abdomen that dominates the first three scenes is replaced in the final scene by a huge, bellylike baptismal font that almost seems to envelop the mother and her older child, as well as the newly baptized baby.[56] Of course, not all babies were healthy enough to risk waiting to be baptized at church; thus emergency baptism by the midwife was sanctioned by the church as early as the seventh century. "The midwife was bound under peril of mortal sin to know and to use the proper ritual when she baptized an infant, and the clergy was specifically charged with instruction of midwives in the administration of this rite.[57]

As concern about witch-midwives increased, the church not only instructed midwives but also began to certify them. Although this certification focused primarily on the prospective midwife's good character rather than on her ability and experience as midwife, Peter Palladius (1503–60), for example, advises that the oldest and most respected women in the parish should approve the person desiring to be a midwife. Palladius, who was the first Lutheran bishop of Denmark, noted that it is in everyone's best interests that midwives are "competent, enlightened, and God-fearing."[58] The specifics varied from place to place, but generally midwives were taught to provide for emergency baptisms;[59] they took oaths in which they swore to make themselves available to rich and poor alike, to refrain from employing sorcery or superstitious methods, and to not destroy or dismember any child.[60] Several ordinances also dealt with the proper burial of stillborn children and prohibited the use or sale of fetal membranes, placenta, or umbilical cord as these might be used for superstitious practices.[61]

Through all this, the church prayed. The church prayed publicly for women in childbirth, and people prayed privately in all circumstances of daily life. A sixteenth-century devotional book for women contains no less than thirty-eight prayers devoted to childbirth.[62] Prayers were not just spoken and written down, some were written on parchment scrolls and used almost as amulets.[63] Surviving examples of such prayer amulets for use in childbirth include riddles as well as words of invocation. A hauntingly beautiful example from 1475 invokes the Father, the Son, and the Holy Spirit; prays that the cross, passion, and five wounds of Christ may be a source of healing; calls to mind the holy mothers Mary, Ann, Elizabeth, and Cecilia; proclaims that Christ rules and had once called forth Lazarus. Then the prayer entices and warns the infant: "Christ calls thee.† The world delights in thee.† The covenant longs for thee.† The Lord of vengeance is God.† Lord of battles, God, free thy servant N.† . . . Oh infant, whether alive or dead, come forth.† Christ calls thee to light.† . . . Christ the Nazarene† King of the Jews, Son of God† have mercy on me.† Amen."[64]

The holy mothers Mary, Ann, Elizabeth, and Cecilia were not the only saints invoked to aid birthing women. The aid of the virgin Saint Margaret, patroness of childbirth also was widely sought. Saint Margaret's picture also was inscribed on birth charms to be worn during pregnancy, and sometimes a copy of her biography was placed on the birthing woman's chest.[65] It may seem odd that this patroness of childbearing, like Artemis and Diana, was a virgin. Saint Margaret's character, however, is quite unlike that of her Greek and Roman counterparts. Legend has it that while Saint Margaret was in prison for her faith, she encountered the devil in the form of a dragon that swallowed her. The cross that she carried in her hand so irritated his throat that he disgorged her. The next day attempts were made to execute her by fire and drowning, but she was miraculously saved. When she finally was executed, she died praying for mercy for all the birthing women who would invoke her aid.[66] In contrast, Artemis was called on by women in childbirth because no pain attended her own birth, and she apparently resented her resulting involvement in birthing.[67]

At least by the eighteenth century, "the Church took a dim view indeed of all such charms—'vanity, illusion, and folly,' to quote one distinguished authority."[68] Even so, such practices continued into the nineteenth century. The tenacity of these customs points to the healing power that women have found in tangible reminders of their faith. Today, too, a candle, a cross, a rosary, or an icon can provide a focal point and comfort during labor, transforming an otherwise unfamiliar and impersonal birthing room into a holy space. Such visible and tangible faith symbols offer a woman the peace of her faith and set her labors and suffering in a sacred context.

Similarly, modern health-care professionals may learn from the Ulster midwives who "marked every outside house corner with a cross, then recited the following prayer before crossing the threshold: 'There are four corners to her bed, Four angels at her head: Matthew, Mark, Luke, and John; God bless the bed that she lies on. New moon, new moon, God bless me, God bless this house and family.' "[69] In our pluralistic society, finding ways to mark the birthing room off as sacred space will usually be the prerogative of the family. Still, the prayers of nurses, doctors, and midwives as they enter the birthing room might well make birthing a more gracious experience for everyone involved.

The church also included in its public prayers a rite for reintroducing parturient women into society. This rite seems to have been related to the Jewish purification rite for women following childbirth, though the earliest extant Christian reference to the rite is from about 400. In that reference, the purification theme with its temporary exclusion of parturient women from full membership in the church is clear: Parturient women are indeed "unchurched," consigned to a place among catechumens.[70] Most Jewish ritual laws had been abandoned by early Christians; why, then, was this rite retained or reintroduced? Part of the rationale may lie in the Virgin Mary's purification, although the parallel instance of Jesus' circumcision did not lead to a Christian rite of circumcision. Kristolaitis suggests that the rite "was kept because it contributed to the continuation of male/female roles in society."[71] This is not a completely satisfying explanation; circumcision would have been a still clearer demarcation of male and female from a religious point of view. Perhaps this rite was continued, in spite of the problems it posed for Christian theology, because people continued to have a deeply engrained feeling that sexuality was somehow unclean. Perhaps, too, the rite was kept because it filled an equally deep human need to articulate communally the life-shaking crisis that childbirth continued to be, both for the mother and for the entire community.

Although Pope Gregory the Great (540–604) taught that neither pregnancy nor childbirth was to be treated as pollution,[72] the purification of women following childbirth became an accepted part of medieval church usage. In the influential medieval English Sarum rite,[73] for example, it is clear that the unchurched woman is considered ritually among the unbaptized. The first part of the rite was said at the church door; then the woman, wearing a veil similar to that worn at confirmation, was sprinkled with holy water and, holding the priest's stole, led by him into the church. During this procession the priest read the prayer used for carrying an unbaptized child into church. Once inside the church, the woman made an offering of the chrism or baptismal gown of her child, who had usually already been baptized, and communicated in the Mass that followed.[74] Psalms 24 and 51 were included as optional parts of the service; the use of Psalm 51, with its recurrent reference to sin and even bloodguiltiness (v. 14), might well leave the impression that reproduction was somehow sinful in itself: "Wash me thoroughly from mine iniquity, and cleanse me from my sin. . . . Behold I was shapen in iniquity; and in sin did my mother conceive me." (v. 2, 5, KJV)

Palladius's journal gives us a glimpse of the common conceptions that had come to accompany this rite by the time of the Reformation, at least in Denmark. He writes that under the papacy, people "spoke derisively of the woman in childbirth. They said she was unclean and defiled, and that she had more to do with the devil than with Our Lord. With candles and holy water she was supposed to hold the devil at a distance when, clad in a gray cloak, she went to church for the first time" after giving birth. Palladius has no patience with such attitudes and customs: "That kind of Mardi Gras foolery is plain evidence. We have certainly been way out."[75] Rather than seeing the churching rite as a matter of exorcism or purification, Palladius interpreted it as marking the end of a kind of maternity leave: "The reason that the woman must manage for so long [six to seven weeks] without attending church, is solely that she may see to her own health and that of the child." He counsels husbands to see to it that the new mother is able to rest; and counsels strong women not to press themselves—if not for their own sake, then for the sake of their weaker sisters who might not have an understanding and helpful husband.[76] The rite itself consisted of prayers of thanks for a safe delivery, prayers for help in the responsibilities of motherhood, and prayers for other pregnant women. After these prayers were said at the entrance to the church, the pastor offered a blessing, and led the woman into church; whereupon her family and female friends followed her up to the altar to present her thank offering. Palladius made a point of encouraging women to show one another this honor, not least to the poor among them.[77]

Similar tendencies are apparent in the rite of purification for women following childbirth that Thomas Cranmer and associates included in the 1549 Anglican *Book of Common Prayer*. The entire service took place within the church, and the sprinkling with holy water was dropped. Thus, although the service was still titled "The Order for the Purification of Women," the parturient woman was no longer treated as one unbaptized. Indeed, in spite of the title, the theme of purification already was being replaced by an emphasis on the preservation of the woman from the dangers of childbirth by the Lord's goodness.[78] This refocusing of the rite was clarified in the 1552 revision of the prayerbook, which renamed the service "The Thanksgiving of Women after Childbirth, commonly called the Churching of Women." In this service the woman gave thanks for safe deliverance from "the great pain and peril of childbirth,"[79] heard the encouragement of Psalm 121, and was prayed for in her vocation as mother. Pastoral guidelines for the use of this service noted that unmarried mothers were to be denied its benefits until they had done appropriate public penance; thus the rite served to promote lawful wedlock, as well as to mark a woman's safe passage through a dangerous crisis and to lift up the vocation of motherhood.

This new emphasis on the vocation of motherhood reflects the new view of family that emerged with the Reformation. To the implications of this new worldview we will turn next.

Notes

1. Eleanor McLaughlin, "Christ My Mother: Feminine Naming and Metaphor in Medieval Spirituality," *The Saint Luke's Journal of Theology* 17 no. 4 (September 1975): 245.

2. Leo Steinberg, *The Sexuality of Christ in Renaissance Art and in Modern Oblivion* (New York: Pantheon, 1983), 72.

3. Caroline Walker Bynum, *Holy Feast and Holy Fast: The Religious Significance of Food to Medieval Women* (Berkeley: University of California Press, 1987), 268f., cf. 296.

4. Caroline Walker Bynum, *Jesus as Mother: Studies in the Spirituality of the High Middle Ages* (Berkeley: University of California Press, 1982), 140f.

5. *The Prayers and Meditations of St. Anselm with the Proslogion,* trans. and intro. Sr. Benedicta Ward (London: Penguin, 1973), 153, cf. 155f.; cf. Matt. 23:37.

6. *Prayers and Meditations of St. Anselm,* 153. Compare Acts 2:24, and discussion above, 163ff.

7. Ibid., 154.

8. A. Duraffour, P. Gardette, and P. Durdilly, *Les Oeuvres de Marguerite d'Oingt* (Paris: 1965), 33–36, quoted in McLaughlin, "Christ My Mother," 235.

9. *Les Oeuvres de Marguerite d'Oingt,* 31f., cited in McLaughlin, "Christ My Mother" 235 n.

10. McLaughlin, "Christ My Mother," 236; cf. *Buch besonderer Gnade, in Leben und Offenbarungen der Heiligen Mechthilds und der Schwester Mechtildis,* ed. J. Müller (Regensburg, 1880), 166.

11. *The Dialogue of Catherine of Siena,* trans. Algar Thorold (London, 1907), 68f.; quoted in McLaughlin, "Christ My Mother," 244.

12. McLaughlin, "Christ My Mother," 236; cf. *The Monk of Farne,* ed. Hugh Farmer, The Benedictine Studies (Baltimore, Md.: Helicon Press, 1961), 69.

13. *The Monk of Farne,* 64, quoted in McLaughlin, "Christ My Mother," 237.

14. Bynum, *Holy Feast,* 270f.

15. Bynum, *Holy Feast,* 271f., and accompanying plates. Compare "The Mass of St. Gregory," ca. 1483, by Master of Westphalia, reproduced in *A History of Private Life,* vol. 2: *Revelations of the Medieval World,* ed. George Duby (Cambridge: Harvard University Press, 1988), 621.

16. Bynum, *Jesus as Mother,* 115.

17. Francis of Assisi, *Opera omnia,* ed. J.J. von der Burg (Cologne, 1849), 5; quoted in McLaughlin, "Christ My Mother," 242. Compare the apostle Paul, Gal. 4:19.

18. Letter 342, Catherine of Siena, Letters, ed. Misciattelli, (Siena, 1913–1922) vol. 3, 174, quoted in Bynum, *Holy Feast,* 179.

19. McLaughlin, "Christ My Mother," 245.

20. Ivone Gebara, for example, asserts that "the spiritual motherhood practiced by women consecrated to God . . . starts with the authority and power structures obtaining in society and in the hierarchical-clerical Church." "The Mother Superior and Spiritual Motherhood: From Intuition to Institution," 42–51, in *Motherhood; Experience, Institution, Theology,* ed. Anne Carr and Elisabeth Schlüssler Fiorenza, Concilium (Edinburgh: T & T Clark, 1989), 206:42.

21. *The Liber Celestis of St. Bridget of Sweden,* ed. Roger Ellis (Oxford: Oxford University Press, 1987), 1:460; quoted in Clarissa W. Atkinson, *The Oldest Vocation: Christian Motherhood in the Middle Ages* (Ithaca: Cornell University Press, 1991), 181. For other instances of mystical pregnancy, see Atkinson, 163, 185f.

22. Atkinson, *Oldest Vocation,* 164f. The Beguines of the Low Countries, for example, included widows and wives (with their husbands' permission) as well as virgins. These service-oriented religious communities valued voluntary poverty in goods and family relationships, rather than sexual status per se.

23. Ibid., 163f.

24. Ibid., 182f.

25. Julian of Norwich, *Showings* (1373), trans. and ed. Edmund Colledge and James Walsh (New York: Paulist Press, 1987), 298.

26. Julian, *Showings,* 297.

27. Bynum, *Holy Feast,* 266.

28. Atkinson, *Oldest Vocation,* 186.

29. Charles de La Ronciere, "Tuscan Notables on the Eve of the Renaissance," in *A History of Private Life,* 2:223.

30. See Alan C. Kors and Edward Peters, "Introduction: The Problem of European Witchcraft," in *Witchcraft in Europe 1100–1700: A Documentary History,* ed. Kors and Peters (Philadelphia: University of Pennsylvania Press, 1972); Thomas Rogers Forbes, *The Midwife and the Witch* (New Haven and London: Yale University Press, 1966); Christina Larner, *Witchcraft and Religion: The Politics of Popular Belief* (Oxford: Basil Blackwell, 1984); and Jeffrey Burton Russell, *Witchcraft in the Middle Ages* (Ithaca: Cornell University Press, 1972) for various views. Russell contains an overview of the history of interpretations, 27–43. See notes in Atkinson, *Oldest Vocation,* 230–234, for a selection of recent articles on the subject.

31. Atkinson, *Oldest Vocation,* 232.

32. Heinrich Krämer and Jacob Sprenger, "Malleus Maleficarum," in *Witchcraft in Europe, 1100–1700,* ed. Kors and Peters, 130.

33. Krämer and Sprenger, 129.

34. Ibid., 134.

35. James Hastings, ed, *Encyclopedia of Religion and Ethics* (New York: Scribner's, 1910). Quoted in Forbes, *Midwife and Witch*, 129.
36. Krämer and Sprenger, "Malleus Maleficarum," 188.
37. Larner, *Witchcraft and Religion*, 3f.
38. Forbes, *Witchcraft and Witch*, 68–79, esp. 77; 80–90. In Italy, for example, "the Fifty-first Psalm was written on paper with pen and ink as far as the words, 'O Lord, open thou my lips.' Then the writing was rinsed off, and the water was swallowed by the parturient woman," 80.
39. Forbes asserts that the midwife's position, especially in rural areas was generally a lowly one, 112f. On the other hand, a recent analysis of an early English devotional book for women suggests that midwives (at least those who worked among the urban and educated women for whom the prayerbook was intended) exhibited a high degree of professionalism and enjoyed considerable respect. See Colin B. Atkinson and William P. Stoneman, " 'These griping greefes and pinching pangs': Attitudes to Childbirth in Thomas Bentley's *The Monument of the Matrones* (1582)," *Sixteenth Century Journal* 21 no. 2 (1990): 199ff.
40. Barbara Ehrenreich and Deidre English, *Witches, Midwives, and Nurses: A History of Women Healers* (Old Westbury, N.Y.: Feminist Press, 1973), 7–17; and *For Her Own Good: 150 Years of the Experts' Advice to Women* (New York: Doubleday, 1978), 31–35. Ehrenreich and English are widely cited. Barbara Rothman, for example, refers uncritically to their theory: "When midwives did organize, earlier in European history, they were burned as witches." *In Labor: Women and Power in the Birthplace* (New York: W.W. Norton and Co., 1982), 76. So, too, a 1985 Canadian Broadcasting Corporation "Doctoring the Family" series referred to their work.
41. Larner, *Witchcraft and Religion*, 149. Larner points out that official medicine did tend to be more interventionist and heroic.
42. Darrel W. Amundsen and Gary B. Ferngren, "Medicine and Religion: Early Christianity Through the Middle Ages," 93–131, in *Health/Medicine and the Faith Traditions: An Inquiry into Religion and Medicine*, ed. Martin E. Marty and Kenneth L. Vaux (Philadelphia: Fortress Press, 1982), 119. Inspired by the New Testament injunction to minister to the sick, the church had from the beginning offered charitable healing assistance, especially for the destitute. Amundsen and Ferngren note that "there is abundant and irrefutable evidence that in the early Middle Ages . . . monasteries became the refuge of the sick, the poor, and the persecuted," 116. On the other hand, while the church accepted secular healers insofar as they were beneficial, there was a

concern that their attempts to heal the body might be detrimental to the soul. Unfortunately, this essay does not explore how midwifery fit into the overall picture.

43. Larner, *Witchcraft and Religion*, 152.

44. Although Russell does not mention midwifery specifically, he does suggest that the "witches Sabbath" and wild night rides that later entered the tradition can be understood from this perspective. See *Witchcraft in the Middle Ages*, 245; cf. 47ff., 78–81, and 115f.

45. The Hippocratic oath, in which the physician promises to heal and not hurt, is the classic effort to deal with this concern. The prevalence of malpractice suits (especially frequent in obstetrics) and public debate of euthanasia and abortion indicate that ambivalence regarding the healer is far from a thing of the past. The importance of this factor in the witch-hunts is illustrated in Iceland's reversal of the standard European pattern. In Iceland, which had a tradition of cunning men and male magicians, twenty-two men and only one woman were burned as witches as a result of the 120 trials conducted between 1604 and 1720. Grethe Jacobsen, "Nordic Women and the Reformation," 47–67, in *Women in Reformation and Counter-Reformation Europe: Private and Public Worlds,* ed. Sherrin Marshall (Indianapolis: Indiana University Press, 1989), 60.

46. The tale of the faithful Hebrew midwives (Ex. 1:15ff.) both shows childbirth as a point of vulnerability and suggests that the pharaoh, at least, viewed midwives as dubious characters who might be willing to do his dirty work for him. The midwives proved him wrong; they emerge as model healers who were courageous and smart enough to protect the lives entrusted to them.

47. See Allison P. Coudert, "The Myth of the Improved Status of Women: The Case of the Witchcraze," in *The Politics of Gender in Early Modern Europe,* ed. Jean R. Brink, Allison P. Coudert, Maryanne Horowitz (Kirksville, Mo.: Sixteenth Century Journal Publishers, 1989), 61–89; Larner, *Witchcraft and Religion*, 58, 84; Atkinson, *Oldest Vocation,* 233.

48. Forbes, *Midwife and Witch,* 113, cf. 117, 119, 129, 132.

49. Larner, *Witchcraft and Religion,* 47.

50. Russell, *Witchcraft in Middle Ages,* 88–92, notes that early Christians too, like the Jews before them, had been accused of ritual human sacrifice. Christian polemicists not only refuted these charges, but made similar accusations against pagans and heretics. Russell, however, apparently believes that there may have been factual basis for this concern: "Witches sacrificed or ate children or made them into magical salves or powders, but they did not abuse them sexually," 263.

51. Kors and Peters, ed., *Witchcraft in Europe,* 12.

52. It may come as a surprise, for example, to learn that the clergy was the other group most often charged with witchcraft. Bynum, *Jesus as Mother,* 20 n.

53. Russell, *Witchcraft in Middle Ages,* 145f., and 280f. associates the rise of the courtly love ideal and its opposite, the fear of women as witches.

54. Previously women had been kept out of court because their misdeeds had been viewed as the legal responsibility of their fathers or husbands; at this time, "women suddenly appeared in the courts in large numbers, the old women as witches, the young as infanticides." Larner, *Witchcraft and Religion,* 60. Larner observes that the obvious gender-related character of witchcraft has yet to be adequately explained, 61f.

55. Peder Palladius, *En Visitats Bog,* retold in modern Danish by Egon Nielsen (Ringkøbing, Denmark: Forlaget Aros, 1981), 74f. Originally written about 1544, this "visitation book" was published after its author's death in 1560. Palladius's warnings against witches are part of his comments on the importance of finding a good midwife. He goes on to encourage people not to be overly afraid of troll-women, and when they have found a good midwife to "pay her decently, for she is well worth her salary. One might wish that the authorities would exempt her from paying taxes," 76.

56. Illustration in Alphonse the Wise, *Cantigas,* reproduced in *A History of Private Life,* 2:81. This acclaimed history of private life in medieval times does not describe birthing practices, but it does reproduce several pictures of women gathering around a mother and her newborn child: 2:221, 247, 248, 532, 540.

57. Forbes, *Midwife and Witch,* 130f. Small Saint Margaret manuscripts, complete with prayers for pregnant and parturient women, continued to be transcribed right down into the nineteenth century in Iceland. See Jacobsen, "Nordic Women and Reformation," 61.

58. Palladius, *En Visitats Bog,* 74.

59. An English edict of 1577 revoked the right of midwives to perform emergency baptisms in Protestant households, declaring "that no midwifes, nor any other woman, be suffred to minister baptisme." Quoted in Forbes, *Midwife and Witch,* 142.

60. Ibid., 131f.; cf. 141–47.

61. Ibid., 118.

62. For examples and analysis of several of these prayers, see Atkinson and Stoneman, "These griping greefes," 196ff.

63. Philippe Braunstein, "Toward Intimacy: The Fourteenth and Fifteenth Centuries," *A History of Private Life,* 2:625.

124 CHURCH HISTORY: BURDENS AND RESOURCES

64. Forbes, *Midwife and Witch*, 89f. The invocation also includes exclamations of Christ's holiness and eternity and a formula that Forbes believes is an acrostic for Hebrew words meaning "Thou art mighty forever, O Lord," 86–93.

65. Ibid., 88.

66. John J. Delaney, *Dictionary of Saints* (Garden City, N.Y.: Doubleday, 1980), 381; cf. Forbes, *Midwife and Witch*, 88 n.

67. Robert Graves, *The Greek Myths* (New York: George Braziller, 1955), 1:83.

68. Forbes, *Midwife and Witch*, 82. Quote is from J. B. Thiers, 1771.

69. Ibid., 83. Prayer quoted from W. G. Black, *Folk-Medicine: A Chapter in the History of Culture* (London: Elliot Stock, 1883).

70. Cheryl Kristolaitis, "From Purification to Celebration," *Journal of the Canadian Church Historical Society* 28 no. 2 (October 1986): 56. The reference is found in the Canons of Hippolytus.

71. Ibid., 56.

72. Atkinson, *Oldest Vocation*, 79. Gregory makes these points in his correspondence with the missionary bishop Augustine of Canterbury.

73. The Sarum rite was the liturgy used in the diocese of Salisbury (Sarum) from the early thirteenth century on. According to King, it "was the most important factor in the liturgy of the English Church from the 13th century until the change of religion in the 16th." Archdale King, *Liturgies of the Past* (Milwaukee: Bruce Pub. Co., 1959), 292.

74. Kristolaitis, "Purification to Celebration" 56f. Compare Marion Hatchett, *Sanctifying Life, Time and Space: An Introduction to Liturgical Study* (San Francisco: Harper & Row, 1976), 88.

75. Palladius, *En Visitats Bog*, 72.

76. Ibid., 77.

77. Ibid., 78. Elsewhere in Denmark churching celebrations apparently drew a large crowd; a 1561 ordinance forbids too many women from accompanying the churching woman and urges those who do so to give their collects together rather than one at a time, so as not to delay the service. *Ribe Bys Historie*, repr. ed. Ole Degn (Århus: Jysk Selskab for Historie, Universitetsforlaget, 1985), 93–96; summarized in Jacobsen, "Nordic Women and Reformation," 61.

78. Hatchett, *Sanctifying Life*, 121. The theme of uncleanness did not disappear completely. *The Monument of Matrones* (1582) contains a prayer in which a postpartum woman refers to herself as God's "most defiled and polluted hand maid" and bewails her "vnworthines, vilenes,

and vncleannes." The *Monument*'s alternate prayer for such women is a prayer of thanks closely modeled on the prayer of thanks in the 1559 version of the *Book of Common Prayer*. Atkinson and Stoneman, "These griping greefes," 198.

79. *Book of Common Prayer 1559: The Elizabethan Prayer Book*, ed. John Booty (Charlottesville, Vir.: 1976), 283, quoted in John Booty, "The Anglican Tradition," in *Caring and Curing: Health and Medicine in the Western Religious Traditions*, ed. Ronald L. Numbers and Darrel W. Amundsen (New York: Macmillan, 1986), 245.

7

Reforming Conceptions of Childbirth

The Protestant Reformation shook the celibate ideal that had held sway in the church for over a thousand years. In Protestant lands, the two-tiered model of a celibate elite and a married, procreative majority collapsed, and a new family-centered religious ideal emerged. Churchmen, who in an earlier age would have sung the praises of virginity, turned their rhetorical skills to exhortations to marriage and childbearing. In doing so, they reclaimed the Hebrew Bible's emphasis on childbirth as a blessing and on sex as an aspect of creation. This new focus on the family increased respect for childbearing and rearing and for women's procreative capacities. It did so, however, at the expense of reducing vocations for women to one: marriage and motherhood. For better or for worse, it also increased theological and pastoral interest in childbirth itself.

Martin Luther's life and teaching exemplify the enormous transitions that were under way in this period. In 1525, the former monk Martin Luther married the former nun Katharina von Bora, thus putting into practice the reformers' conviction that sexual drives are a gift of the Creator and that marriage is as holy as celibacy. Their marriage caused consternation even among some of Luther's closest associates, who feared that this taboo-shattering marriage of a former monk and a former nun might jeopardize the cause of the Reformation itself;[1] and the birth of their first child was awaited with more than the usual suspense. According to superstition, a two headed monster could be expected to issue from such a "sacrilegious" union.[2] Imagine, then, the relief and joy that must have attended the birth of the Luthers' healthy baby!

The Reformation survived Luther's marriage, and indeed Luther's bold affirmation of human sexuality and marriage is one of the lasting benefits of the Reformation. The cloud of suspicion that had cast such a long shadow over everything associated with procreation began to lift. Of course Luther was a child of his times as well as a herald of a new era; more than a decade after he had boldly argued that "the estate of marriage and everything that goes with it in the way of conduct, works and suffering is pleasing to God,"[3] he still referred to sexual intercourse after the fall as shameful and infected by lust, far from the delightful intimacy God envisioned for man and woman.[4] Nonetheless, Luther vigorously proclaimed the goodness of sexuality as a God-given gift. His contemporaries, schooled to view sex in terms of sin rather than in terms of creation, must have been astonished and even offended at Luther's insistence that procreation was among the most delightful and sacred aspects of the created order.[5] "For truly," he wrote, "in all nature there was no activity more excellent and more admirable than procreation. After the proclamation of God's name it is the most important activity Adam and Eve in the state of innocence could carry on."[6]

Luther insisted that even in a sinful world, sexuality is to be respected as a vital aspect of God's creative power. We "should distinguish vices, which original sin brought on, from the creation and works of God. I am sure that I was created a male."[7] So, too, original sin is the "source of the aspersions against the female sex, aspersions which ungodly celibacy has augmented."[8] Like all human faculties, sexuality has been affected by sin: "The passion of lust is indeed some part of original sin. But greater are the defects of the soul: unbelief, ignorance of God, despair, hate, blasphemy."[9] Thus Luther unmasks the celibate ideal and its pretensions of special holiness. Indeed he holds "ungodly celibacy" responsible for *augmenting* the effects of original sin by disparaging God's creation. He proclaims that the sexual instincts that the monastic tradition feared as especially sinful, and strove to prevent, have been ordained and blessed by God from the first chapters of Genesis.[10] These created and creative drives are not to be suppressed, but rather domesticated in marriage and fulfilled in procreation. As Martin Marty puts it, for Luther "the God who forgives smiles more on the Christian parents-to-be who are begetting than on the monk who prattles prayers."[11]

Luther did not rule out celibacy as a God-given calling, but he pointed out that such cases are rare. Even before his own transition from monk to married man was complete, he questioned the motives of those who were tempted to reject marriage and parenthood. He poked fun at those who choose the cloister in order to avoid the inconveniences of married life; seduced by natural reason they think: " 'It is better to remain free and lead a peaceful, carefree life; I will become a priest or nun and compel my children to do likewise.' "[12] Cloisters began to close throughout Protestant areas, treatises and sermons that had detailed the pain and peril of motherhood while extolling virginity fell into disuse, marriage and motherhood became the main Christian vocation for women.

Luther's esteem for procreation led him to question the desire to remain childless wherever he met it. Luther had harsh words for those, found "chiefly among the nobility and princes, who often refrain from marriage for this one single reason, that they might have no offspring. It is even more disgraceful that you find princes who allow themselves to be forced not to marry, for fear that the members of their house would increase beyond a definite limit." Luther saw selfish political and economic interests at work in "this callousness and inhuman attitude" and viewed such calculated childlessness as a barbarous rejection of one of God's most wondrous gifts; such attitudes "serve to emphasize original sin."[13] This severe assessment of those who base procreative decisions on economic considerations might seem naive or even heartless, were it not for the fact that by this time Luther was personally acquainted with the demands and delights of a growing family. At the time he delivered this critique, he and Katharina were the parents of five children under the age of ten (a sixth child had died in infancy), and were living within very modest means.[14] What is more, Luther's critique focused primarily on the wealthy and powerful, the very persons who had the means to support children.

In an era of concern for overpopulation, such a vigorous acclamation of procreation may seem outdated at best. Indeed, Luther did live in a very different era, both with respect to the size of the human population and with respect to the demands the human population placed on the earth. And yet his words still prod persons, especially the world's affluent, to examine their motives when deciding whether to have children. Is the decision not to have children an expression of caring for the earth and its capacity to sustain its inhabitants, or is it more directly related to the burdens of maintaining children in the style customary in a consumer society? Luther's insight into the ways egotism may motivate the decision not to have children challenged his era's notion that celibacy and childlessness represented admirable self-sacrifice. Today our ready association of "Christian" and "family values" attests to the success of the reformers' struggle to renew appreciation for procreation and to elevate the vocation of Christian parenthood. Rhetoric aside, however, the actual level of appreciation and practical support American society offers children and their parents suggests that the struggle to rightly value procreation and parenthood is still pertinent today.

Luther's emphasis on parenthood as vocation was particularly significant for women, not only because it honored the work of bearing and raising children that women had done throughout the generations, but also because the new emphasis on motherhood as vocation would soon practically eliminate all other vocations for women. Luther himself has been accused of arguing "that women's justification and salvation lay in her womb."[15] This assertion is based on Luther's commentary on the promise of 1 Tim. 2:15 that "woman will be saved through bearing children." In fact, Luther's response to this problematic text is considerably more circumspect. He approaches the verse in light of the penalties woman has suffered ever since Eve (distress in childbearing and domination by man), observing that though the blame passed over, the penalties imposed in Gen.

3:16 will continue until the final judgment and must be endured. (Although he doesn't mention man's punishment in this context, presumably it, too, continues and must be endured.) Having endured these penalties, woman will be saved, a phrase Luther explains here in terms of social status, not in terms of eternal salvation; he takes "saved by bearing children" to mean that "she has an honorable and salutary status in life if she keeps busy having children."[16] We may find this comment offensive and outmoded, but it is hardly a position paper arguing that woman's salvation lay in her womb, or that "the ability to give birth enabled women to atone for their responsibility for the Fall."[17]

Elsewhere it becomes clear that Luther respected woman for a wide range of talents, not just for the procreative capacities of her womb. Luther's own wife Katharina was an independent and capable woman who managed the Luther family finances and property. Although he took for granted the traditional division of labor, which assigned women to the domestic sphere, Luther clearly respected the range of talents required to run a pre-industrial household: "Even if men could bear children the world would go to rack and ruin without women, because they know all about 'spending and saving'—and that is what politics and government are all about."[18]

Furthermore, although the work of child rearing fell primarily to women, Luther envisioned parenthood as a shared endeavor. In a 1522 treatise affirming the estate of marriage, he repeatedly mentions the diaper washing and other "insignificant, distasteful, and despised duties" family life may involve—each time pointing out that no Christian *man* should turn up his nose at such tasks. Instead, faith enables the Christian family man to look on everything from sleepless nights spent caring for a crying child to days spent laboring at his trade as duties that are precious in God's sight. Indeed, such a Christian father confesses his unworthiness to perform the humblest of services for the family with which God has blessed him: "O God, because I am certain that thou hast created me as a man and hast from my body begotten this child, I also know for a certainty that it meets with thy perfect pleasure. I confess to thee that I am not worthy to rock the little babe or wash its diapers, or to be entrusted with the care of the child and its mother."[19] And when in Christian love a father "goes ahead and washes diapers or performs some other mean task for his child . . . God with all his angels and creatures is smiling—not because the father is washing diapers, but because he is doing so in the Christian faith." On the other hand, those who ridicule such a man as an effeminate fool "are ridiculing God with all his creatures . . . indeed they are only ridiculing themselves; with all their cleverness they are nothing but devil's fools."[20]

Of course the disadvantages of dirty diapers and extra work that might dissuade men from marriage pale in comparison to the pain and life-threatening danger that childbearing meant for women. In spite of the suffering and danger, Luther affirmed woman's work in childbearing: "If you were not a woman you should wish to be one for the sake of this very work alone, that you might thus gloriously suffer and even die in the performance of God's work and will. For here you have the word of God, who so created you and implanted within you this extremity."[21] This view has offended at least one writer, who interprets Luther to mean that it doesn't matter if a woman dies in childbirth, because it is for this that she is created.[22] No one who has read Luther's descriptions of Tamar's difficult childbirth,[23] or his insights into Jacob's "bitter grief" at Rachel's death in childbirth[24] could imagine that he thought "it didn't matter if a woman dies in childbirth." To the contrary, he wrote that "among all the various kinds of death I consider it the saddest sight when a mother dies with her unborn child."[25]

A death met in the midst of working with God to bring forth new life is both sad and noble, akin to the death of the martyr who dies witnessing to the Gospel's life-giving message. A birthing woman can face the possibility of her own death in the confidence that even such a sad turn of events will not separate her from God's creative purposes. From this perspective the specter of death begins to lose its power, and the woman is released to immerse herself in the work of giving birth. Thus Luther suggests that the best way to comfort and encourage a woman in labor is not by repeating "St. Margaret legends and other old wives' tales," but by reminding her that she is engaged in noble and God-pleasing work.[26] According to Luther, even an unwed woman in childbirth can boast that what she is doing is pleasing in God's sight.[27] "Contemplation of and respect for this work have remained even among the heathen;"[28] Christian women, moreover, have God's word of promise as well as punishment. Their pains are not only evidence of sin and divine judgment, but also "a sure sign of divine blessing that through birth the human race and the very church of God are being rebuilt."[29] Thus the birthing woman should be encouraged to "trust joyfully in [God's] will, and let him have his way with you. Work with all your might to bring forth the child. Should it mean your death, then depart happily, for you will die in a noble deed and in subservience to God."[30]

The sexual overtones of "letting God have his way with you" and the reference to "subservience to God" are troubling because they imply such a masculine God and because they suggest a picture of sexual relations as domination—one partner gets "his way," the other is subservient. In spite of its patriarchal expression, however, this passage offers the intriguing suggestion that the religious dimension of letting oneself go in birthing may be akin to the delights of marital intimacy. Nor should reference to "subservience to God" obscure how this speech builds up the birthing woman—building up her appreciation of her own childbearing capacities, building up her joyful faith in the God who will remain with her throughout this demanding experience, and strengthening her to give herself over to the task at hand.

In accordance with the traditional interpretation of Gen. 3:16, Luther sees the suffering and danger involved in childbirth as a punishment for sin. He emphasizes that this punishment is "a happy and joyful punishment," because it is so limited. The punishment is a sign that the woman's relationship to God has been damaged by sin, but not destroyed. "Eve hears that she is not being repudiated by God. Furthermore, she also hears that in this punishment she is not being deprived of the blessing of procreation, which she was promised and granted before sin." Nor does the woman's punishment mean complete alienation from her partner: "She sees that she is not being separated from Adam to remain alone and apart from her husband."[31] Indeed, in marriage part of woman's punishment is transferred to her husband, "for he cannot without grief see those things in his wife."[32] Thus even though it is marked by the effects of sin, childbirth provides the couple an opportunity to form new bonds of shared suffering and joy. The husband's active participation in his wife's travail also is suggested in Luther's comments on Micah 4:9. There he likens the prophet to a labor companion; "writhe and groan" is not a word of woe, but a word of encouragement, "as we generally help women in childbirth with our cries of encouragement."[33] Here Luther gives us a glimpse of birthing as a communal event, the laboring woman surrounded by friends and family who cheer her on and suffer with her, encourage her to express her distress physically and orally, and remind her that the release of birth is close at hand.[34]

Luther also sees the suffering of childbirth as a help to keep woman humble,[35] in that it reminds her that she, too, is a sinner, and that she is privileged to be God's coworker in the miracle of bringing forth new life. Indeed, all persons should approach a newborn child with awe and humility: Luther approvingly cites Cyprian, who "wrote that one should kiss the newborn infant, even before it is baptized, in honor of the hands of God here engaged in a brand new deed." Furthermore, "all nuns and monks who lack faith, and who trust in their own chastity and in their order, are not worthy of rocking a baptized child or preparing its pap, even if it were the child of a harlot."[36] Luther reminds his reader that however commonplace it may be, childbirth remains a miracle:

> The birth of a human being . . . is just as miraculous today as was the birth of Isaac. But because of their frequent occurrence these great miracles have become commonplace. Therefore God sometimes puts forth a new work, not that it may be a greater one but to show that those common and ordinary works which happen among us are similar to those extraordinary ones and are derived from the same source, that is, from the Almighty Word of God.[37]

According to Luther, attention to God's Word clears human eyes to "see that the entire world is full of miracles." And one senses the miracle and joy of birth ready to burst forth, even in Luther's discussion of birthing danger and suffering. He sees God's mercy, even in the midst of punishment. So, too, the experience of giving birth may be an occasion for a woman to strengthen her relationship to the " 'God who hides himself.' For under the curse a blessing lies hidden; under the consciousness of sin, righteousness; under death, life; and under affliction, comfort."[38]

In the wake of the Reformation, new attention was focused on conception and birth. The reformers' efforts to rid the populace of the "papist" practice of venerating the saints extended into the birthing room with admonitions against invoking Mary and the saints for their help in childbirth. Luther advised reminding women of the nobility of their birthing work rather than telling them Saint Margaret's story; his successors more vigorously set about correcting birthing customs. The Danish bishop Palladius, for example, inveighed against "old monks' women" and their incantations invoking the virgin, Saint Anne, and Saint Margaret; prelates continued to argue against such practices well into the eighteenth century.[39] Churchmen gave advice regarding midwives, and assisted in licensing them until that function was taken over by the civil authorities.[40] This focus on procreation was not limited to church officials; civil authorities enacted and increasingly enforced strict laws governing sexual activity.[41]

In colonial America this interest in pregnancy and childbirth found new expression in the preaching of the renowned Puritan, Cotton Mather (1663–1728). In contrast to Luther, who saw childbirth as evidence of God's ongoing creative power and compassion for sinful, suffering human beings, Mather considered pregnancy an opportune time for women to consider the wrath of God, and repent. In a widely distributed published sermon, Mather admonished, "for you ought to know, your Death has entered into you, and you may have conceived that which determines but about nine months at most, for you to live in the world. Preparation for death is that most reasonable and

most seasonable thing, to which you must now apply yourself."[42]

To facilitate this preparation, Mather depicted the "place of
dragons and of Torments," which he foresaw as the lot of the
unregenerate, and urged the expecting mother to ponder her
own sorry, sinful state in light of the hellfires that might be her
fate. He admonishes her to "be as much afraid of leaving any Sin
unconfessed, as [she] would be of having the *After-birth Left in
[her]*, after [her] Travail." Moreover she should bewail her
inborn sinfulness—both her share in the sin of her first parents
and "that Corrupt Nature which by a Derivation from your Next
Parents you brought into the World with you."[43] Having been
brought to utter contrition and despair, the woman is told to
"behold the admirable SAVIOUR provided for you: The JESUS
who is *God manifest in Flesh:* God and MAN in one Person: the
SAVIOUR who is *Able to save you unto the uttermost.*" She is
enjoined to resign herself up to the Holy Spirit, and to "take up
the *Resolutions* of universal and perpetual PIETY. Thus the New
Birth is carried on."[44]

According to Mather, this new birth is the only birth that is
really worthwhile: "Except you are *Born again,* it had been *good
for you that you never had been born* at all: The *Sorrows of
Childbirth,* will be to you, but the *Beginning of Sorrows,* and of
such as know no *End.*"[45] If, on the other hand, a woman
undergoes the soul-searching travail that culminates in her
rebirth, that is, the conquest of her soul by the Holy Spirit, death
will be disarmed of all its terrors; even "if you should now be
Teeming with your Death, yett you may keep Rejoicing in the
Hope of the Glory of God."[46] In this way the "Curse" associated with childbearing "is turned into a Blessing," as fear of
trauma and death lead to spiritual rebirth. Mather saw this
salvific effect of facing the hazards and hardships reflected in the
fact that more women than men were apparently pious and
"partakers of a *New Birth.*"[47]

Mather's sermon highlights in drastic terms the proximity of
life and death in birthing and the opportunity this presents for
spiritual growth. It is true that childbirth would not be necessary
if it were not for human mortality; and even today mothers do

risk their lives to give birth to their children. Still, Mather's words strike the modern ear as excessively morbid and terrifying, also when compared to the views Luther had expressed almost two centuries earlier. Does Mather's emphasis on death reflect a greater physical risk to birthing women in colonial America than had been the case for women in sixteenth-century Germany? Possibly, although studies have shown that colonial American women were actually less likely to die in childbirth than were their English contemporaries.[48] Perhaps the difference between Luther and Mather is more directly related to their theological views; the Puritan tendency to admonish by emphasizing God's righteous judgment might well lead Mather to dwell on the distressing and dangerous aspects of procreation. Indeed, Mather's emphasis on the seriousness of a pregnant woman's situation precludes much appreciation of the joy of childbirth. He assumes that women need to be convinced that they are supposed to regard their pregnancy as a blessing,[49] and although he cites John 16:21[50] as a word that once dropped from Jesus' lips, he quickly tempers its joyful proclamation with reminders of Rachel's death in childbirth.[51]

What were the effects of such preaching? Did it promote healthy self-examination, so that women were at peace with themselves and their world as they began their birthing labors, or did it simply instill a morbid fear that increased the distress of childbirth? How could a woman know for sure that she had confessed every last remnant of sin and that her soul had been completely conquered by the Holy Spirit and was thus safe from a fate worse than death? Mather enjoined the regenerate pregnant woman to exercises of piety including earnest and constant prayer, scripture reading, psalm singing ("considerately alone by yourself"), and alms giving (distributed with a special eye for needy childbearing women and for the poor who could pray for her during her pregnancy and confinement). These exercises may have provided women with assurance of the Spirit working through them, in addition to the inherent benefits of increased prayer, Bible study, and ministry to and from others.

Perhaps such preaching and piety helped women approach childbirth spiritually prepared to face possible death; it does not seem to have helped them relish the joyous accomplishment of childbirth. Colonial women's diaries do not record feelings of joy and ecstasy in giving birth; more prevalent are sentiments such as Anne Bradstreet expressed in her poem, "Before the Birth of One of Her Children." Bradstreet contemplates her own eventual death and takes the precaution of bidding her husband farewell:

> All things within this fading world hath end,
> Adversity doth still our joys attend; . . .
> How soon, my Dear, death may my steps attend,
> How soon't may be thy lot to lose thy friend,
> We both are ignorant, yet love bids me
> These farewell lines to recommend to thee. . . .[52]

One searches Mather's sermon in vain for a glimpse of the Creator who brought forth all creation and affirmed its goodness. The first person of the Trinity is vividly depicted as angry, powerful, and easily offended—hardly the sort of companion most women would desire to have by their side in childbirth. No wonder Mather directs women to Christ as their mediator. Christ, in turn, is depicted both as the compassionate son who, having been born of a woman, will hear childbearing women's cries for protection and assistance[53] and as the "mighty and most gracious *Husband*" who is both willing and able to give a woman a happy travail. Mather tells the pregnant woman to face labor with courage and supplications, confident that her omnipotent Redeemer will send good angels to help her. Although Mather exclaims that "no Midwives can do what the Angels can," he does recognize the need for tangible assistance to deal with the suffering of childbirth and attaches a list of remedies for child-bearing maladies to the end of his sermon.[54] Notably, these remedies do not draw upon spiritual resources for healing, such as prayer, laying on of hands, or even confession and absolution. Instead, they are mostly potions attributed to medical doctors. Thus the spiritual and physical crises of childbirth are largely separated, and in both crises, women are dominated by male saviors. It is ironic that the respect for medical authority promoted by Mather's appended list of remedies would eventually divert attention almost completely away from the spiritual opportunity that was his sermon's main concern.

Between Luther and Mather stands the American religious leader and midwife Anne Hutchinson (1591–1643). Like Mather two generations later, Hutchinson viewed childbirth as an appropriate time to consider the state of one's soul. Her ministrations as midwife to the women of the Massachusetts Bay Colony included not only herbal remedies and practical help, but also pastoral care. John Cotton, the Puritan pastor caught between Hutchinson and her religious and political opponents, observed later, "She did much good in our town, in woman's meeting and at childbirth travails, wherein she was not only skilful [sic] and helpful, but readily fell into good discourse with the women."[55] Unfortunately, the details of that "good discourse" may be lost to history; to this author's knowledge, no study of this subject has yet been done. Presumably she spoke of "the covenant of grace" as opposed to the "covenant of works" and encouraged women to rely on God's grace rather than on their own piety for the assurance of their salvation.

Hutchinson was not just a mother and midwife. She had received training in theology and Scripture from her father, an English parish priest whose outspoken criticism of the church hierarchy put him out of a parish for a number of years. Her teaching emphasized "the covenant of grace" and was grounded in the belief that the Spirit could directly inspire the faithful, without recourse to the guidance and approval of church authorities. These ideas struck a responsive chord with many of Boston's leading citizens; up to eighty people, men as well as women, would gather weekly at her home for reflection upon the week's sermon. As might be expected, Hutchinson's ideas and popularity brought her into conflict with the colony's hierarchy. Under more favorable circumstances, Hutchinson might have developed and articulated connections between her theology and her experience of birthing fifteen children and attending the births of many more. As it was, her energies were taken up in a struggle that eventually ended with her banishment and excommunication.

Hutchinson's competence as midwife was admitted by even

her adversaries; according to John Winthrop, it was precisely Hutchinson's skills as midwife and healer that enabled her to "easily insinuate herself into the affections of many."[56] Another observer found a more sinister reason for Hutchinson's popularity: "Midwives . . . not only have familiarity with the Devil, but also in that service commit devilish malefices."[57] Subsequent events were taken as proof of God's judgment upon Hutchinson and her followers. First, one of Hutchinson's supporters miscarried at the time of her civil trial. When news of this reached Winthrop some months later, he had the remains exhumed, and then described the stillborn child in terms befitting a devil's offspring. For Winthrop, this "monster" was a clear sign of the "monstrous errors" of Anne Hutchinson.[58] Second, Hutchinson herself miscarried shortly after going into exile. Although she had previously borne fifteen healthy children and was of menopausal age, the details of her miscarriage were taken by her adversaries as a sign of God's displeasure with her teachings. "See how the wisdom of God fitted this judgment to her sin every day, for look as she had vented misshapen opinions, so she must bring forth deformed monsters."[59] Similarly, Hutchinson's death in an Indian massacre was viewed as divine punishment.

Times have changed—few twentieth-century Americans are inclined to interpret natural disasters as expressions of divine wrath, much less to attribute a woman's miscarriage to the defects of her theology. The secular view of nature and natural processes that has replaced the Puritans' thoroughgoing religious worldview has undoubtedly served to minimize unnecessary guilt in the face of suffering. Less happily, it also has tended to develop an increasingly secular practice of medicine, in contrast to Anne Hutchinson's ministry to body and spirit.

This new situation challenges the church to reclaim childbirth as spiritual event. The paternalistic tendencies Palladius and fellow reformers show in attempting to direct childbirth practices rightly give us pause, but should not dissuade us from prodding health-care professionals today to expand their understanding of childbirth to include its spiritual dimensions. So, too, the manipulative underpinnings of Cotton Mather's effort to

scare religious commitment into pregnant women should cau-
tion us, but not prevent us from shaping more appropriate
models for pastoral care to the childbearing. The church has a
responsibility to affirm childbearing as a spiritual, as well as a
physical and social, experience, and to work with the healers in its
midst to recover the holistic strength that characterized Anne
Hutchinson's ministry as midwife.

Similarly, the secular view of nature and natural processes
today challenges the church's pastors, theologians, and birthers
to find meaningful ways to articulate God's presence in childbearing and to reexamine the relationship between sin and
procreative difficulties ranging from infertility or miscarriage to
the pain of travail. Can we speak meaningfully and gracefully
about the effects of sin as mirrored in such difficulties, or has the
connection between sexuality and sin been so grossly misused
that we must seek new language with which to probe the
spiritual meaning of such experiences?

Odd as it may seem, Søren Kierkegaard (1813–1855), the
Danish thinker whose pseudonyms expressed some utterly out-
rageous views of women,[60] struggled with this latter problem in
The Concept of Anxiety, and in so doing he displayed remarkable
insight into the psychological and spiritual dynamics of childbearing. Kierkegaard was not writing for or about women, he
was simply trying to make sense of Augustine's doctrine of
inherited (that is, original) sin with the help of modern psychological categories. Following Augustine's lead, he reflects upon
procreation as related to the solidarity of sin. Birth is ideally
suited to expressing human solidarity: human beings' life stories
are many and varied, but we are all born of a mother's womb.
Thus to say we are all born in sin clearly states the solidarity of
human sin—and leads to thinking about how this might be. The
problem with linking the transmission of sin to birth as Augustine does is the resulting tendency to practically equate sex
with sin, a tendency Kierkegaard takes pains to reject.[61]

Kierkegaard seeks to avoid this misunderstanding of inherited sin and to allow for individual responsibility by introducing
the psychological category of anxiety (*Angest*) as an intermediate
disposition between innocence and sin. Anxiety is the fundamen-

tally human experience of being both attracted to and repelled by something.[62] This ambivalent experience reflects the nature of the human synthesis that comprehends both necessity and freedom, a synthesis that is poised between blind instinct and sheer transcendence. Sin is one possible outcome of this anxiety; wholeness through faith is the other. Thus sin is not simply equal to concupiscence or lack of control, and the inevitable involvement of sexual arousal (concupiscence from Augustine's viewpoint) in procreation does not adequately explain the transmission of sin.

Kierkegaard proposes a theory of the procreative experience that avoids defining sexual arousal per se as sinful and that does not depend on viewing a bodily fluid like semen as the source of spiritual contamination. He reflects on the interplay of body and spirit in both sexual intercourse and birthing and finds that both moments evoke heightened anxiety: "In the moment of conception, the spirit is farthest away and therefore anxiety is the greatest. . . . In birthing, woman is again at the outermost of one of the extremes of the synthesis, so the spirit trembles."[63] The parents' anxiety is communicated at these two points to the unborn child. Kierkegaard does not stop to explain just how the parents' anxiety is communicated to the child. Somehow the anxiety that arises from the interplay of body and spirit during conception and birthing is communicated to the child from the moment it comes into being, and the anxiety becomes a hallmark of its humanness—its capacity for faith and freedom as well as for sin.[64]

Kierkegaard's introduction of anxiety as an intermediate disposition avoids linking sexual processes directly to sin and helps interpret the anxiety that often surfaces during pregnancy and childbirth. Far from being a sign of weakness or pathology, such anxiety is a fundamentally human experience that reflects the complexity of the human condition. Seeing anxiety as a normal response to the challenges of childbearing frees women to face and voice the ambivalence they often experience. Birthing is a body-dominated experience that the spirit is hard pressed to assimilate. The anticipation and experience of pain, the fear of death, and the loss of self are in constant tension with the promise of new life and motherhood. Whereas Mather had practically reduced this anxiety to its negative elements in order to fit the requirements of his strategy for salvation, mainstream contemporary American culture tends to do the opposite, showing little tolerance for expressions of pain or the struggles of the maternal role. Kierkegaard's model reminds us that both attraction and antipathy are fundamentally human responses to the situation, and that facing both responses encourages spiritual maturity and renewed health.

More than a woman's intrapsychic and interpersonal struggles are involved in this anxiety. Society's assessment of the value of woman's procreative task also enters the picture. In keeping with the general assumptions of his day, Kierkegaard wrote that from an ethical point of view, woman culminates in procreation.[65] Although many will find this view offensive, it continues to linger, though it is rarely expressed so bluntly. Thus while many women still experience motherhood as the threshold into adulthood, fatherhood is seldom such a dominant aspect of male identity.[66] Anthropologist Helen Callaway observes that "to be a female is first to be identified with biological reproduction— 'the most essentially female function of all.' In contrast to a woman, a man is likely to be designated as father of a family only incidentally to the list of public activities and achievements which proclaim his identity."[67]

There is no indication that Kierkegaard found this notion even potentially offensive; he minced no words in explaining that though the man's desire is for the woman, "his life does not culminate in this desire, unless his life is either foolish or lost."[68] In what, then, does man's "ethical culmination" lie—his work? his civic duties? Kierkegaard does not address that question here, but leaves one wondering if these spheres of activity are really so much more valuable than family life. In any case, this idea leads to curious complications in his view of birthing. Only a few pages after noting the ethical significance of procreation for woman, he explains that in birthing, the spirit trembles "for in that moment it does not have its task, which is as it were suspended."[69] Normally, the ethical is characterized by the spirit's involvement in deliberation and in the exercise of the will; according to Kierkegaard's model, woman reaches a peak of her ethical culmination while the spirit is "as it were suspended." How are we to understand this? Apparently Kierkegaard views birthing as so body-dominated that there is little the spirit can do; indeed both conception and birthing would seem to test the resilience of the body-spirit synthesis that he takes to be the structure of the human self. Is this because in procreative acts human beings show most clearly their kinship to animals? Like all female animals, women expel their babies from the womb as a result of powerful, involuntary uterine contractions. Perhaps this lessening of the will's ability to direct body processes is what Kierkegaard had in mind when he wrote that the spirit's task is suspended in birthing. There is a sense in which a birthing woman needs to trust her body and her Creator enough to relinquish deliberate control of the process to the innate ability and wisdom of her body.

It also is possible that Kierkegaard took the guttural cries and moans that replace conversation during birthing to be a sign of the spirit's suspension. He had just explained "as a Greek" that the spirit cannot really take part in the culmination of the erotic: "The spirit is of course present; because it is that which constitutes the synthesis, but it cannot express itself in the erotic, it feels foreign."[70] Reflecting on this passage, Birgit Bertung notes the speechlessness of the sexual act itself: "One does not speak during orgasm, and speech is an integrated part of the spirit, actually the expression of the spirit."[71] Kierkegaard cautions that he is "speaking as a Greek" here, and it may well be that from the viewpoint of classical Hellenism, the spirit cannot express itself in the erotic. According to Christian teaching, however, the finite is capable of bearing the infinite, and no aspects of human life remain unclaimed by the spirit. Moreover, only months before writing *The Concept of Anxiety*, Kierkegaard had memorably depicted father Abraham responding to God's command in *Fear and Trembling*. During this experience of the most extreme spiritual testing, Abraham exhibits surprising parallels with the birthing woman. He, too, is intrinsically speechless during the time of trial; his ethical obligations are "suspended" for the duration.[72] Kierkegaard highlights the contrasts between Abraham viewed from the outside, and his experience perceived from the inside. So, too, there may be a considerable contrast between the sounds and appearance of a laboring woman and her internal world. What may look like an utterly physical, almost animal experience, may well be imbued with a sense of the presence and creative power of God as a woman's unspoken prayers mingle with the Spirit's "sighs too deep for words" (Rom. 8:26). Obviously there are differences between Abraham and the birthing woman: His is an exceptional case; hers is common to women throughout the generations; his involves potential sacrifice of progeny, hers involves potential sacrifice of herself. And yet the parallels point to birthing as a profound spiritual as well as physical trial.

Giving birth may present an important spiritual trial, but procreation is by no means the epitome of the Christian life, according to Kierkegaard. Indeed, Kierkegaard may be Protestantism's most vigorous defender of the celibate ideal. As part of his polemic against the domestication of Christianity, Kierkegaard decries clergy self-interest in encouraging procreation:

> For "the pastor" only one thing is important: in every way (by virtue of his oath upon the New Testament) to do exactly the opposite of what the New Testament does; in every way to preserve, cultivate, and encourage in people the desire for the propagation of the race, so that there may constantly be provided battalions of Christians, which is of course a completely vital necessity if thousands of vigorously breeding pastors with families are to live off them.[73]

He is appalled that pastors of the established church use religion to "cement families more and more egotistically together, and to arrange family festivities, beautiful, splendid family festivities"[74] rather than prodding individuals to take their own spiritual development seriously. The temptation Kierkegaard sees is that people will allow their family responsibilities to distract them from seeking eternal happiness.

Kierkegaard's critique of "familyism"[75] is definitely written from a male perspective—he tells, for example, how Frederick [a newly certified pastoral candidate] was diverted from his honest questioning of Christianity by his girlfriend Juliane's desire to get married and by his ensuing family obligations. Juliane's story gets short shrift, though both of them seem to experience a vague sense of loss in later years.[76] Is this critique of "familyism" simply sour grapes from a man who broke his own engagement and remained single to the end of his life? Was Kierkegaard indeed something of a misogynist? The cutting words he tried out on maternal love in his private papers of this period must give one pause: "For as wife, as mother—whew! it is an egotism which man has no inkling of. Society has privileged it under the name of love—good night! no, it is the most violent egotism, in which I daresay she does not first love herself, but through <'egotistically'> loving what is hers, she loves herself."[77] Abrasive as such comments are, they might actually free women to healthier and more thorough self-examination by pulling motherly love down from its pedestal. Still, he decides not to publish such harsh invective, warning instead that "even if all were unmarried, yet everyone has within himself something which more artfully and more urgently and more persistently than a woman can, will cause a person to forget the eternal."[78] When the dust of Kierkegaard's passionate polemic settles, the reader is left facing the pathos of lives circumscribed by family affairs, and perhaps provoked enough to test those bounds.

Thus in Kierkegaard the Reformation Luther touched off comes full circle. Whereas Luther had held up the dignity of procreation and unmasked the sinfulness that might reside in celibacy, Kierkegaard protested the cult of the Christian family that followed in the wake of the Reformation and exposed the self-deception and egotism that allowed family ties to flourish at the expense of the single person's discipleship. Today the challenge remains—to affirm the dignity of procreation as a God-given gift while also affirming the value of each person and the variety of ways in which persons may grow in grace.

Notes

1. Heiko A. Oberman, *Luther: Man between God and the Devil,* trans. Eileen Walliser-Schwarzbart (New Haven: Yale University Press, 1989), 281f.

2. Oberman, *Luther*, 278.

3. *Luther's Works* (St. Louis and Philadelphia: Concordia and Fortress, 1955–76), 45:38 ["The Christian in Society," 1522].

4. Ibid., 1:116f. In a world tainted by sin, man experiences sexual passion almost as a disease (1:119), and woman is used by her husband to a great extent as "a medicine against the sin of fornication" (1:118).

5. Compare Oberman, *Luther*, 273.

6. *Luther's Works*, 1:117f.

7. Ibid., 4:6.

8. Ibid., 1:118.

9. Ibid., 1:114.

10. Compare D. Martin, *Martin Luthers Werke: Kritische Gesamtausgabe, Abteilung Werke* (Weimar, 1883), 18:275, lines 19–28; 1525. Quoted in Oberman, *Luther*, 273f.

11. Martin E. Marty, *Health and Medicine in the Lutheran Tradition: Being Well* (New York: Crossroad, 1983), 127.

12. *Luther's Works*, 45:39. Noble families longed for heirs to preserve their lineage, but once several sons had survived to adulthood, it was advantageous to limit the number of families in the next generation, so that the family's wealth and power need not be spread too thin.

13. Ibid., 1:118; cf. 3:135.

14. Oberman, *Luther*, 279.

15. Allison P. Coudert, "The Myth of the Improved Status of Women: The Case of the Witchcraze," in *The Politics of Gender in Early Modern Europe*, ed. Jean R. Brink, Allison P. Coudert, Maryanne Horowitz (Kirksville, Mo.: Sixteenth Century Journal Publishers, 1989), 80.

16. Luther on 1 Tim. 2:15, as quoted by Coudert, "Myth of Improved Status of Women," 80.

17. Coudert, "Myth of Improved Status of Women," 80.

18. Oberman, *Luther*, 277. As the basis of this passage, Oberman cites D. *Martin Luthers Werke: Kritische Gesamtausgabe, Tischreden* [Table Talk], (Weimar, 1912–21), vol. 1. no. 1006; 505, lines 22–25, from the first half of the 1530s.

19. *Luther's Works*, 45:39.

20. Ibid., 45:40f.

21. Ibid., 45:38.

22. Rosemary Radford Ruether, *Women-Church: Theology and Practice of Feminist Liturgical Communities* (San Francisco: Harper and Row, 1985), 71. Although Ruether does not cite Luther directly, this is presumably the passage to which she refers.

23. *Luther's Works,* 7:47ff.

24. Ibid., 6:268–271. "This end of Rachel is assuredly wretched and sad for both her husband and the rest of the household. . . . All the circumstances of this story increase and emphasize this grief," 270.

25. Ibid., 2:311.

26. Ibid., 45:38; cf. 8:203.

27. Ibid., 45:41.

28. Ibid., 7:46; cf. 4:8.

29. Ibid., 3:134.

30. Ibid., 45:38.

31. Ibid., 1:199; cf. 3:134.

32. Ibid., 1:201.

33. Ibid., 12:243f.

34. Compare Luther's comments on the prudence, courage, and great hope required in a midwife, and the prayers and lamentation of the whole house when mother and child are in life-threatening travail. *Luther's Works,* 7:48.

35. Ibid., 1:201.

36. Ibid., 45:41.

37. Ibid., 4:4f.

38. Ibid., 4:7f.

39. Ibid., 45:38; cf. 8:203; for Palladius and the Scandinavian situation, see Grethe Jacobsen, "Nordic Women and the Reformation," 47–67, in *Women in Reformation and Counter-Reformation Europe: Private and Public Worlds,* ed. Sherrin Marshall (Indianapolis: Indiana University Press, 1989), 61; for other instances, see Thomas Rogers Forbes, *The Midwife and the Witch* (New Haven and London: Yale University Press, 1966), 82. As noted above, p. 115, women resisted these changes and continued to practice traditional birthing practices in spite of clerical prohibitions.

40. Compare above, p. 114.

41. For examples, see Christina Larner, *Witchcraft and Religion: The Politics of Popular Belief* (Oxford: Basil Blackwell, 1984), 60f; Jacobsen, "Nordic Women and Reformation," 62.

42. Cotton Mather, *Elizabeth in Her Holy Retirement* (Boston, 1710), 7, quoted in Richard Wertz and Dorothy Wertz, *Lying-In: A History of Childbirth in America* (New York: Schocken, 1979), 21. The sermon is available as "Retired Elizabeth," in Cotton Mather, *The Angel of Bethesda,* ed. Gordon W. Jones (Barre, Mass.: American Antiquarian Society and Barre Publishers, 1972), 235–48.

43. Mather, *Angel of Bethesda,* 237f.

44. Ibid., 239.

45. Ibid., 237.

46. Ibid., 239.

47. Ibid., 236.

48. Wertz and Wertz, *Lying-In,* 19.

49. Mather, *Angel of Bethesda,* 236.

50. "A Woman When she is in Travail, hath Sorrow, because her Hour is Come; But as soon as she is delivered of the Child, she remembers no more the Anguish; for Joy that a Man is born into the World."

51. Mather, *Angel of Bethesda,* 244.

52. Quoted in Wertz and Wertz, *Lying-In,* 1, 21.

53. Mather, *Angel of Bethesda,* 240.

54. Ibid., 244ff.

55. John Cotton, "The Way of the Congregational Churches Cleared" (1648), in David D. Hall, ed., *The Antinomian Controversy* (Middletown, Conn.: Wesleyan University Press, 1968), 412, cited in Selma R. Williams, *Divine Rebel: The Life of Anne Marbury Hutchinson* (New York: Holt, Rinehart and Winston, 1981), 97f.

56. John Winthrop, "Short Story," in Hall, *Antinomian Controversy,* 263, cited in Williams, *Divine Rebel,* 97, cf. 98.

57. Robert Baylie, *A Dissuasive from the Errours of the Time* (1645), 65, in Hall, *Antinomian Controversy,* 437; cited in Williams, *Divine Rebel,* 99.

58. Winthrop, "Short Story" cited in Williams, *Divine Rebel,* 186.

59. Rev. Thomas Weld, cited in Williams, *Divine Rebel,* 188.

60. "The Diary of the Seducer" in *Either/Or I* and "in vino veritas" in *Stages on Life's Way* are among the better-known examples.

61. *Søren Kierkegaards Samlede Værker,* 1st ed., ed. A. B. Drachman, J. L. Heiberg, and H. O. Lange (Copenhagen: Gyldendal, 1901–06), 4:337. Translations my own.

62. "Anxiety is a sympathetic antipathy and an antipathetic sympathy," Kierkegaard, *Samlede Værker,* 4:313.

63. Kierkegaard, *Samlede Værker,* 4:341.

64. Later, in *The Sickness unto Death,* Kierkegaard returns to the problem of sin, and emphasizes its universality, carefully employing a new metaphor. Sin is described there as a mortal, universal sickness; the birthing process plays no part. *Samlede Værker,* 11:111–241.

65. Kierkegaard, *Samlede Værker,* 4:336.

66. Myra Leifer, *Psychological Effects of Motherhood: A Study of First Pregnancy* (New York: Praeger, 1980), 32; cf. Arthur and Libby Colman, *Pregnancy: The Psychological Experience* (New York: Herder and Herder, 1971), 36.

67. Helen Callaway, " 'The Most Essentially Female Function of All': Giving Birth," 163 185, in *Defining Females: The Nature of Women in Society,* ed. Shirley Ardener (New York: Halsted Press, John Wiley & Sons, 1978), 164.

68. Kierkegaard, *Samlede Værker,* 4:336.

69. Ibid., 4:336.

70. Ibid., 4:341.

71. Birgit Bertung, *Om Kierkegaard, kvinder og kærlighed—en studie i Søren Kierkegaards kvindesyn* (Copenhagen: C.A. Reitzels Forlag, 1987), 37.

72. Kierkegaard, *Samlede Værker,* 3:159f., 163, 104–116. Kierkegaard's exploration of the theological suspension of the ethical includes a passage comparing Abraham with "God's mother, the virgin Mary," 3:114f. "She needs no worldly admiration, just as little as Abraham needs tears, for she is no heroine, and he no hero, but they both became greater than these, not at all by being exempted from the distress and the anguish and the paradox, but they became so through them."

73. Ibid., 14:256 [The Moment].

74. Ibid., 14:263.

75. "Familyism" is borrowed from Kristin M. Foster. Although Foster uses the term to describe the situation of the church today, it is quite applicable to the situation Kierkegaard attacked over a century ago: "Anything done in the name and for the sake of families is unquestionably good . . . Nothing takes precedence over the emotional and material security of the family, certainly not God, the biggest family-backer!" Kristin M. Foster, "Ministry and Motherhood: A Collision of Callings?" *Currents in Theology and Mission 16* (April 1989): 101.

76. Kierkegaard, *Samlede Værker,* 14:175ff.

77. *Søren Kierkegaards Papirer,* 2d ed., ed. Niels Thulstrup (Copenhagen: Gyldendal, 1936), 11:1, A-141, 99.

78. Kierkegaard, *Samlede Værker,* 14:307.

Part 3
Toward a Birthing Theology and Ministry

8
Birthing in a New Era

Kierkegaard or Luther (not to mention Augustine or the person who first inscribed Gen. 3:16 on a scroll) could hardly have imagined the dramatic changes that would take place in the circumstances of birth by the final decade of the twentieth century. At least in technologically advanced countries, birthing circumstances have changed more between Kierkegaard's day and our own than they had changed in the centuries separating Augustine and Kierkegaard. Maternal mortality has declined greatly, and the benefits of medical and technological assistance are taken for granted. "To procreate or not to procreate" is no longer a stark all-or-nothing proposition; women no longer need to choose between a life that revolves around a flock of children and a life completely devoted to other aspirations. Instead planned parenthood and the hope of "having it all" has become a middle way for many—with a resulting drop in the birth rate and an increase in the number of people who "regard becoming pregnant and carrying the fetus to term as voluntary acts."[1]

This chapter considers the theological dimensions of childbirth today under three main headings: the miracle of childbirth; comprehending birthing distress; pregnancy and childbirth as spiritual crisis.

The Miracle of Childbirth

Although the birth rate is falling, public discussion of childbirth has never been greater. As anthropologist Helen

153

Callaway points out, this raises an interesting question: At a time "when more couples are deciding to have only one child or none at all, why should there be such a fascination with the event of birth?"[2] It may well be precisely because childbirth is experienced less often, that it is explained and displayed and pondered in increasing detail. As Luther observed so many years ago, "even in beasts procreation and birth are something great and wonderful . . . But because God has scattered this miracle over the whole human race and over all living things throughout the whole world, it has begun to be regarded cheaply."[3] Perhaps now that this miracle is experienced only a few times in a couple's life we may better appreciate it.

Pregnancy and childbirth themselves evoke wonder: wonder at the intricacy and elegance of our body processes, wonder at the mystery of two becoming one flesh, wonder at participating in a vital process much larger than oneself. This wonder is in one sense open to all: It is an experience of general revelation similar to the wonder that a glorious mountain vista, a functioning polis, or the sight of a flower blossoming from a crack in the pavement may evoke, even among people who have never laid eyes on Genesis 1. In the past, the church itself has tended to take this procreative miracle for granted, "regarding it cheaply" in its rush to proclaim the urgency of new birth and to explore the meaning of the special revelation in Jesus Christ. In our increasingly secular world, it is more important than ever that the church take time to explore the contours of this generally accessible miracle, both as a sign of God's blessing in its own right and in its intimate connection to the specifically Christian revelation.

In another sense, of course, the miracle of childbirth is not completely open to all. Only women are physically able to give birth, and even they are able to do so for only part of their lives. Moreover, this miracle is indeed "scattered" throughout the human population; in spite of a variety of fertility-enhancing techniques, conception is still not available on demand, and some couples still suffer childlessness not of their own choosing. This, too, causes us to wonder—and confronts us with the limits of being human: We cannot make our bodies do everything we please. Those hoping against hope to conceive often feel painfully left out in the presence of another's blossoming belly or newborn child; yet even this hard experience of human limits can engender awe at God's capacity to do what we alone cannot.

Childbirth brings the fertile, too, to their limits. A woman who has given birth may feel at a loss to communicate her experience to others. As one glowing new mother said to a hospital chaplain who had no firsthand experience of birth, "Then I guess you wouldn't understand." The overwhelming experience of childbirth reminds us that we are limited creatures: The most attentive listener cannot get inside another's skin and experience; our most vital experiences leave us groping for words. Even more powerfully, however, childbirth bears an impulse to transcend limits. The birth of a baby reminds us not only of our own mortality but also of connections that transcend our lifespan, reaching back generations into the past and forward into the generations to come. In pregnancy and childbirth even the usual interpersonal boundaries are transcended for a time as mother and child share the same body space and influence one another's well-being. And while the full import of childbirth may be beyond what words can express, researchers as well as friends and family have found most new mothers eager to relate their birth stories. Especially when a listener shows genuine interest, a new mother's urge to relate her trials and joys, and to comprehend this tremendous experience for herself, generally overwhelms any concern she might have about her listener not being completely able to understand.[4]

Many of these stories are formulated largely in the language of the hospital and medical procedures. The trip to the hospital, the kinds of medical interventions that were employed or avoided, the length of time involved in the various stages, the measurement in centimeters of the cervix's dilation—such information forms the backbone of the story. As one anthropologist observed, "Even the language in which most Americans discuss birth events is predominantly medical rather than familial, religious or otherwise couched in intimate terms."[5] The human and communal components of the experience are often phrased in sports terminology, with the birthing woman feeling like part of the delivery room "team," her husband cast in the role of "labor coach." Compared to the sophistication of the medical terminology that many lay people readily use, religious language seems sparse and almost formulaic—perhaps because we approach the limits of what language can express, perhaps because we have not developed our language for religiously appropriating the experience, perhaps because religious experience is generally viewed as a very private matter.[6]

The bits of religious language that do make their way into these stories point theology to miracle rather than sin as a starting point. The Christian tradition from Genesis 3 and Psalm 51 onward has repeatedly pondered how to properly articulate the connection between birth and sin, yet "sin" rarely, if ever, comes up in modern American birthing narratives. The words that do come up again and again are words like "miracle," "delivery," and "joy." Thus not least in our era, a birthing theology will do well to begin in wonder at the miracle of birth.

"Miracle" itself requires some discussion. For one thing, "miracle" is defined primarily as *extraordinary* divine intervention in the course of human events. From this perspective only virgin births or postmenopausal births would seem to qualify. Still people readily describe the birth of their child as a "miracle"; on the stage of one's own life, even the most normal, uncomplicated birth *is* an extraordinary event, a window through which divine participation in human lives may be glimpsed. More problematic is the common figurative application of "miracle" to extraordinary *human* interventions and accomplishments. This occurs frequently in the field of health, where technological advances and success stories are regularly labeled "miracles," and broadcast as such through the media. Such usage is problematic, both because it tends to deify technology, and because it saps "miracle" of its numinous, awe-inspiring quality. Exploring childbirth in terms of miracle helps reclaim the religious power of "miracle." One pastor, who regularly brings "miracle" into visits with new parents, finds that even persons who generally put miracles in the same category as spaceships can see the miracle in their child's birth. Lifting up the miracle inherent in the earthy grandeur of childbirth reminds us of our roots in the natural world and our kinship with all living things, and helps us see straight, so that we do not overlook the liberally distributed miracle of God's procreative blessing in our amazement over the feats of modern medical wizardry.

We may begin sketching the features of the miracle of childbirth by drawing attention to the created elegance and intricacy of the human body. The miniature perfection of a newborn child captivates adults, who may completely lose track of time gazing at tiny fingers already able to reach out and hold on, little ears able to hear, delicate lids and fine lashes already protecting wide baby eyes. In most cases everything works, with no need for technical assistance—all limbs are properly joined, lungs and vocal cords work together to add a new voice to the human chorus, even the gold deposit in the newborn's diapers is a sign that, inside as well as out, everything is working properly. The baby may be wrinkled, its feet bent forward from months in tight quarters, its head may still be shaped by its journey through the birth canal—and yet we see in this tiny new creature all the magnificence of the human body. At the same time, this little bundle of flesh and bones (that would die of starvation if no one had compassion upon it) also confronts us with our inborn human vulnerability—vulnerability that may lessen with years, but never completely disappears. Part of the miracle of birth lies in the newborn's very ordinariness: We recognize ourselves in the tiny newcomer. We are struck by the magnificence and the frailty of human being and confronted by our need to help and to be helped.

Even when something goes wrong, and the frailty of human being is made especially evident in the person of a baby born with severe health problems, we still find ourselves in the presence of the miracle of new life. Perhaps the most awe-inspiring aspect of the miracle of birth, after all, is that there is now something where there once was nothing; some*one* where there once was no one. Children reflect this wonder from a very early age when they ask, "Where was I before I was born?" And though adults know that each parent contributes a bit of themselves to start a new life, it is still astonishing to contemplate the unique new human being who eventually emerges. The whole is so much more than the sum of the two parts that had united months earlier in the hidden regions of the womb—one plus one equals three. And only God knows why this new individual received its unique combination of maternal and paternal traits, why it was precisely this sperm that united with this egg and, nourished and protected in its mother's womb, developed from a collection of cells into a viable human being. The wonder of this new person may be particularly apparent to parents who love one another and who see this tiny new individual as a living and tangible expression of their love and union. But in every case, a newborn is ultimately a gift— a gift that may be appreciated or not, a gift in whose making parents play a part, but do not determine the result. This gift may be received by parents with joy and thanksgiving, or it may be rejected as an impossible burden. Often it will be received with mixed feelings—wonder and pride tempered by tremors of awe at the enormous responsibility that comes with the gift. Parents may well exult with Eve, "I have produced a man with the help of the LORD!" (Gen. 4:1b, NRSV) and still murmur a fervent prayer for the Lord's continuing help through the challenges yet to come. The newborn is also a gift to the community; indeed a newborn can create glimpses of community where there once was none. Perfect strangers will break through the invisible bubble of propriety to inquire how old the baby is or to talk and play with him or her. Babies offer even strangers a promise of the future. They embody a fresh start in the midst of a messy, troubled world and present a reminder of what has been called "our original goodness."[7]

This view of children as a gift of God is challenged by the increasing tendency in our society to regard pregnancy and carrying a fetus to term as voluntary acts. Childbirth historians Richard and Dorothy Wertz observe that "a woman who believes that children are the result of her own free choice rather than a gift of God or the involuntary product of nature feels more responsibility for ensuring the best possible outcome, the most perfect child."[8] It might be added that a society that regards childbearing as a couple's free choice may quite consistently also regard children as a private luxury, thus abdicating its responsibilities for supporting children and the families who raise them. The burden of producing the "perfect child" falls on both the parents and the health-care system—increasing both the technological monitoring and intervention in childbirth and the pressure on health-care providers to use such technology, even when the risks to the child may be minimal.[9] According to the Wertzes, "Most women agree with the medical view that the route to the child's perfection—and their own empowerment— lies in the use of more technology in pregnancy and birth."[10] This faith in medical technology has led to increasing surveillance of the fetus from the earliest weeks of pregnancy. Increasingly routine amniocentesis and other forms of prenatal screening present parents with difficult moral dilemmas even before birth: Should we undergo such screening? What will we do if the results are bad?[11] Others wonder whether the existence of screening procedures will result in pressure to use them and in correspondingly less sympathy for the parents of children born with handicaps.[12] Are we entering an era in which birth defects may again be seen as a sign of the parents' lacking faith, only this time the god in question is the "god" of technology? Never has it been more important for the church to lift up children and the capacity to bear children as gifts of a gracious God.

Indeed, childbearing may evoke wonder not only at the gift and giftedness of the newborn, but also at the unsung splendor of the adult human reproductive system. Seen through the eyes of faith, the data of biology textbooks come alive in praise of the Creator. God did create us male and female and gave each sex a vital role in reproduction. (We may take this fact for granted, people in other times and places have not always done so.[13]) The physiological fact that the angle of the human female's vagina favors face-to-face sexual intercourse and that human sexual instincts are not limited to brief estrus periods can be seen as the work of a loving Creator engendering intimate and ongoing human community, as well as providing a means for the reproduction of the human species. The features of human reproduction that more closely resemble those of other mammals are no less awe-inspiring. The capacity of a woman's womb to expand in the course of a few months from an organ about the size and shape of a pear to one that reaches from the pelvis to the rib cage and accommodates several pounds of baby and amniotic fluid is in itself astonishing; the purposeful power the womb musters at the height of this distended state is even more so. The nurturing discrimination of the placenta, which replenishes fetal blood with nutrients and oxygen and carries away its waste products without mingling the blood of mother and child; the continuous renewal of cleansing and protective amniotic fluid, the delicate and mysterious interaction between mother and child that governs the onset of labor—all these details evoke wonder at the excellence of our reproductive systems. Our bodies are indeed God's temple, in their physical elegance as well as in their spiritual capacity, and the experience of pregnancy and child-birth may serve to draw attention to the created beauty of that temple.

Comprehending Birthing Distress

Important as it is to celebrate our God-given reproductive capacities, a birthing theology also must comprehend the distress and pain involved in giving birth. Although exclamation at the wonder of birth flows freely in the rejoicing of new parents, pain, too, figures prominently in many women's birth stories. Penelope Washbourn, for example, finds herself apologetic for writing extensively of the enjoyment and graceful dimensions of child-birth because so many women had told her "of loneliness, intense pain and horror associated with childbirth. In fact, it seemed to me that women made a point of telling me about the pain."[14]

Most women do experience pain in labor, but the degree varies enormously. One woman rather embarrassedly compared the pain of her uncomplicated home birth to the discomfort of passing a large bowel movement. At the other extreme, some women describe in excruciating terms their feeling of being ripped apart underneath. Where do these vastly different perceptions of childbearing pain come from? Is the emphasis on pain a female rendition of the war story that magnifies the enemy and thus also the glory of victory? Does it reflect a preoccupation with pain, or do many women simply experience lots of pain as they give birth? While all these factors may play a role, it is clear that we live in a culture that does not readily accept pain as a natural part of life and that does not greatly value the ability to endure pain. Instead of encouraging people to find ways to live through pain, our culture teaches us to avoid it at all costs.

Paradoxically, this all-out avoidance of pain may itself lead to a heightened perception of the pain that does come. A study of four different groups residing in Western Canada (Ukrainian Orthodox, Hutterite, Anglo-Canadian, and East Indian) suggests that perceptions of pain in childbirth are closely related to the culture's perception of childbirth as a natural event. The Ukrainian and Hutterite cultures view childbirth as a natural, though somewhat painful, event. Yet women from both these cultures perceived considerably less pain in their birthing than women from either of the other two groups. The East Indian women (for whom even the mention of childbirth is taboo) experienced the most pain, followed by Anglo-Canadian women (who view childbirth as potentially pathological). The East Indian women approach childbirth completely unschooled in what to expect and thus find the pain overwhelming. The Anglo-Canadian women, on the other hand, had participated in childbirth classes and were prepared for some pain. The study found, however, that these women took a relatively passive attitude toward the expected pain, knowing they could always fall back on medication if they found the pain too severe.[15]

Just as cultures variously affect the way birthing pain is experienced and expressed, so, too, cultures vary in the way birthing pain is interpreted. The East Indian women see their great pain as initiation into the mysteries of the universe. The Orthodox Ukrainian and Hutterite women, like traditional Christians more generally, understand the pain of childbirth as a punishment for human sin; thus they, too, connect their personal experience of distress with distress of cosmic proportions. This connection of the individual's pain with an overarching religious drama is a strength of the traditional interpretation, though too often that interpretation has implied—contrary to the biblical witness—that childbirth per se is a punishment for the exercise of female sexuality. That the church has allowed this mistaken interpretation to flourish is coming back to haunt it today, as writers like Kathryn Rabuzzi question the integrity of biblical religion: "Even the most sacred mystery of the Goddess, the act of giving birth, an event no man has ever yet experienced, has been defined for us. In Western cultures childbirth is the painful wages of our original sin"[16]

Few women in this author's acquaintance perceive their childbearing pains (much less childbirth itself) as the wages of sin. Modern Americans, like the Anglo-Canadians in the aforementioned study, are influenced rather by the prevailing biomedical model of childbirth and are thus more likely to regard labor pain as a problem to be remedied, or a test to be passed. From this perspective, pain becomes a sign to a woman that she is by nature weak, disposed toward disease, and in need of the blessings medical science and experts can provide: "Whereas few but fundamentalist believers are likely to feel 'sinful' about their birth-related functions today, many women do feel 'sick' rather than 'sacred' when they 'suffer' from them."[17]

Whether this is any kind of an advance is debatable. Christians may agree that birthing is sacred work and still find ample evidence of human sin multiplying distress in labor. Consider the anxieties that, instead of being resolved in trust of a graceful Creator, impede labor; or the biomedical structures that tend to define a woman as a patient rather than as God's gifted, capable coworker in blessed labor; or the expectations and social and legal structures that jeopardize the crucial element of trust between birthing women and their attendants.[18] The list could go on; each of these examples illustrates how even the greatest human capabilities and achievements are fraught with negative potential.

The challenge to contemporary Christians is to affirm modern medicine in its efforts to alleviate human suffering, while also articulating a more wholistic response to pain. Christians can encourage one another to receive birthing pain as a reminder of our body's creative power and strength, as well as a sign of our vulnerability and need for one another's help. Christians can lift up birthing travail as a reminder of our participation in the sorrows and travail of all creation—and of our exalted standing as responsible human beings, living in the presence of a just and compassionate God. A meaningful spiritual framework enhances the birthing process; research shows that women with a strong religious faith tend to have happier birth experiences, characterized by "fewer obstetrical complications in general and fewer caesarean sections in particular."[19]

For the sake of our theology, too, it is vital that Christians clearly proclaim that women are not paying for sin, even in their labor pains. Jesus Christ has once and for all paid the price of human sin through his own birthing travail and shares in our travail as we struggle to bring forth new life. Indeed, for a Christian woman, the agony as well as the ecstasy of birth can be an occasion to draw closer to Christ. As one recent new mother exclaimed, "I never really understood the crucifixion until I gave birth!" Seeing birthing travail in terms of Christ's birth work on the cross not only puts women's travail in a meaningful religious context and honors this powerful female experience, it offers a fresh and intimate metaphor for God's way of bringing healing into a world marred by sin.[20]

Finally, even birthing pain bears within it gracious potential. Washbourn writes that for her at least, the intense bodily experience of pregnancy, labor, and birth "were worth it for their own sake, and not just bearable because of the desire for the end result—the child." She even goes so far as to say, "Even if the baby had died at birth, it would not have changed the experience."[21] This shocking statement may be only partly true—a baby's death at birth would probably raise all sorts of questions and guilt feelings that would cast a shadow back on the experience itself. Still, Washbourn makes a vital point: Giving birth, pain and all, is such an intense experience of life, creation, and meaningful struggle that it is good in and of itself. I know women who, half an hour after giving birth, were ready to go back and do it all over again—not because they wanted another child, but because the process had been so exhilarating.

Furthermore, whether or not it is such a gracious experience, the travail of childbirth does come to an end, usually in the joyous satisfaction of nestling a newborn to the breast. Anne

Eggebroten points out that from this vantage point, the suffering and pain involved in childbirth are like the wounds of Christ.[22] Just as the wounds visible on the risen Christ's body serve as a mark of identity, and thus promote Thomas' faith, so too the wounds of childbirth can be a sign of a trial endured and a reminder of the preciousness of life brought into the world at such cost. Looking back on the suffering one has endured, and through which one has been blessed, can transform those wounds into a source of empowerment that a woman can draw on in facing other challenges in her life.

As sociologist Ann Oakley points out, however, such a graceful transformation does not necessarily occur. Oakley warns that much about the current medicalized model of childbirth militates against such a transformation: "Institutional delivery, epidural anesthesia and technology in general interpose medical intervention as a condition for the successful delivery of mother and baby from the perils of childbirth." She argues that medical control encourages birthing women to feel dependent and helpless; thus "they receive a sense of failure in the one activity they are demonstrably able to claim as their own. But more simply than this, they are deprived of one form of achievement human beings are able to experience: the achievement of producing another human being." Oakley sums up her assessment of the psychological and sociological impact of contemporary hospital childbirth practices in words that bear eerie comparison with the views held by medieval monks: "It is because they are so useful as manifestations of human weakness and vulnerability that women are so useless to themselves."[23]

Women have looked to medicine to remedy the physical distress and danger of childbirth; but as Oakley's remarks show, help for the body can have a profound impact on the soul. Indeed, the complex interrelationship of body and spirit is set in sharp relief throughout pregnancy and childbirth.

Pregnancy and Childbirth: A Spiritual Crisis

According to Penelope Washbourn, the experience of pregnancy and birth is a spiritual crisis that both challenges and contributes to a woman's identity.[24] Washbourn emphasizes the essentially ambivalent character of pregnancy and childbirth—the conflicting emotions, the symbolic death of an old sense of self and the birth of a new one, the demonic as well as graceful possibilities opened up by this multifaceted experience. She directs attention to the many challenges of pregnancy and childbirth: A woman has to deal with dramatic changes in her own body; she experiences awe-inspiring, but essentially impersonal forces of nature at work within her, and lives with the immediate evidence of her own fertility and femaleness. She faces new chapters in personal relationships and is reminded of her own mortality; she wonders how the birth will go, if the baby will be healthy, how she will deal with pain, and manage as a mother—all in the space of a few short months.

Pregnancy's most obvious challenge to a woman's identity lies in the rapid change of her body's shape. This is especially true at the time of a woman's first pregnancy. During the initial stages of her first pregnancy, a woman often will look at her body with a mixture of pride and disbelief for signs that will confirm her own fertility. Even for a woman who has hoped to become pregnant, these feelings of pride and wonder may well be mingled with sadness at the loss of her prepregnant figure, particularly in a culture that highly values slenderness.[25] These physical changes portend a significant change in a woman's self-image and social status: A woman's first pregnancy means more than a change from a youthful to a more matronly figure; for many it is perceived as the transition to adult womanhood, and even the transition to adulthood per se.[26] Thus the physical changes of pregnancy usher in a time of grieving for a woman's loss of her carefree, youthful self, as well as a time for expanding her self-image to include the joys and responsibilities of motherhood. As Washbourn puts it, in every pregnancy there is a symbolic death of the old, prepregnant self, and the birth of a new, pregnant one. Initially, the woman can exercise considerable control over the situation; she can choose whom to tell of the secret unfolding in her womb, she can decide to terminate the pregnancy before outsiders are even aware of it. By the second trimester, though, a woman's pregnant appearance is more obvious, and she may begin to feel dominated or even defined by her body. Women will sometimes experience the sudden largeness of their bodies as "almost ego-alien," hardly recognizing themselves when they catch a glimpse of their pregnant figure in the mirror. At the same time researchers have found that women have many positive feelings about their pregnant shape, especially during the middle months of pregnancy.[27] Many women express "a sense of being in a special 'state of grace' " as their bodies blossom and they experience the wonder of life quickening in their wombs, as well as increased care and attention from other people.[28] Some women will enjoy the attention they and their bodies receive, others will resent or resist it, particularly if they sense that the multifaceted personal identity that they have acquired over the years is suddenly being swallowed up in the prominence of their body.[29]

At the same time, a women is herself usually focused on her body to a much greater extent than at other times—she pays special attention to diet and exercise, waits for the first flutter of the baby's movements, and watches with some awe as her waistline and navel disappear, and her belly continues to swell. Pregnancy is a living reminder of our embodiedness—of our physical connectedness with one another, of our body's effect on our self-image and the image others have of us. Pregnancy reminds us in a very bodily way of our inborn potential for hospitality and nurture and of the burdens and blessings of self-giving. Pregnancy and childbirth surprise us with direct evidence of our body's elasticity, flexibility, and strength as well as of its givenness and its limitations. The very physical nature of procreation also calls attention to our kinship with all other creatures. Indeed, the elemental experience of begetting, bearing, and birthing offspring may be one of the few points at which modern city dwellers experience the animal power and creativity of their bodies. Both parents may sense, at least for a moment, a solidarity of birth that transcends the limits of time, space, and even species. For women tired of being relegated to second class as the more physical, earthy sex, however, this kinship with the animals is problematic. Too often in human history, the female alone has symbolized human weakness, vulnerability, and bodiliness. Who wants to be compared to a cow, or a mother bear or hen, when society so clearly rewards the intellect and artifice that project themselves as being unencumbered by passions or bodies? And yet as human exploitation of mother earth reaches ever more dangerous proportions, a healthy acceptance of human kinship with the rest of creation has never been more vital. Perhaps the shared experience of birth could help *both* men and women begin to accept their common kinship with and dependence on the rest of creation, *as well as* their shared ability and responsibility to transcend biology and to steward creation in a God-pleasing manner.

A theology of giving birth will prod us to lift up both these aspects of the human synthesis. Childbearing is itself so much more than the unfolding of a simple biological process: This intense experience of embodiment is also a time of great spiritual ferment. Pregnant women are traditionally pictured pensively knitting baby clothes—immersed in thoughts and dreams even as they make practical preparations. So, too, psychologists find pregnant women "far more open to their inner experiences, more willing to discuss dreams and anxieties than most normal women in a nonpregnant state."[30] Some of these anxieties concern the health of the baby, her relationship to it and its father, and the irreversible changes the child will bring into her life. Women will wonder and pray about their babies' health and very ability to survive.[31] Other anxieties focus on the challenge to a woman's identity and sense of vocation—her feelings about her body and her sexuality, her prospects as a mother, and in many cases, decisions regarding work outside the home.

Women also may be anxious about their own health and well-being. Even a woman who is basically happy to be pregnant may at times be startled to find herself thinking of the baby as a parasite sapping away her strength from within.[32] Childbearing does include elements of sacrifice, even for healthy women—so much so that Patricia Jung compares continuing a pregnancy to donating an organ to save the life of one's child.[33] Some of the sacrifices, such as the fatigue and strain on muscles and circulatory system, are involuntary. Others, like the time spent attending prenatal clinics and classes, and abstinence from alcohol, nicotine, and caffeine, are voluntary sacrifices that can be likened to the fasting of a saint or the regimen of an athlete. Increasingly, these voluntary sacrifices are being shared by men as an expression of solidarity with their wives.[34]

The sacrificial aspects of pregnancy and childbirth become more pronounced as a woman's "estimated delivery date" approaches. By this time many women experience increasing physical discomfort and negative feelings about their bodies[35] and by the time the baby is due, most are more than ready to hold their baby in their arms rather than in their wombs and to get their bodies back to "normal." At the same time, women feel increasingly vulnerable and are concerned about the impending delivery—in particular about the treatment their body might endure in the hospital.[36] This can be a time of considerable emotional and spiritual struggle as a woman prepares herself to confront the unknowns of labor, seeks to come to terms with the legacy of any prior birthing experiences, and perhaps encounters new "risk" factors, such as a baby in breech position, toxemia, or signs of premature labor. Her struggles with the stranger within and the unpredictable challenges awaiting her may be surprisingly akin to those of Jacob, who on the threshold of returning to his family of origin, wrestled through the night with a stranger who left him wounded but blessed, and with a new identity (Gen. 32:24–32).

A woman on the threshold of labor also may be compared to Jesus in Gethsemane, well able to foresee the violation and suffering she may have to endure if the new life within her is to be born. Assault by an external, malevolent force is a common theme in dreams during this time.[37] There is a realistic element to these fears—injury at this time would have greater than usual consequences. The fear of assault also may be related to the prospect of "losing control" of one's body during labor—not only to the body's own involuntary processes, but also to the doctors and other strangers who will "precisely at this most vulnerable time, be probing into the very center of the woman's body."[38] Moreover, the very intensity of a woman's fears "may be related to her positive feelings, to her sense that she is charged with something extremely valuable."[39]

Thus, too, the relationship of death and new life comes very close to the surface during pregnancy, not least as the crisis of birth approaches. Psychologists Arthur and Libby Colman note increased interest in the topic of death and dying among the pregnant women with whom they spoke: "It was as though, by being closer to birth, to the beginning of life, these women were automatically closer to death."[40] One pastor tells of a special bond that developed when she was expecting a baby and a parishioner was dying of cancer: "We talked about how we were both on the threshold of something radically new. When the baby was born, I sent her a picture, which she put on her bedpost. A few days later she died. It was as if she was waiting for that baby to be born."

This concern with death is another sign of childbirth as a spiritual crisis. Whether or not a woman has realistic grounds for concern, her body confronts her with her own mortality and vulnerability. And although maternal and infant mortality rates continue to decline, there are still realistic grounds for concern. Poor women are most vulnerable, but no one is immune.[41] Each year a variety of parents will experience the sorrow of a miscarriage or stillbirth, or the early death of a severely handicapped child.[42] The grief families experience at these times is very real, and perhaps more difficult to bear as such deaths become increasingly exceptional.[43] A birthing theology, then, also must face death and comprehend it as part of life.

Furthermore, even when all goes well, the birth of a child involves a second symbolic death and rebirth for the mother. In a matter of hours, her pregnant self is lost, and a new, postpartum self begins to emerge.[44] The way this "death" and birth occur varies considerably, even within a single woman's experience. Thus there is an element of surprise involved in each birth: Will the birthing process begin in a sudden gush of amniotic fluid in a public place, or will contractions begin so calmly that even the mother herself may not know just when her labor begins? Will labor be straightforward and unmedicated, or will it encounter complications, difficult decisions, and interventions? Will a woman emerge feeling exhilarated, strong, and affirmed after successfully negotiating the ordeal of childbirth, or will she feel betrayed, disappointed, or incompetent if the birth failed to live up to expectations?

Both graceful and demonic possibilities are present throughout this experience of waiting, squeezing and stretching, panting and pushing. The sudden rush of amniotic fluid, for example, can be received with embarrassment as a kind of defilement, with joy as a sign that the drama of birth has now begun with a splash or with some combination of the two. So, too, the powerful waves of contractions can be resisted or welcomed—responded to as pain, or received "as intense energy directed toward an end."[45]

The childbirth education movement has done much to lift up the important role a woman's mental preparedness plays in making birthing a graceful experience. For example, childbirth educators advise women to greet each contraction with a cleansing breath. This encouragement to greet the contraction as a friendly force rather than resisting it as an enemy provides a grace-filled interpretation of the body's birthing work that can promote the integration and cooperation of body and spirit, thus reducing tension and the pain it causes.

Moreover, the idea of a *cleansing* breath reframes in psychosomatic terms the uncleanness associated with childbirth in cultures around the world. It is a breath, that is, a physical action, but its cleansing action presumably has to do with the mind and soul—whisking away the memories of previous physical pain that might cause a woman to tense up. This psychosomatic ritual of cleansing may remind us of the age-old sense of childbirth as taboo work, involving the human in dangerous intimacy with the divine.

Otherwise this primal experience of uncleanness is very limited in our culture. Much of the blood and mess of childbirth is usually caught on a disposable pad and efficiently removed before it makes much of an impression; newborns are often wiped clean and even wrapped before being given to their mothers. Still, even if a woman never has the opportunity to touch and explore her newborn's body while it is still freshly damp and blood-streaked, childbirth cannot help but assault our conventional expectations of cleanliness, propriety, and control.

Bladder and bowel control are temporarily out of the question, a woman's "private parts" are exposed, in some cases to quite a large public of strangers, the bleeding that begins with birth will continue for some time afterward. Childbirth requires letting go of some of the control we normally exercise—indeed, childbirth may teach us the healing power of accepting ourselves, mess and all. As one midwife has observed, "Once a birthing woman lets go of all the reins, all the inhibitions . . . then there is not long left" before delivery.[46] It may be that the sterile hospital environment not only serves to minimize risk of infection[47] but also provides what is perceived to be a pure, set-apart place in which that letting go can happen safely, and the chaos, spilled blood, and dangerous uncleanness of childbirth can be contained.

From a Christian perspective, the healing power of meeting contractions with a cleansing breath might renew our appreciation of the work of the Holy Spirit in our lives—whisking away whatever burden of anxiety, shame, or guilt we may carry in body or soul, so that we are free to respond anew to the next challenge that faces us.

For some, the crisis of birth goes quickly; for others it involves many, many cleansing breaths and contractions that squeeze breathing techniques right out of the picture. Somewhere in their birth story, many women come to a point at which the body is more than willing, but the spirit is weak. At such a moment a woman feels like calling it all off and going home, only to realize that there is no turning back; at that moment it becomes clear that there is no way out but to follow the body's lead through the tumult and struggle. And then, at this point of extremity, perhaps crying out, "I can't do this"—she does it. At this moment, letting go and trusting her body, her birthing attendants, and her God, a woman may experience a glorious surge of new strength, energy, and purpose as body and soul unite in a common endeavor, vagina and uterus become one birth canal and, massaging and squeezing, push a new person out into the world.

This is life, this is a glimpse of resurrection, this is the miracle of birth—for the husband who holds his wife's hand, rubs her back, and weeps for joy, as well as for the woman who is amazed at strength and endurance she did not know she had. And just as her colostrum already springing to meet her baby's needs and the rich milk supply building in her breasts are living reminders of God's overflowing abundance and sustenance, so too the wounds her body has endured may be transformed by grace into the intimate, irradicable bonds of compassion that bind mother and child and into a new, stronger sense of self.

We turn now to ways in which the church can promote such a gracious negotiation of this significant spiritual crisis.

Notes

1. Richard W. Wertz and Dorothy C. Wertz, *Lying-In: A History of Childbirth in America,* expanded ed. (New Haven: Yale University Press, 1989), 240.

2. Helen Callaway, " 'The Most Essentially Female Function of All': Giving Birth," 163–185, in *Defining Females: The Nature of Women in Society,* ed. Shirley Ardener (New York: Halsted Press, John Wiley & Sons, 1978), 167.

3. *Luther's Works* (St. Louis: Concordia; Philadelphia: Fortress, 1955–76), 7:46f.

4. Myra Leifer, *Psychological Effects of Motherhood: A Study of First Pregnancy* (New York: Praeger, 1980), 58; and Arthur and Libby Colman, *Pregnancy: The Psychological Experience* (New York: Herder and Herder, 1971), 10.

5. Karen L. Michaelson, et al., *Childbirth in America: Anthropological Perspectives* (South Hadley, Mass.: Bergin and Garvey, 1988), 10.

6. I am unaware of any studies of religious language in the telling of birth stories, or even studies of birth stories as a literary genre. This is probably not surprising, since until very recently, birth stories have been almost exclusively an oral tradition.

7. Rosemary Radford Ruether, *Women-Church: Theology and Practice of Feminist Liturgical Communities* (San Francisco: Harper & Row, 1985), 200f.

8. Wertz and Wertz, *Lying-In,* 240.

9. Obstetricians know that increasingly they may be sued if a baby does not meet its parent's expectation of a "perfect baby." The obstetrician who does not make full use of the available array of tests and treatments risks being found negligent, even if these very interventions may actually negatively affect not only the woman's experience of

childbirth and the normal, though unpredictable unfolding of the birth but also the health of mother and child. Compare Wertz and Wertz, *Lying-In*, 244, 255–59.

10. Wertz and Wertz, *Lying-In*, 243.

11. These difficult decisions often will be lonely ones; if parents choose to terminate the pregnancy, they may keep their decision hidden from even family and friends. The grief that accompanies any loss of a fetus can only be compounded under such circumstances, the quantity and quality of grief support drastically limited.

12. Linda Hughey Holt, "Medical Perspective on Pregnancy and Birth: Biological Risks and Technological Advances," 157–75, in *The Transition to Parenthood: Current Theory and Research*, ed. Gerald Y. Michaels and Wendy A. Goldberg (Cambridge: Cambridge University Press, 1988), 169. Compare Wertz and Wertz, *Lying-In*, 249ff. for other potentially negative effects of extensive prenatal testing.

13. "In anthropology 'the denial of physiological paternity' has been a recurring area of discussion since Malinowski asserted . . . that 'knowledge of impregnation, of the man's share in creating new life in the mother's womb, is a fact of which [the Trobriand Islanders] have not even the slightest glimpse'. . . . If 'the denial of physiological paternity' has been the basis for vigorous discussion in the anthropological journals, 'the denial of physiological maternity' has received little notice. . . . Joseph Needham calls our attention to ideas held in Greece before the time of Aristotle . . . that the father alone was the 'author of generation' while the mother provided only the 'nidus and nourishment for the fetus.' " Callaway, "Most Essentially Female Function of All," 167f., quotes Joseph Needham, *A History of Embryology*, 2d ed., rev., A. Hughes, (Cambridge: Cambridge University Press, 1959).

14. Penelope Washbourn, "My Body/My World," 87–94, in *Male and Female: Christian Approaches to Sexuality*, ed. Ruth Tiffany Barnhouse and Urban T. Homes III (New York: Seabury Press, 1976), 91. Compare Anne Eggebroten, "The Cost of Life: A Mother Experiences Incarnation," *The Other Side* 25 (May/June 1989): 44–46, which emphasizes the pain and suffering of childbirth as illuminating the preciousness of life.

15. Janice M. Morse and Caroline Park, "Differences in Cultural Expectations of the Perceived Painfulness of Childbirth," 121–29, in Michaelson, et al., *Childbirth in America*, 127f.

16. Kathryn Allen Rabuzzi, *Motherself: A Mythic Analysis of Motherhood* (Bloomington, Indiana: Indiana University Press, 1988), 203.

17. Rabuzzi, *Motherself*, 201.

18. As one doctor put it, "In the current obstetrical climate, every

174   TOWARD A BIRTHING THEOLOGY AND MINISTRY

patient is approached as a potential litigant." Dr. Roger Rosenblatt, University of Washington Department of Family Medicine, quoted in "Despite Criticism, Fetal Monitors Are Likely to Remain in Wide Use," *New York Times,* 27 March 1988, cited in Wertz and Wertz, *Lying-In,* 260.

19. Frances Kaplan Grossman, Lois S. Eichler, Susan A. Winickoff, *Pregnancy, Birth, and Parenthood: Adaptations of Mothers, Fathers, and Infants* (San Francisco: Jossey-Bass, 1980), 68.

20. See p. 64ff.; cf. p. 202ff.

21. Washbourn, "My Body/My World," 91.

22. Eggebroten, "The Cost of Life," 45f.

23. Ann Oakley, *Women Confined: Towards a Sociology of Childbirth* (New York: Schocken; 1980), 272f. See also Sheila Kitzinger, *Women as Mothers: How They See Themselves in Different Cultures* (New York: Vintage Books, 1980), 74ff; and Barbara Katz Rothman, *Recreating Motherhood: Ideology and Technology in a Patriarchal Society* (New York: W.W. Norton, 1989), 55ff.

24. Penelope Washbourn, *Becoming Woman: The Quest for Wholeness in Female Experience* (San Francisco: Harper & Row, 1977), 94–112.

25. Leifer, *Psychological Effects of Motherhood,* 32; cf. Colman and Colman, *Pregnancy,* 36.

26. Oakley, *Women Confined,* 186, cf. 75; Leifer, *Psychological Effects,* 168ff.

27. Leifer, *Psychological Effects,* 34.

28. Ibid., 56, cf. 34.

29. Childbearing women may well have a special affinity for the story of Jonah—alternately seeing themselves as the individual being swallowed up by motherhood; and as the great fish who protects and carries a little stranger in its body until the Lord says that it is time to expel the precious cargo.

30. Leifer, *Psychological Effects,* 43.

31. Compare Leifer, *Psychological Effects,* 48f.

32. That a pregnant woman should express her concerns in this way is one thing; that such a negative image can find its way into supposedly "objective" medical texts is quite another. Such language defines pregnancy as pathology and completely ignores the benefits that pregnancy may confer on women. Compare Barbara Katz Rothman, *In Labor: Women and Power in the Birthplace* (New York: W.W. Norton, 1982), 135, 154ff., 275. Rothman sees the "parasite" metaphor informing much of the medical model.

33. See Patricia Beattie Jung, "Reconceiving Pregnancy," *Currents*

in Theology and Mission 18 (August 1991): 256–62. Jung points out the deficiencies of the popular "spaceship/astronaut" and "child rearing" metaphors for the relationship between a pregnant woman and her fetus and admits that her organ donor model also presents (unspecified) problems. It is a sad commentary on our society that the sacrificial side of childbearing can so completely overwhelm the blessedness of being God's procreative coworker. A better model for articulating a mother's sacrifice might be that of a prophet or a priest—called to do a holy work and enabled to do this holy work in spite of dangers and sacrifices.

34. Tribal cultures often clearly define expected participatory behavior for the expecting father. According to the Colmans, these "couvade" customs "serve an important psychological function for the husband and wife. Perhaps our own rituals (or lack of rituals) for the pregnant husband are limiting a potentially rich experiential event, or causing harm to the individual and his family." Colman and Colman, *Pregnancy*, 105.

35. Compare, for example, Leifer, *Psychological Effects*, 35f.

36. For the first-time mothers in Leifer's study, "fear of the hospital often far outweighed concerns regarding the birth process itself." Episiotomy, in particular, was viewed with dread, *Psychological Effects*, 127. The fear of violation and surgical defacement represented by episiotomy all too often proves warranted: episiotomies are performed on no less than 90 percent of women having their first vaginal delivery in a U.S. hospital. One in four women entering a U.S. hospital to give birth will be left with the scars of a cesarean section, Wertz and Wertz, *Lying-In*, 255. Oakley discusses the emotional ramifications of the surgical aspects of most hospital births, *Women Confined*, 220–24.

37. Colman and Colman, *Pregnancy*, 23f. Compare Leifer: at this time "women commonly began to view the outside world as being potentially threatening," and expressed fears that their husband might die or abandon them, *Psychological Effects*, 48.

38. Colman and Colman, *Pregnancy*, 25. Simply entering the hospital implies a loss of control. Leifer found that most of the women she interviewed experienced their entry into the hospital as an abrupt shock that "radically changed their perception of birth as a natural event to a view of birth as a medical event or operation," Leifer, *Psychological Effects*, 137.

39. Colman and Colman, *Pregnancy*, 26.

40. Ibid., 13f.

41. "In 1985, the United States ranked seventeenth in the world in infant mortality, down from fifteenth in 1973." Wertz and Wertz, *Lying-In*, 303. According to Ellen S. Lazarus, the decline in the national

infant mortality rate leveled off in 1985 and "infant morality is now actually increasing in some cities," in "Poor Women, Poor Outcomes: Social Class and Reproductive Health," 39–54, in Michaelson, et al., *Childbirth in America*, 39. By 1991, experts were informing Congress that the United States had slipped to nineteenth in infant mortality rates. "Experts: Prenatal care isn't only problem," *Bellingham Herald* [Bellingham, WA] 13 Sept. 1991. Compare Wertz and Wertz, *Lying-In*, 270ff., 297.

42. According to Sheila Kitzinger, "one in every five pregnancies probably ends in miscarriage." Stillbirth is much more rare, but does still occur. *The Complete Book of Pregnancy and Childbirth* (New York: Alfred A. Knopf, 1982), 291.

43. Increasingly, the church is formulating pastoral responses to the grief of miscarriage and stillbirth. See, for example, Ruether, *Women-Church*, 162f.; David Presky, "An Often Neglected Loss," *Your Church* 33 (March/April 1987): 36–39; Janet S. Peterman, "A Pastoral and Theological Response to Losses in Pregnancy," *The Christian Century* 104 (Sept. 9–16, 1987): 750–53; Victor M. Parachin, "Helping Families Survive Stillbirth," *The Christian Ministry* 22 (July/August 1991): 19–20.

44. From this perspective, the increased dissatisfaction with their physical appearance experienced by many women after birth may be seen as an expression of grief at the loss of the pregnant self with its sense of fullness and intimate connection with the baby. Interestingly, Leifer found that the two women who were consistently satisfied with their pregnant and postpartum appearance were also the women who nursed their infants beyond six months, *Psychological Effects*, 36. Oakley points out the similarities between postpartum grief and the grief experienced at the loss of a body part, *Women Confined*, 212. Indeed, Oakley finds that under present social conditions in the industrialized world, women often experience more loss than gain at the birth of a child—including loss of status, independence, and many peer relationships.

45. Washbourn, "My Body/My World," 90.

46. Dorthe Taxbøl, "En nat i oktober," 107–123, in *Forløsning: Ni kvinder skriver om at føde* (Copenhagen: Rosinante, 1991), 115; translation my own.

47. The need for antiseptic precautions is crucial in the hospital environment, where women would otherwise meet a host of microbes to which their bodies were unfamiliar. Such concerns are much less important in home births, where unfamiliar sources of infection are much fewer. Currently, it is probably the hospital technology rather than antiseptic conditions that gives birthing women a sense of security

there. Still, the various machines and uniformed personnel project the impression of efficiency and the ability to control the vagaries of the birthing process. Few studies have been done of the experiences of women who have given birth at home, although there are indications that for healthy women who have had a normal pregnancy it is a safe (perhaps even safer) alternative with considerable personal and family benefits. See Wertz and Wertz, *Lying-In*, 284–91, esp. 288f. Compare Rothman, *Recreating Motherhood*, 171ff.

9

Birthing Ministry

How can the church promote the graceful aspects of giving birth and better incorporate the gifts of birthing into its life and teaching? Opportunities abound in all aspects of the church's life: pastoral care and prayer, support for health-care vocations, justice and advocacy, worship life, proclamation and education.

Pastoral Care and Prayer

Worlds do turn topsy-turvy during pregnancy, childbirth, and new parenthood, and as the previous chapter noted, these dramatic changes present spiritual as well as physical and emotional challenges for the childbearing woman and her family. This is an important time for pastoral care in people's lives. For church members who already enjoy multifaceted relationships with their pastor and other members of the congregation, the church community can be both a good source of practical help and a trustworthy ear to bend as they sort through the many issues confronting them. Research indicates that such a combination of practical and emotional support is especially salutary.[1]

Some of this ministry probably has always occurred informally in Christian congregations. Church women who share maternity and baby clothes with one another, give baby showers, and bring meals in for families of newborns often take time to minister to the emotional needs of the childbearing woman while offering these practical signs of support. Professional church workers may enhance these informal ministries by lifting up the spiritual challenges of childbearing through sermon illustrations and educational opportunities, thus encouraging congregational members to offer an especially attentive listening ear to the childbearing woman and her family.

In addition, congregations might offer a more intentional form of pastoral care for the childbearing. Some congregations already link expecting mothers with lay ministers who have received training in pastoral visitation. The Stephen Ministries program, for example, provides laypersons with training in the area of pregnancy and birth, as well as in other life crises.[2] The advantages of an intentional program are several. First, it better ensures that all childbearing women in the congregation are included. Informal networks may overlook persons less prominent in congregational life; a well-publicized, intentional program has a better chance of reaching those on the outskirts of the congregation. Such a ministry might also be offered as a service to those beyond the bounds of the congregation.

Second, the very presence of a regular visitor coming on behalf of the church calls attention to the spiritual dimensions of childbearing. The woman who receives regular visits from such a minister may be more likely to see the spiritual dimensions of her experiences, feelings, and decisions. Seeing and hearing about pastoral care to the childbearing also may prompt members of the congregation to broaden their appreciation of this time in life.

Third, trained pastoral visitors would be alert to the interplay of psychological, social, physical, and spiritual dynamics in childbearing. Thus a pastoral visitor could assure a pregnant woman that her mood swings are quite normal,[3] as well as give her an opportunity to lament, rejoice, or think about the shape of her Christian vocation and express both hopes and fears in terms of her faith. Such visits might include time for confession and forgiveness, sharing joys and concerns, prayer, storytelling and shared reflections on Bible readings; singing hymns, or perhaps even gentle massage. The frequency of visits will depend on the schedules of the persons involved and on the rapport they are able to build. Considering the intensity of the experience, however, it would be wise to plan on visiting every two or three weeks initially, more often as the birth draws near, and during the first few postpartum weeks.

In many cases, parish pastors will not be able to devote so much visitation time to one family.[4] What is more, the church must resist the temptation to add a spiritual "expert" to the range of professionals who already tend to mold and direct childbirth.[5] Thus lay ministers, especially women who have themselves experienced childbirth, may be the most helpful pastoral caregivers at this point in a woman's life. In either case, it is critical that the pastoral caregiver refrain from assuming the role of expert, whether on the basis of office or of prior experience. Ministers might better think of themselves as pastoral midwives (literally "with-women"), whose wisdom and compassion enables them to attend and support the childbearing woman as she does her spiritual and physical work, catching and holding up the spiritual insights to which she gives birth. Clergypersons who are willing and able to devote some time and energy to such visitation will almost certainly be blessed by insight into this important time in the lives of their parishioners, as well as be struck by the sheer miracle, the stirring life, and the drama of it all.

Reaching out with pastoral care to women who are not affiliated with a congregation presents more challenges. Some congregations already minister in practical ways to childbearing women in their neighborhoods, perhaps by maintaining a "bank" of maternity and baby clothes for poor women, perhaps by offering community childbirth education classes in their buildings. Such service projects also may open avenues to offering more specifically pastoral care; at least they offer an opportunity to extend an invitation. Childbirth classes, for example, not only are beneficial in and of themselves but also can gracefully offer a Christian perspective on childbirth, even in classes that are open to the general public.[6] Although care needs to be used in such cases, Christian instructors can surely find appropriate ways to offer suggestions for enhancing the spiritual dimensions of childbirth.

The practice of prayer is one obvious way to increase awareness of God's presence in the birthing room. Pastors or chaplains may be present and able to offer prayer, occasionally even a midwife or a doctor will do so. Increasingly husbands pray aloud for their wives during labor, and women pray themselves, often silently. Childbirth instructors might also suggest breathing prayers as an alternative to the regular Lamaze lingo. For example, the classic Jesus prayer ("Lord Jesus Christ, Son of God," as the breath is slowly inhaled, "have mercy on me, a sinner," while slowly exhaling) can be a meaningful, relaxing form of breathing and praying during the early part of labor. This prayer might be modified to "Lord Jesus Christ, Child of God; have mercy on me as I suffer;" or even "Lord Jesus Christ, who gave birth on the cross; have mercy on me as I labor." One woman noted that as her labor intensified, this breathing prayer shortened to "Lord, have mercy," and then to simply "help me."[7] Finally, there may come a point at which a woman will be unable to pray as she would like, only to find herself supported by the Spirit who "helps us in our weakness, . . . [interceding] for us with sighs too deep for words" (Rom. 8:26). Such prayers become much more than a breathing technique; they enfold the struggle to birth in prayer. Indeed they remind us that the childbearing labor can itself be an act of prayer. Later, too, these breathing prayers can link the powerful experience of childbirth with challenges in other areas of life. As a woman again breathes this prayer, she may be strengthened by its reminder of how she lived through labor by the grace of God, as well as its reminder that God's presence is as near and life-giving as every breath she draws.

Childbirth instructors usually suggest that a birthing couple take some object along to the hospital to serve as a focal point during labor. Often this object is recommended as a diversion from the pain that accompanies contractions. A Christian childbirth instructor might suggest that a cross, a picture of the virgin Mary, a candle, or other faith symbols be displayed prominently in the labor room, not so much as an attempt to divert attention from the body's exertions, but more as an aid to putting the suffering of childbirth in the context of Christ's being born and giving birth, suffering with and for us, and drawing us through even our suffering to release and joy. Similarly, a Christian instructor might suggest playing tapes of appropriate religious music as a source of comfort and inspiration. These tapes might include a variety of instrumental and vocal music—gentle hymns and spiritual songs, such as "Amazing Grace," "Children of the Heavenly Father," "Simple Gifts," "Swing Low, Sweet Chariot," and "Lord of All Hopefulness" to aid relaxation during labor; and on the other side, more energetic hymns of praise, such as "Joyful, Joyful, We Adore Thee," "Thine Is the Glory," and "Now Thank We All Our God," to accompany the exertions of pushing. A congregation could put together such a tape and make it available to couples for use during pregnancy and childbirth, thus extending something of corporate worship into the birthing room. The result may even be a form of witness to hospital personnel: One doctor tells of the moving experience of attending a birth surrounded by religious music. Throughout labor and delivery the woman and her husband were so peaceful and calm that the doctor felt as if she had "touched the center of peace on earth."

Prayer, religious symbols, and music cannot guarantee such a peaceful birth, of course, but they can contribute to a good birth and extend the church's birthing ministry into the birthing room itself. Providing hands-on pastoral care during the birth itself may be more complicated. Traditionally, hospital labor and delivery rooms have not been open to clergy, although this has begun to change as husbands and friends gain access to birthing rooms and as more female pastors are available. Still, even female chaplains on maternity wards are not regularly expected to attend normal, healthy births. Perinatal chaplains are more likely to see their work as providing "pastoral care and grief services in the hospital for people who are experiencing a high-risk pregnancy" or other childbearing difficulty or tragedy.[8] Thus the healthy woman giving birth often receives no pastoral support beyond that which her husband (who faces challenges of his own) is able to offer her. Indeed, many staff people will come in and out of the birthing room at this intensely intimate and stressful moment in a woman's life, but there is little likelihood that any of them will have her emotional (much less her spiritual) well-being as their chief concern.[9] The very woman who experienced pregnancy as a special state of grace may find herself ignored as a person at precisely the moment she is engaged in some of the most vital, personally meaningful, and powerfully creative labor done by human beings.

The importance of intentional pastoral care during childbirth has never been more important, as increasing reliance on technological assistance tends to replace the human contact involved in simpler practices like massage, change of position, or help with breathing techniques. The birthing woman may be left with little or no genuine emotional reassurance, support, and encouragement from the staff.[10] This is not to imply that hospital staff people are negligent or intentionally callous; as hospitals become larger and more centralized, and hospital staff increasingly specialized, opportunities for staff members to build a relationship with the birthing woman diminish. Chances are that the person who comes in to draw the birthing woman's blood has never seen her before and probably will never see her again; similarly the nurse who does internal pelvic exams to check a woman's cervix during early labor may well finish her shift and go home before the baby is born. The birthing woman often has to cope with a series of strangers observing and examining her most private parts, and the medical staff tends to be distanced from the fullness of the miracle being experienced in the lives of individual birthing women and their families. Thus the experience that serves to forge and enrich communal bonds in most traditional societies is characterized by disconnectedness in our own.[11]

This situation can be beneficially addressed in several ways. Congregations and chaplains can make pastoral care and prayer support tangibly available during birth; they can also uplift and encourage birthing attendants to nurture the pastoral dimensions of their vocation. The congregation that provides pastoral care to a childbearing couple at the time of birth helps make connections, strengthening communal bonds as well as calling attention to God's presence. As one father told his pastor, months after the birth of his children: "I will always remember how you came and prayed with us; I know God was there with us in that hospital room." This pastoral care, too, may be given either by the parish pastor or by a layperson. Male pastors often will find that their gender hinders them from ministering to birthing women, although a visit early in labor might be appreciated and often can be accomplished without anyone feeling awkward.

Generally speaking, female pastors and laywomen will probably feel more comfortable and be more welcome in the midst of birthing. Researchers have found that even an untrained and previously unknown person can greatly enhance the course of a birth by simply providing friendly, supportive, and consistent companionship;[12] how much greater might be the blessings when the supportive companion is familiar to the birthing woman, represents her church, and has ministered to her during her pregnancy? The pastoral caregiver might bring a symbol of the congregation's prayer support, for example, a multicolored "friendship bracelet" for the woman to wear during childbirth as a reminder of the prayers that encircle her and in celebration of her own multifaceted identity as a beloved child of God.[13] The pastoral caregiver may serve in a variety of ways: offering a hand to hold or a shoulder to lean on as well as a prayer, listening to the concerns of the father as well as of the mother; serving as a buffer between the hospital environment and the birthing woman if necessary; cheering the woman on, as well as affirming what she is already accomplishing.

The church is also in a position to extend its pastoral care for the childbearing into the early postpartum period, a time that is especially trying in our culture.[14] Many women experience becoming a mother as a "shock."[15] For some the birth itself is experienced as a shock; for many the fatigue, the sheer amount of work, and feeling of being tied down present another shock, particularly because so many newborn mothers feel alone in trying to deal with their baby's needs. Fledgling public attempts to improve preparation for parenthood and to enhance parents' support networks have shown promising results.[16] The church, as a community traditionally interested in ministering to families' practical as well as spiritual needs, is ideally suited to contribute in this area. Congregations can continue to offer a listening ear as newborn families move toward a new equilibrium. They can offer occasional child care, so that new mothers can take some time for themselves.

Support for Health-care Vocations

Hospital chaplains are especially important as bearers of Christian witness for those among the hospitalized who do not already have a strong church affiliation. Thus it is important that chaplains, too, find ways in which to minister to those who experience the trials and joys of healthy birthing, as well as to the grieving. A chaplain might serve as a guest speaker in the hospital's maternity orientation class, lifting up the spiritual dimensions of birthing and offering to make visits during labor. The chaplain also might meet birthing women at the admissions office, offering support and, when appropriate, a word of prayer. More indirectly, too, the chaplain may minister to birthing women—by challenging hospital administrations to provide person-centered birthing care; by strengthening programs to train and make labor companions available; and not least, by ministering to the obstetrical staff. Respected and known as a member of the staff, the chaplain is in a position to challenge birthing attendants to better appreciate and support the holiness of the birthing woman's work, as well as to support those same staff people in their struggles to balance conflicting demands and to cope with the stress of difficult situations in their healing work. The chaplain can help staff face the ethical questions that arise, hear confessions when something goes wrong, and share in the rejoicing when difficult births turn out well.

Similarly, a congregation also may indirectly bless childbearing women by alerting the health-care professionals in their midst to the pastoral possibilities in their daily work and by supporting them in their efforts to contribute to graceful birth experiences. Local congregations can pastorally challenge and care for the caregiver, not least by bringing together, on neutral ground, persons who provide obstetrical care and families like those they serve. Opportunities to share birth experiences from various perspectives may lend insight into the constraints under which health-care professionals work and the impact their actions have on those they serve. These insights, in turn, may suggest ways to enhance the birthing process. The joy of new life coming into the world may prevent work in a maternity ward from ever becoming just a series of bloods to be drawn or cervixes to be checked. Still, staff members' connections inevitably tend to be with one another and the facilities, not with the families who come and go. They may have little idea how offensive it can be for a laboring woman to hear her nurse bantering with a colleague while holding the birthing room door ajar, or how rude and even sacrilegious a woman struggling to push her child out into the world may find waiting neonatal nurses' chatter about last night's party. Perhaps it is too much to expect that human beings can experience the full wonder of birth day after day. Still, the experience of a child's birth is never routine for the parents, and even the simplest expressions of respect and human attention will greatly enhance their experience. One researcher was both touched and saddened "to see how extraordinarily grateful women were for any sign of personal interest, consideration, or respect from the staff. One woman spoke warmly about a medical student who . . . took the time to discuss with her how her labor was progressing. 'It really made a big difference to me,' she recalled, 'though it was such a small thing. It was as though he was the first person to treat me as an intelligent adult and not as a body to be examined.' "[17]

On the other hand, such sharing also may dispel some myths that surround the medical profession, not least the obstetrician. Open discussion will reveal that obstetricians are neither more divine nor more demonic than other people. They do wield disproportionate power within the hospital setting and are subject to the temptations that accompany power, but they too are affected by the underlying mistrust that is often present between them and the people they serve. Moreover, open, honest discussions can reveal the efforts that some doctors, nurses, and midwives make to enhance the birthing process—in spite of the threat of malpractice, conflicting desires, and impossible expectations. A family doctor works consciously to empower the women she assists in birthing; an anesthesiologist voluntarily undergoes preparation for surgery, so he will be better able to understand the feelings of surgical patients; a midwife anoints a woman's stretched perineum with oil, and later blesses the newborn child and parents with prayers of thanks and prayers for healing of any birth trauma—all these persons are ministering to the spiritual as well as physical needs of the people they serve.

On a larger level, the church might lift up the variety of birthing vocations and alternatives by sponsoring occasional symposiums including doctors and nurses, hospital and birthing center administrators, lay and certified midwives, pastors and chaplains, as well as interested members of the public. Such a symposium could focus on the possibilities for ministry in each of these occupations; participants could consider together how the Christian faith might inform birthing practices, whether in the hospital, in a birthing center, or at home. "Midwifery as a Ministry" was the most requested workshop option at a recent homebirth conference;[18] other childbirth professionals may show a similar interest.

Justice and Advocacy

The church as a community of people from all walks of life can significantly contribute to public debate and policy formation on a whole range of childbearing issues, first by wrestling through the issues themselves, then by carefully articulating the moral issues involved. One such issue is the extent to which the health-care beliefs of the majority should be imposed on minorities with differing beliefs. For example, is it appropriate for government to require heroic measures to prolong the life of severely handicapped newborns or for judges to grant court orders permitting drastic interventions in the labor of women who refuse them, in spite of doctors' warnings of possible danger to their baby?[19] At issue is the extent of persons' freedom to make health-care decisions for themselves and their babies.

Nor is the relevance of this issue restricted to exceptional situations that may require interventions; even such common decisions as the selection of a birth attendant are limited by the assumptions of the medical mainstream.[20] Thus, until recently, women choosing to use the services of certified nurse midwives often had difficulty being reimbursed by their health insurance companies. While certified nurse midwives are now gaining hospital privileges and acceptance by insurance carriers in many parts of the country, expenses for lay midwives assisting at home births are rarely reimbursed. The church would do well to explore the issues involved in such decisions and to support the availability of appropriate birthing options. Indeed, it may be increasingly important for the church to work for the very availability of appropriate childbirth care and to voice insights into proper allocations of obstetrical resources. Trends toward hospital centralization and obstetric specialization, for example, are not necessarily in the best interest of the public. These trends may or may not be reversible. In either case, the church community should be deliberating the personal and communal consequences of such decisions and doing what it can to envision and to encourage the healthiest possible way forward.

Furthermore, the church should continue to raise its voice on behalf of the disadvantaged. Sometimes that will mean standing with an unwed mother, helping her to communicate her reservations about proposed therapies; sometimes it will mean lobbying for more available prenatal care and healthier living circumstances for poor women. That a wealthy, health-conscious country like the United States should continue to slip in world rank in its infant mortality rates is disgraceful. That so many of these infant deaths are directly related to their parents' poverty stands as a word of judgment on our entire society. The sources of this injustice are beyond the scope of the present study,[21] but a church committed to justice for all God's children will explore the issues and actively promote ways to give each newborn child an equal opportunity to survive and thrive.[22] Indeed, the church, as a compassionate community that crosses all socioeconomic lines, may be uniquely positioned both to

advocate healthy change and to incarnate the healing power of
hope in these distressed communities.

Finally, the church can advocate improving structural social
and economic supports for new parents. Making and strengthening provisions for parental leave is one obvious area in which
society should show its shared interest in, and commitment to,
the well-being of children and families. The church, composed as
it is of both employers and employees, young and old, married
and single, is a good place to renew a vision of shared responsibility for our children, as well as to work together on ways to
implement that vision in practical terms.

Worship Life

Public worship can indirectly strengthen women for childbirth and all other challenges by consistently proclaiming the
Christian message of life's victory over death and by assuring all
people of God's presence with them as they face life's challenges.
Public worship also offers more direct opportunities to
strengthen women in their childbearing and to bring the gifts of
childbirth into the life of the church.

The public prayers of the church are one simple and regular
place to begin. Many congregations already offer prayers of
thanks for newborn children and prayers for women in the final
weeks of their pregnancies. Childbearing women and their
families might be included regularly in a congregation's public
prayer throughout their pregnancies and early weeks of parenthood. Prayers also may be offered more generally for all expecting mothers and their babies, especially for those in difficult
circumstances. So, too, prayers that use maternal metaphors for
God are lending new vitality to our prayer life, as well as
increasing women's appreciation of God's presence with them in
their childbearing.

Semiprivate, as well as more public rites of passage also may
help acknowledge and resolve the spiritual crisis presented by
childbirth. Appropriate liturgies might complement the traditional baby shower's signs of communal support by articulating

the spiritual dimensions of giving birth. Rosemary Radford Ruether proposes a birthing preparation liturgy to be observed in its own right in a circle of family and friends. This "Women-Church" liturgy centers on a myth that weaves together biblical and extrabiblical themes and links the religious meanings of creation and procreation. This new myth of creation, fall, and redemption makes prominent use of birth imagery:

> In the beginning was the egg . . . and the Mother-Spirit moved within the egg, shaping and forming all the living things that grew within the egg . . . And men forgot the Mother-Spirit and sought to become themselves eternal Creator and the Lords of creation. And they looked on woman's body as a tool to be enslaved and used, through which they could create life by command, rather than giving and receiving life from one another as a gift from the Mother-Spirit . . . But each new child brings to us the promise of restoration of our original goodness and harmony with all living things . . . every mother repeats the primal mystery of the Mother-Spirit of the original creation and the Mother-God who nurtures a redemptive people. . . .[23]

This myth presses disconcertingly against the limits of traditional Christian theology; and yet it is precisely this myth with its tremendous scope that gives the ritual its power. It vividly connects the miracle occurring in the woman's womb to the miracle of all creation, to the drama of human life, and to biblical maternal images of God working in human history. Can Christians retell the traditional biblical account of creation, fall, and redemption in an equally powerful and liberating way?

Marge Sears's "Celebration of Pregnancy" is less jarring to the sensibilities of many Christians, relying as it does upon a biblical version of cosmic creation to furnish the context for the miracle of a child's conception and growth: John 1:1, 4, 14 is read, then the pregnant woman says: "In the beginning was the seed, in the beginning was the egg that teemed with life. The fertilized egg grew and expanded, full of God's power and mystery, yet dependent on the womb, the mother for nourishment and shelter . . ."[24] This is a gentle celebration of the joy of childbirth; it does not relive the drama of fall and redemption or call to mind the elements of struggle involved in pregnancy and birthing. In its own gentle way, though, it does guide attention to a new identity in the offing: "Now is the season of the secret, the secret that new life is transforming our lives. It is not shape, movement, body, person that is within the dark confines of ourselves, but it is the Mysterious Creator unfolding in life's experiences, treasuring the discovery of a new self in each of us, gentling our own living with the touch only the Wondrous One gives."[25]

There is also an important place for a public rite celebrating a woman's successful negotiation of the challenges of childbirth. Rites of seclusion and purification such as those embodied in an earlier era's practice of "churching" women reflect a genuine need for "a ritual to allow the death of the old self through the ordeal and transformation into a new state."[26] The suggestion that purification is needed following childbirth will strike modern readers as foreign and distasteful, not to mention theologically suspect. Still, the abandonment of this rite, or its transformation from the churching of *women* into a "Thanksgiving for the Birth or Adoption of a *Child*"[27] misses an important point, that is, the significance this transition has for the mother. Indeed, it could be argued that our culture already practices rituals of seclusion and purification—in the hospital rather than in the church. One significant disadvantage of this development is that these ritual moments are concentrated into an increasingly shorter time frame. No longer does a woman's first postnatal foray into the public sphere lead her to church. Instead her reentry into the public sphere is signaled by her discharge from the hospital—days, or even hours after the birth of her child, long before her body has had an opportunity to heal.

The church could address the need for a later ritual closing to childbirth by encouraging the new mother to rest at home with her newborn as much as possible during the infant's first few weeks of life (offering her practical assistance with shopping and household chores, opportunities for companionship and rest), and then, six weeks or so after the birth, inviting the new mother to church for a rite of thanksgiving for the childbearer.[28] In addition to offering women an opportunity to bring their childbirth experience to a ritual close, such a rite also would help the community do what other cultures do more clearly, namely thank a woman for her childbearing work.[29]

Episcopalians could develop such a rite by expanding their own prayer book's service of thanksgiving for the birth of a child by including prayers of thanks for the woman's birthing labors.[30] Other traditions might build on the common practice of giving a rose in celebration of a child's birth. Such a rite of thanksgiving for the childbearer might look like this: a representative of the congregation invites the new mother and her family to the altar at a prearranged point in the worship service and gives the woman a rose as a token of the community's appreciation of the suffering and struggle she has endured in bringing new life into the world. The congregation then offers a prayer of thanks for her work and asks God's blessing on her and her husband as they care for the gift of life that God has given them. The parents and older siblings offer a prayer of thanksgiving that includes thanks for the God-given creative powers of the human body, for God's presence with the woman and her birthing assistants through the dangers of labor, for the gift of the child, and that concludes by asking for continued healing and for the wisdom, grace, and strength to care for this child. The parents then place the rose on the altar for the remainder of the service, as a symbol acknowledging that they are stewarding "their" child for its heavenly parent. The rite might conclude with the congregation reading Ps. 121 or the Magnificat and singing such a song as "I Was There to Hear Your Borning Cry."

Public rites celebrating God's creative work in childbirth also might help put baptism in a healthier perspective. As noted at the end of chapter 5, describing baptism as a "new birth" has suggested to some that baptism is a new and improved version of birth in which a patriarchal church corrects the imperfections of mother-given birth. Uplifting, praising, and thanking women for their work in childbearing is one way to counter this impression. Honoring and developing the birthing symbolism of baptism also can help reclaim the life-affirming power of the metaphor. For example, a baptismal prayer might well refer to the waters of the womb, which cleansed and protected each of us before we had even seen the light of day, as well as to the waters of creation, drowning, and renewal. Teaching and preaching can lift up the narrowness of the passage into life, as well as the naked equality with which we enter both God's world and the body of Christ. We might explain that only the drama and miracle of birth gives a metaphor radical enough to express the meaning of initiation into the body of Christ. In baptism we receive new life and a new identity, which is not to denigrate our natural life any more than being born implies there is something wrong with fetal life. One is the precondition for the other, and both are God-given.

Today baptism is less clearly a rite of birth than it has been in the past. The urgency with which medieval Christians hastened to baptize their children within the first few days of life is rare, even among members of traditions that practice infant baptism. Is this because infant mortality is generally low, and parents believe their child to be at least physically protected by the rituals that take place in the hospital (drops in the eyes, bathing, blood testing, weighing and measuring, registering, and in most cases the naming of the child, and in some cases circumcision)? Does it reflect increased secularization of society or less fear of the evil one's power over vulnerable infants? The tendency to see baptism as more an initiation into Christ than as a cultural rite associated with birth may perhaps loosen the association between birth per se and human sinfulness as well as diminish any tendency to see baptism as a ritual improvement upon natural birth.[31]

Education and Proclamation

Baptismal instruction, in particular, benefits from exploring what birthing symbolism means (and does not mean) about baptism. Some infant-baptizing churches already encourage parents to attend baptismal classes even before the baby is born. Such classes give parents the opportunity to think about their child's spiritual welfare as they begin giving their child an identity and envisioning themselves as parents. And, like child-birth education classes, baptismal education groups might give rise to lasting supportive relationships between members.

Indeed, the church's education program might minister to families by offering lifelong preparation for the joys and cares of parenthood as well as childbirth. In contemporary society, so much attention is focused on getting through childbirth that women often are quite unprepared for the challenges of new motherhood. Congregations might offer prebirth parenting classes[32] as well as find ways to include childbirth and parenting in their educational program. In our day and age few people know much about what to expect in childbirth and early parent-hood before pregnancy sends them dashing to the bookstore, library, and prenatal classes.[33] The intergenerational community of the church offers great potential for sharing experience, concerns, and insights, for helping one another learn what childbirth and parenting might entail, and also for liberating birth stories from the closet where they often have been lan-guishing—encouraging people who may have little or no idea of the circumstances of their own birth to ask their mothers about it; encouraging parents to tell their children the story of how they were born. There are few stories more dramatic or relevant! And in the process, stories and wisdom will be shared, challenges explored, strengths and weaknesses acknowledged, blessings recounted, and God's work in human lives lifted up.

In turn, these stories of struggle and euphoria (literally, "good-birth" or "well-borne"), shock and surprise, and disap-pointment and delight may lend new insight into Bible study, sermon preparation, and even into the way we envision and address God. Groups or individuals may want to weave personal and biblical perspectives, along with space for reflection, into devotional journals to be given to childbearing couples; or they may want to share birthing metaphors with the entire congrega-tion in Advent or Lent devotional booklets. Preachers may pay closer attention to maternal metaphors in Scripture and in the rhythms of the church year. Some care should be exercised here, however, so that Advent, for example, does not become the "childbirth season." One pastor was so inspired by his experience at the side of a parishioner during childbirth that the birth dominated his Advent sermons. One parishioner was so relieved when Christmas arrived that she exclaimed, "I think I would have blown up if I'd heard one more sermon about that birth!" The risk is well worth taking, however, for even shock at the unfamiliar and the intimate, the earthiness and the passion, may open up new approaches to glimpsing God's ways and God's works. Of this, more in the next chapter.

Notes

1. Benjamin H. Gottlieb and S. Mark Pancer, "Social networks and transition to parenthood," 235–269, in *The Transition to Parenthood: Current Theory and Research,* ed. Gerald Y. Michaels and Wendy A. Goldberg (Cambridge: Cambridge University Press, 1988), 254. Compare Karen L. Michaelson, "Bringing Up Baby: Expectation and Reality in the Early Postpartum," 252–260, in *Childbirth in America: Anthropological Perspectives,* Karen L. Michaelson, et al. (South Hadley, Mass.: Bergin and Garvey, 1988), 258.

2. For information regarding the Stephen Ministries training program, write: Stephen Ministries, 1325 Boland, St. Louis, MO 63117.

3. Psychologists say that pregnant women experience increased "emotional lability," i.e., they tend to experience stronger emotional responses than usual and more fluctuation in their moods. Arthur and Libby Colman, *Pregnancy: The Psychological Experience* (New York: Herder and Herder, 1971), 7f. Compare Myra Leifer, *Psychological Effects of Motherhood: A Study of First Pregnancy* (New York: Praeger, 1980), 43, 55f. Most pregnant women are relieved to learn that these disconcerting changes are not unusual. Colman and Colman, *Pregnancy,* 24, cf. 12.

4. Most pastors and congregations probably prioritize visitation of sick, shut-in, dying, and bereaved members above ministry to the childbearing. What do these priorities say about the church?

5. Ann Oakley writes persuasively of the power relations and social control involved in modern obstetrics and of the subtle ways in which the medicalized experience of childbirth reinforces women's acceptance of their subordinate social status. *The Captured Womb: A History of the Medical Care of Pregnant Women* (Oxford: Blackwell, 1984); and *Women Confined: Towards a Sociology of Childbirth* (New York: Schocken, 1980).

6. Independent childbirth classes per se seem to have a salutary effect: Leifer found that women who had participated in Lamaze classes in addition to the classes offered by the hospital, had strikingly more positive responses than those who had no preparation or only the hospital-sponsored class. They tended to have shorter labors and coped more successfully with labor, Leifer, *Psychological Effects,* 139f. Oakley, too, stresses the importance of independent, well-rounded childbirth education. Indeed, she finds hospital-based childbirth classes geared primarily toward the socialization of women into model patients, *Captured Womb,* 262–65, and sees prenatal care in general "as a strategy for the social control of women," ibid., 250, cf. 252ff.

7. Anne Eggebroten, "The Cost of Life: A Mother Experiences Incarnation," *The Other Side* 25(May/June 1989): 44–46. Eggebroten also describes replacing the Lamaze "hee-hee-hee-ho" pattern with "Jesus, Jesus, Jesus, Lord."

8. Linda Francisco Bets, "Perinatal Chaplaincy: How Do You Do What You Do?" *Lutheran Partners* 7 (March/April 1991): 15.

9. Compare Leifer, *Psychological Effects,* 145, cf. 239.

10. Compare Leifer, *Psychological Effects,* 146. Nurses no longer even need to ask the woman about the strength of her contractions, since she is probably connected to a machine that provides a printout of the interplay between her womb's actions and her baby's heartbeat; attention is diverted from the woman to the machinery monitoring and moulding her "progress." The intravenous setups and electronic fetal monitors that are becoming an increasingly routine part of hospital birth may give a sense of security, but they also hamper a woman's freedom of movement, define her as "sick" rather than healthy, and capture the attention not only of the hospital staff but often of the birthing parents as well. As if this were not enough, Oakley argues that few studies have demonstrated the effectiveness of many of these technical procedures. *Captured Womb,* 287.

11. The main exception to this trend results from the increased number of men who witness the birth of their children. Initial studies suggest that such fathers feel closer to both the child and its mother, though this does not necessarily translate into increased involvement with the actual care of the baby. Men often have little or no child-care experience, and childbirth classes rarely (if ever) give any practical child-care instruction to either parent. Compare Frances Kaplan Grossman, Lois S. Eichler, Susan A. Winickoff, *Pregnancy, Birth, and Parenthood: Adaptations of Mothers, Fathers, and Infants* (San Francisco: Jossey-Bass, 1980), 167; and Leifer, *Psychological Effects,* 74.

Furthermore, society offers little support for those fathers who do try to take a more active role in child care, Leifer, 244

12. Benefits included fewer complications, shorter labors, and increased mother-child interaction following the birth. Gottlieb and Pancer, "Social Networks," 263f. This study was done in a Guatemalan hospital, hence cross-cultural factors need to be considered. The positive effects were, however, dramatic—both the incidence of complications and labor time were reduced by almost half.

13. Young people in the congregation would probably enjoy braiding such bracelets; symbolic colors might be chosen and the significance of the armband explained on an accompanying card.

14. Oakley found varying degrees of postpartum blues and anxiety so common that she terms them "normal concomitants of first-time motherhood" in the specific cultural context of "institutionalized childbirth and socially isolated motherhood," *Women Confined*, 137f.

15. Oakley, *Women Confined*, 181; cf. Leifer, *Psychological Effects*, 137.

16. Gottlieb and Pancer, "Social Networks," 260ff.

17. Leifer, *Psychological Effects*, 146.

18. "I'm not able to have all Christian speakers and I'm not trying to shove Christianity on anyone, but I really hope to turn the table on new age midwifery. There are a lot of Christian midwives but almost everything offered for or by midwives is new age. Our most requested workshop option is Midwifery as a Ministry." The conference chairperson of the "Healing Hands Homebirth Conference," as quoted by Helen Wessel, *Bookmates International/Apple Tree Family Ministries Prayer Letter*, March–May 1988, 3.

19. Up until this point, court orders mandating obstetric interventions have been sought and granted primarily in cases involving women outside the mainstream of middle-class America. There is no way of knowing how many middle-class women have been influenced in their "election" of, say, cesarean section, by the mention of such legal recourse. See Barbara Katz Rothman, *Recreating Motherhood: Ideology and Technology in a Patriarchal Society* (New York: W.W. Norton, 1989), 160–68 for the implications of court involvement in obstetric interventions and 185ff. for the parallel case of court-mandated neonatal treatment.

20. This is not the place to consider the pros and cons of midwives or physicians as birth attendants. For the benefit of those not familiar with modern midwives, the following description of the midwifery model in contrast to the medical model may be helpful.

The most widely accepted distinction is that midwives see pregnancy and birth as normal processes, as part of the life cycle, not as
illnesses or disease states. In practice, midwives allow nature to run
its course unless intervention becomes a necessity. Most midwives
consider psychological, emotional, interpersonal, family and spiritual needs as essential parts of health care. Finally, most believe in
each woman's right to maintain control of her body and her care.
This is accomplished through informed decision making, which
mandates a great deal of teaching and information giving by
midwives.

Ronnie Lichtman, "Medical Models and Midwifery: The Cultural
Experience of Birth," in Michaelson, et al., *Childbirth in America*, 130.
Lichtman is a certified nurse midwife (i.e., a registered nurse with
specialized training and experience in midwifery) who practices in a
hospital setting. Lay midwives share the same general philosophy, but
are not trained or licensed by any medical establishment. Barbara
Rothman argues that midwifery (at least as practiced outside of medical
settings) offers a more woman-centered "reconceptualization of the
'facts' of procreation," *Recreating Motherhood*, 172.

21. Among the factors that have been cited: inadequate prenatal
care and education; use of alcohol, drugs and tobacco; and poor
nutrition. Poor and working-class women are less likely to attend
prenatal classes or to go for prenatal checkups, even in Britain where
costs are borne by the national health service. Oakley, *Captured Womb*,
266ff. American researchers find similar results: See Ellen S. Lazarus,
"Poor Women, Poor Outcomes: Social Class and Reproductive
Health," 39–54, in Michaelson, et al., *Childbirth in America*, 41f., 52;
and Marilyn Poland, "Adequate Prenatal Care and Reproductive Outcome," 55–65, in Michaelson, et al., *Childbirth in America*, 61f., 65.
The tendency not to seek prenatal care may reflect a more general
mistrust of institutions, as well as logistical difficulties with attendance
and frustration with the impersonal care and long waiting times often
experienced at public clinics. Thomas Coyle, director of a Baltimore
program to fight infant mortality, told the House Select Committee on
Hunger, "Many poor women do not see public health programs as in
their best interests. . . . They see these programs as punitive." At the
same hearing, health experts noted that "Other problems include
homelessness, lack of transportation to health-care centers, lack of
reliable baby-sitting and perhaps most importantly, the sense of hope-
lessness in inner city neighborhoods." Quoted in *Bellingham [WA]
Herald*, Sept. 13, 1991.

22. Efforts to overcome barriers and bring good prenatal care to disadvantaged women show promising results: When hospital-based midwives visit women in their homes rather than seeing them in clinics, mortality and surgery rates drop sharply. For example, the maternity service of the North Bronx Hospital has the lowest rates of cesareans and neonatal intensive care in New York City, "Although four-fifths of the mothers are medically at high risk and a third are drug addicts," Wertz and Wertz, *Lying-In*, 299.

23. Rosemary Radford Ruether, *Women-Church: Theology and Practice of Feminist Liturgical Communities* (San Francisco: Harper & Row, 1985), 200–203.

24. Marge Sears, *Life-Cycle Celebrations for Women* (Mystic, Conn.: Twenty-Third Publications, 1989), 5–8. Sears also includes a "Healing Ritual following Stillbirth or Miscarriage," 12–14, and a "Ritual for a Nursing Mother and Child," 15–18, as well as a "Celebration of a Newborn," 9–11.

25. Ibid., 7.

26. Penelope Washbourn, *Becoming Woman: The Quest for Wholeness in Female Experience* (San Francisco: Harper & Row, 1977), 99.

27. *The Book of Common Prayer and Administration of the Sacraments and Other Rites and Ceremonies of the Church, According to the use of the Episcopal Church* (New York: Church Hymnal Corporation, 1979), 439ff.

28. It is probably no accident that the forty days of ritual impurity in Hebrew practice coincide with the mother's final postnatal examination in our culture. By this time postnatal bleeding should have stopped and the uterus should be back to its nonpregnant size.

29. Compare, for example: Oakley, *Women Confined*, 87.

30. Cheryl Kristolaitis finds the service of "'Thanksgiving for the Gift of a Child'" in the Canadian Book of Alternative Services particularly helpful. She notes that this "service was revised, in good measure, because of its continuing use in Newfoundland. Input in both opinion on the service and the writing of it was given by women. . . . The service acknowledges the crisis nature of childbirth and realistically provides a sensitive and compassionate prayer for the needs of parents who have a handicapped child." Cheryl Kristolaitis, "From Purification to Celebration: The History of the Service for Women after Childbirth," *Journal of the Canadian Church Historical Society* 28, no. 2 (Oct. 1986): 61.

31. There may still be a need for a more general religious rite celebrating a child's birth. Compare David Rathgen, "First Steps" (Hokitika, New Zealand: David Rathgen, 65 Stafford St., 1986); and

John Simpson and Christopher Byworth, "A Service of Thanksgiving and Blessing" (Bramcote, Nottingham, U.K.: Grove Books, 1974).

32. Some congregations already offer such classes, as well as prebaptism classes. See, for ex., Charlotte E. Erlandson, "Affirmation of Baptism in the Midst of Life-Long Learning," *Word and World,* 11 (fall 1991): 359, for a short description of "Parenthood and Your Marriage Classes" offered by a congregation in conjunction with Lutheran Social Service.

33. According to Niles Newton, "Most women in our culture grow up basically uninformed about important aspects of female sexuality, such as pregnancy, childbirth, and lactation." Niles Newton, "Interrelationships Between Sexual Responsiveness, Birth, and Breast Feeding," in *Contemporary Sexual Behavior: Critical Issues in the 70s,* ed. Joseph Zubin and John Money (Baltimore: Johns Hopkins University Press, 1973), 72–98; cf. Leifer, *Psychological Effects,* 20. Intergenerational learning about childbirth has become an exception rather than the rule. The trend toward hospital birth has resulted in a generation of women who have never seen anything of birth before giving birth themselves. Although a woman may ask her mother about childbirth, her mother's birthing recollections may well be limited by the heavier use of anesthesia common a generation ago. Indeed, birthing customs have changed greatly even within the last decade, so women tend to seek information about it from their peers and/or reading and classes.

10
Reclaiming God Our Mother

Glimpses of God our Mother can be found throughout the Bible. Chapter 3 above includes samples from the psalms, the pentateuch, and especially the prophets. Chapter 4 contains references from Acts, Matthew, and Luke, the gospel and letters of John, and the letters of Peter and Paul. So, too, chapters 5 and 6 show glimpses sprinkled here and there through the church's history, from Clement of Alexandria to Anselm of Canterbury to Julian of Norwich.

Even so, many people today assume that if you want to talk about or pray to a birthing God, you have to look outside Christianity. On the one hand, some Christians fear that addressing God as Mother will import foreign influences into church practice; Elizabeth Achtemeier, for example, worries that the church "may find its liturgy changed by some worship committee into a celebration of a Canaanite, fertility birthing god."[1] At the other end of the spectrum, the contemporary search for "the Goddess" seems to proceed from the same assumption—that maternal expression of the deity is not to be found in Christianity.[2]

This final chapter considers ways to correct this unfortunate assumption and explores the gifts we stand to gain, in light of two contemporary theologians' reflections on the maternity of God.

Choan-Seng Song observes in his *Theology from the Womb of Asia*, "We have barely begun to explore theologically the volcano of passion that a mother experiences at childbirth. Maybe this is the reason why our theology has been without much passion."[3] Why is the theological exploration of childbirth still in its infancy? Is it simply because professional theology has, until recently, been dominated by male teachers who have not connected with female imagery for the divine? Most of us tend to draw on examples and struggles from our own lives in articulating what our faith means; thus it is little surprise that a preponderance of male theologians results in a preponderance of masculine imagery for God. This imbalance is slowly being corrected as more women go to work as theologians and as more men witness the birth of their children and share domestic duties to a greater extent than their fathers did.

But why is the maternal imagery that does exist in the biblical tradition so commonly overlooked? I suspect that many of us have simply been blind to glimpses of a maternal God, even when they have been staring us in the face. To cite one glaring personal example, I almost sent this book out into the world without even mentioning Acts 2:24 and its crucial reference to Jesus' birthing travail of death. I put that verse on my list of biblical birthing terms right at the start of my research, yet it was only after months of writing and rewriting that its significance finally struck me—in spite of the fact that I had been concentrating all the while on childbearing imagery! If we are to recover this neglected imagery, we must be vigilant and imaginative readers; and we must help one another remove the blinders that prevent us from seeing what is written plainly on the page. I hope the resources gathered in the preceding pages will help in that effort.

Song's contrast between the passion a mother experiences at birth and theology's lack of passion suggests another reason that childbearing imagery for the divine has been neglected. From the birth poetry of poor Asian mothers, Song gleans a description of childbirth as a volcano of *passion*—a powerful combination of love and suffering, endurance and exertion—a rock extruding burningly new life. This passion is awe-inspiring, as frightening in its disruptive power as it is overwhelming in its creative possibilities. Especially if we feel in control of our lives (or at least think we have a good handle on the rules of the game), we might prefer that God stay put in our neatly labeled boxes, rather than bursting through our definitions and assumptions with new life.

Moreover, the passion of childbearing implies so much blood and guts and is so closely related to sexual passion, that many people find it difficult to square with their concept of God. Indeed, Sally McFague observes that any female metaphor for God makes people uneasy. She suggests that the most basic reason for this "uneasiness with female metaphors for God is that unlike the male metaphors, whose sexual character is cloaked, the female metaphors seem blatantly sexual and involve the sexuality most feared: female sexuality."[4] And yet, as we have seen, such metaphors are part of our Christian heritage. The Bible itself employs explicit, sensuous metaphors of God giving birth and suckling—and thus honors female experience, including its sexual aspects. So, too, these obviously maternal biblical metaphors may, in turn, help us all to accept our sexuality and our passions, not only as God-given gifts, but also as aspects of ourselves that can communicate something of God's self.

Indeed, the experience of childbirth can be revelatory: Some women find in childbirth a wondrous integration of body and soul, as every fiber of their being participates in the strenuous exhilaration of pushing new life into the world. Such an experience is not only a revelation of human possibilities, but also a glimpse of God, in whom everything in heaven and on earth is integrated.

Even if childbirth is not such a euphoric experience, it offers a glimpse into the struggle and self-giving that go into creation and the joy and bonds of love that emerge. Song reminds us that childbirth begins with the most intimate bonds of blood and flesh, moves through the explosive pains of separation, and ends with "tears of joy at having participated in the creation of life, tears of deep awe at being able to be co-creators of life with God. What an awesome thought it is! And what a revelatory experience it ought to be!"[5] Thus, for Song, childbirth reveals a glimpse of the God who passionately gives birth to creation and passionately loves creation—to the point of personally entering into it in the soul and womb of woman.

Song finds evidence of this mother-God's passion both in Christ's embodiment in Mary's womb and in the passionate "theology of the womb" she bears on her lips. In her Magnificat, Mary proclaims a tumultuous, joyous, passionate womb theology of reversals, justice, new life, and fulfillment. Far from being either a marginal, special-interest theology, or an ahistorical creation theology, Song asserts that Mary's "theology of the womb must be the foundation of all theology—theology of politics, theology of history, theology of cultures—theology of God's saving love for all human beings, all created in God's own image."[6]

Childbirth, of course, is not only a "volcano of passion," but also an integrative social event that builds up families and communities and binds individuals together; thus Song's theology of the womb also stresses kinship. He explores kinship primarily in terms of the incarnation, basing his study on the genealogies of creation and redemption found in Genesis, Matthew, and Luke. These genealogies point to kinship and community as the matrix in which people apprehend and appropriate God's salvation, and they point to a radical expansion of conventional notions of kinship in Christ: "In and through the seed of life conceived in Mary's womb, all men and women are basically blood brothers and sisters. The concept of kinship is therefore fundamental to the biblical understanding of salvation."[7]

One of the great strengths of procreative imagery for God is its ability to articulate the bonds of love and affection that bind us to God and the kinship we have with one another. Thus Job looks to God's work in the womb as the source of fundamental human equality that, in turn, obligates people to treat one another fairly, regardless of social status: "Did not he who made me in the womb make him [that is, Job's servant]? And did not one fashion us in the womb?" (Job 31:15, cf.14, 16ff.). Mary's womb theology lifts up this fundamental human equality in more unsettling fashion:

> [God has] put down the mighty from their thrones,
> and exalted those of low degree;
> he has filled the hungry with good things,
> and the rich he has sent empty away (Luke 1:52f.).

Kinship is also at the heart of Sally McFague's exploration of "God as Mother." The kinship McFague has in mind encompasses all creation, thus she finds this model of God eminently suited to her "theology for an ecological, nuclear age." McFague takes her clue for envisioning God as mother from Paul Tillich's "symbolic suggestion for imaging the ground of being, the depths of divinity, as mother-love, which both gives life to all and desires reunification with all life."[8] Although McFague expands Tillich's insight from its maternal base to include all parental love and makes quite clear that there is more to parental love than giving birth, she explains that the parental metaphor for God derives much of its power from the experience of childbirth: "Becoming a biological parent is the closest experience most people have to an experience of creation, that is, of bringing into existence."[9]

McFague draws out the agapic dimensions of such familiar love: "Parental love is the most powerful and intimate experience we have of giving love whose return is not calculated . . . it is the gift of *life as such* to others."[10] When the accent falls on agape as the love that gives, the very act of creation can be seen to be pure divine agape. Here McFague follows in the tradition of Julian of Norwich, who saw the creator-motherhood of God expressed in the simple fact that we exist: As a mother gives of her being so that her child may receive the gift of life, God gave of Her very substance, that creation might come into existence.

Envisioning God as giving birth to creation expresses the kinship of all creation in the most intimate of terms. Viewed thus, the sun is indeed our brother, the moon our sister, the earth and sea and all their inhabitants our siblings. From the perspective of the tradition, however, this image presents something of a leap. Julian of Norwich spoke of the Creator in terms of motherhood, and isolated Bible verses hint at God's giving birth to "the earth and world" (Ps. 90:2; cf. Job 38:29; Isa. 23:4; 45:10f.). Still, for the most part, Christianity has not described creation in terms of conception, gestation, and birth.

McFague asks why "the birth of the world and all its beings has not been permitted the imagery that this tradition uses so freely for the transformation and fulfillment of creation"[11] and finds reasons in the Christian tradition's alienation from female sexuality, and its Christ-centered tendency to overlook the first birth in its efforts to stress the second. If these are indeed the reasons for the dominant Christian tradition's rejection of birthing imagery to describe creation, repentance and renewed openness to the promptings of the Spirit are in order.

Are there any legitimate concerns about the application of birthing imagery to creation? Imagining God's giving birth once may have risked suggesting a plurality of gods akin to the pantheons of neighboring religions;[12] this is a less pressing danger today. McFague herself warns that any parental model can tend toward infantilism and echoes Tillich's concern that the maternal model in particular can suffocate and "swallow."[13] Other possible concerns include the risk of confusing God our Mother with Mother Nature, the risk of collapsing the distinction between Creator and creature, and the risk of understating the element of divine intentionality in creation.

These are not insurmountable difficulties, however, and indeed any metaphor has its limitations. McFague, for example, points out that the tendency of the Hebraic-Christian tradition to imagine creation as the product of God's speech and handiwork may overemphasize the distance between Creator and creation.[14] McFague sees other biblical values emphasized when God is imagined as the mother who bodies forth and nourishes the world: the imagery of gestation, birthing, and lactation "creates an imaginative picture of creation as profoundly dependent on and cared for by divine life."[15] Thus she proposes a picture of creation as a physical event: the universe bodied forth from God, expressive of God's very being, and claims that this picture is "both closer to the Christian faith and better for our world than the alternative picture."[16] She finds it closer to the Christian faith because it reclaims the biblical sense of God's intimate relationship to the world and better for our world because it undercuts the dualistic thought patterns that have separated God from the world, body from mind, flesh from spirit, nature from humanity.[17]

McFague addresses the risk of infantilism that may accompany a parental model of God by describing this mother-God not only as creator but also as judge, who fights injustice as a mother defends her young.[18] This judge may be as passionate as a mother defending her young, but she is not preferential as creaturely parents tend to be; McFague takes care to point out that mother-God gives birth to all creation, and hence wants *all* forms of life to flourish.[19] The judgments of God as mother proceed from an appreciation of the needs of all her children in the vast household of the universe, thus the primary sin becomes "the refusal to become a part of the ecological whole whose continued existence and success depend upon a recognition of the interdependence and interrelatedness of all species."[20]

Far from provoking an infantile response, McFague believes that picturing God as Mother can inspire quasi-parental responsibility. As God is parent to creation, so, too, "We should become mothers and fathers to our world," extending our natural parental instincts to other human beings and even to other species.[21] McFague believes that this ethic calls on our deepest instincts: "We all want to be life givers, to pass life on, and when we do we can face our own deaths more easily."[22] Thus the cycle of life and death may comfort us and impel us to careful stewardship of life, especially in an era when even that fundamental cycle is threatened.

This cycle of life and death also may well appall us with its impersonal rounds, however, and here the model's potential for suffocating or swallowing surfaces. Indeed, McFague's own redefinition of the primary sin as "the refusal to become a part of the ecological whole" might itself seem to threaten to "swallow" the individual. But is this danger of suffocating or swallowing a function of the maternal imagery? In this case, at least, it seems that McFague's ecological sensibilities might have produced a similar outcome, even if the picture of God as mother had not been introduced.[23]

I suspect that this fear of suffocation has to do with a more familiar maternal metaphor, namely Mother Nature. There is a measure of comfort in viewing nature as a mother from whom we come and to whom we return, but maternal metaphors do not necessarily emphasize the cyclical, nor is Mother Nature's comfort ultimately satisfying. Women may be particularly attuned to the cycles of nature, given their menstrual cycles, their awareness of their "biological clock," and the frequency with which their work involves responsibility for caring for the young and the old. Nevertheless, women are much more than a bundle of cycles. Even in childbirth, one of the very experiences that brings them closest to the cycles of life and death, women are not only connected with all of creation and its cycles, but also intensely personally involved. This is a specific woman, giving birth to a specific baby, under specific circumstances. She may grieve at the loss of her pregnant intimacy with her child, but she is usually also happy to push the baby out into a wider world where she can see and hold her, talk to and play with him, feed and watch the little one grow. Unlike Mother Nature, human mothers do not draw their children back into the womb.

Viewing God our Mother from a mother's perspective can help us avoid several of the possible difficulties with the maternal imagery. The fear of being swallowed is a concern (realistic or not) perceived from the viewpoint of the child struggling to assert its own identity as distinct from that of its parent. From the perspective of a mature mother, however, pregnancy, childbirth, and lactation are the first phases of a relationship that is a gradual process of separation moving toward the maturation of the child. The mother's goal is not the reassimilation of the child, but rather the blossoming of an adult relationship of mutual respect, compassion, and freely given love.

Negotiation of these transitions is obviously neither easy nor foolproof for human parents. Still, the intention embodied in the very progression of pregnancy, childbirth, and lactation may give us a glimpse of how God our Mother relates to the universe. First, we might say that even more than human parents who desire children and come together in hopes of bringing a new person into being, God desired to bring forth a cosmos where there once was none. The creation of the world was not an accidental pregnancy, but rather a love child intentionally conceived of and borne within the mystery of God's self.

Second, the God who conceives the universe and brings forth mountains and wisdom, the entire earth and all life and breath, is also the divine parent who desires the fruit of her womb to reach the fullness of its stature and who nourishes, guides, and prods it along its way toward that goal. Just as giving birth initiates a whole lifetime of giving and caring, the God who intentionally gave of herself to bring forth creation continues to nurture and guide it. The universe, then, can be seen as God's child—distinct from its parent, but intrinsically related, sharing in God's body-spirit substance. God transcends the universe as a mother encompassing a fetus or nursing her child.[24] Paradoxically, the God who as mother desires creation's maturity and freedom, remains her child's only possible source of being and nourishment. Thus freedom and maturity does not mean freedom from God, but rather freedom to enjoy and share and respond to God's plenty.

Within this overarching picture, which may make humans feel insignificant as tiny cells in the body of God's child, we find that God our Mother also brings forth peoples and prophets and graciously participates in the birth of each individual. In these biblical glimpses of God's giving birth to a people, the Creator of the universe is most clearly seen to be also the Redeemer who acts in human history and who, more than any birthing mother, demonstrates incredible endurance, powerful love, and purposive strength. Isaiah 42, for example, shows us a picture of God our Mother whose creative labor cannot be stopped by the results of her people's mistrust and wrongheadedness, by the political powers that be, or even by the structures of creation itself.

Much remains to be done in filling out the features of God our Mother—the mother who both creates and renews and nurtures her beloved child and all its members. If we are to appropriate the strengths of maternal symbolism for God and to pass them on to future generations, we must find ways to dismantle the competition and mistrust that has grown up between advocates of "the first birth," that is, the messy, mundane miracle of childbirth and those who stress "the second birth," that is, the redemption and renewal of creation in Jesus Christ.

I believe the most fruitful approach to this task centers in Christ. Christ's birth has hallowed all human birth, and Christ knows personally what it is to endure birthing travail. To those who assume that this strategy is but another way of focusing on the "second" birth at the expense of the first, I should say that I did not begin this inquiry looking for Christ as the answer. Initially, I was simply fascinated with Old Testament maternal metaphors; in my own childbearing, however, it was Christ who came to me. Long before I noticed that Acts 2:24 had anything to do with birth, before I had even heard of Julian of Norwich, I knew that the distress of giving birth was like Jesus' crucifixion.

Strapped to an operating table, with my arms stretched out and bound to crosspieces on either side, I felt as if I was on the cross, naked and vulnerable under the sterile sheets. Some years later, while laboring with another child, I tried to focus my breathing and prayers by visualizing a peaceful risen Christ, or Mary, throned in glory—only to find that all I could see was Jesus on a cross, struggling for every breath. Nor is my experience unusual; many women have found a sense of kinship with the suffering Christ through their own struggles to give birth.

Christ's birth work on the cross means that women suffering in childbirth can look to Jesus as their sister in meaningful, life-giving suffering; the point of comparison, of course, is not only the suffering but also the creative purpose and the joy of accomplishment. The suffering of childbirth is real, but in the end it is worth it all—both because it is such an intense experience of life and because of the beloved children who emerge. Lifting up this point of connection between female experience and Christ's saving work gives women a resource for dealing with their travail, and equally important, shows Christ as fully human, a person who is not limited to male experience.

Christ entered fully into our world and at the same time gave us insight into the God who is neither male nor female, but encompasses both. Thus, too, we may look to Christ as the mother of our faith. Indeed, following medieval mystics' lead, we may see Jesus' entire life as a bringing to birth of new life, new kinship networks, new joy for all people. From this perspective God-in-Christ's birthing work began with the incarnation. As a woman gives of herself so that the vulnerable new life in her womb may

survive and thrive, so too, God-in-Christ relinquished the preroga-
tives of divine power and took on the vulnerability of human flesh.
This movement is in itself life giving and relationship renewing. In
it God disarms human mistrust and fear and reveals the depths of
divine love for creation by willingly and fully entering the creaturely condition. In Christ we see that God is the mother who
lovingly gives birth and rejoices in the child's blossoming; a mother
who bends down, even lies down to talk face to face with her
child—a mother who far from swallowing her child, risks being
swallowed by it—in order to reestablish their relationship. This
God Incarnate does not abhor or fear a woman's womb, but enters
into it, and quite possibly enjoys experiencing creation from the
inside out![25]

God-in-Christ did not abhor or fear a woman's womb, but
entered into it—and enjoyed the experience. God-in-Christ did
not treat women as walking wombs, but regarded them as full
human beings. God-in-Christ did not shun the birthing travail of
death, but lived through it, and in so doing transformed it to joy
for all the people. From this perspective, birth from on high does
not denigrate birth from the wombs of women, but reaffirms it.

Proclaiming this aspect of the Christian message requires
you and me to do our best to articulate and embody a balance
that generations before us have found difficult to achieve. We are
called to appreciate and honor women's capacity to give birth
and to value childbearing as a significant moral, physical, and
spiritual life experience, while resisting the temptation to define
women primarily in terms of their childbearing abilities.

We can set about rising to this and all life's challenges with
the joy of expecting parents. Not only do we have the buried
treasure of maternal metaphor to cherish, ponder, and share; but
we also have God's promise of nourishment at the breast of
Christ and the assistance of the Spirit's midwifery as we struggle
to give birth to Christ in our lives, to give birth to justice in our
world, and to share the glimpses of God that we have ourselves
received.

Lord Jesus Christ, who gave birth on the cross; bless us as we
labor!

Notes

1. Elizabeth Achtemeier, "Renewed Appreciation for an Unchanging Story," *The Christian Century* 107 (June 13–20, 1990): 597.
2. For one example, see Kathryn Allen Rabuzzi, *Motherself: A Mythic Analysis of Motherhood* (Bloomington, Ind.: Indiana University Press, 1988), 203–209.
3. Choan-Seng Song, *Theology from the Womb of Asia* (Maryknoll, N.Y.: Orbis, 1986), 115.
4. Sally McFague, *Models of God: Theology for an Ecological, Nuclear Age* (Philadelphia: Fortress Press, 1987), 98.
5. Song, 115.
6. Ibid., 119.
7. Choan-Seng Song, *Third Eye Theology: Theology in Formation in Asian Settings* (Maryknoll, N.Y.: Orbis, 1979), 139.
8. McFague, *Models of God*, 101f. Compare Paul Tillich, *Systematic Theology* (Chicago: University of Chicago Press, 1963), 3:293f.
9. McFague, *Models of God*, 104.
10. Ibid., 103. Finding signs of divine agape in parental love obviously involves an understanding of agape that (in contrast to many definitions) does not see disinterestedness as a key characteristic. McFague argues that seen in the context of creation, rather than in the more usual context of redemption, agape "need not be disinterested; in fact it should not be" (102). To the contrary, the divine creative agape is the freely giving love that properly includes both intense interest and impartiality, similar to the love of parents who care passionately for each of their children and, at the same time, strive to love them all fairly and equally.
11. Ibid., 105.
12. See p. 45f.
13. McFague, *Models of God*, 116; cf. 101.
14. Both, however, clearly portray God's intention to create. Pregnancy, on the other hand, may be unintended, even unwanted. Therefore, it is important to articulate clearly that this conception and bringing to birth was God's wholehearted intention and the work of God alone.
15. McFague, *Models of God*, 106.
16. Ibid., 110.
17. McFague's maternal model is complicated by her simultaneous view of creation as God's body, and she acknowledges the nonsensical side of the proposed model that emerges at this point—mothers (at least as we know them) do not give birth to their own bodies. Even so,

McFague thinks "the picture of God giving birth to her 'body,' that is, to life . . . provides a model of kinship, concern, and affinity" that can describe God as the source of all life in terms well suited to today's holistic, evolutionary sensibilities. Ibid., 111.

18. Ibid., 113.
19. Ibid., 108.
20. Ibid., 114.
21. Ibid., 119.
22. Ibid., 120.
23. This tendency is compounded by McFague's view of all creation as God's body, of which any creature is but a small part.
24. I find picturing the cosmos as God's child more helpful than McFague's view of the cosmos as God's body. The scriptural hints lead in that direction (cf. Ps. 90:2; Prov. 8:24f.; Isa. 45:10f.). Moreover, envisioning God transcending the universe as a mother encompasses a fetus, rather than as a person transcending her body, avoids reintroducing a dichotomy between body and self, as well as better preserving the distinction between Creator and created.
25. Leo Steinberg, *The Sexuality of Christ in Renaissance Art and in Modern Oblivion* (New York: Random House, Pantheon, 1983), 126, notes that the nursing baby Jesus is often portrayed turning his head to the viewer, as if God is relishing this opportunity to enjoy creaturely delight. Might God, then, not also have enjoyed a sojourn in the human womb?

Index of Scripture

Index of Names and Subjects